SPIRIT AS SCULPTOR
OF THE HUMAN ORGANISM

SPIRIT AS SCULPTOR
OF THE HUMAN ORGANISM

Sixteen lectures given in Stuttgart, Dornach, The Hague, London and Berlin in 1922

TRANSLATED BY MATTHEW BARTON

INTRODUCTION BY MATTHEW BARTON

RUDOLF STEINER

RUDOLF STEINER PRESS

CW 218

The publishers gratefully acknowledge the generous funding of this publication by the estate of Dr Eva Frommer MD (1927–2004) and the Anthroposophical Society in Great Britain

Rudolf Steiner Press
Hillside House, The Square
Forest Row, RH18 5ES

www.rudolfsteinerpress.com

Published by Rudolf Steiner Press 2014

Originally published in German under the title *Geistige Zusammenhänge in der Gestaltung des menschlichen Organismus* (volume 218 in the *Rudolf Steiner Gesamtausgabe* or Collected Works) by Rudolf Steiner Verlag, Dornach. Based on shorthand transcripts (not reviewed by the speaker). This authorized translation is based on the latest available (third) edition, 1992, edited by Dr H.W. Zbinden

Published by permission of the Rudolf Steiner Nachlassverwaltung, Dornach

A catalogue record for this book is available from the British Library

ISBN 978 1 85584 408 7

Cover by Mary Giddens
Typeset by DP Photosetting, Neath, West Glamorgan
Printed and bound in the UK by 4edge Limited

CONTENTS

PART ONE

LECTURE 1

STUTTGART, 9 OCTOBER 1922

Experiences During Sleep: Their Spiritual Context and Significance for our Daily Life

Knowledge of the 'unconscious'. Sleep and dream. First stage of sleep: from a nebulous sense of self to search for the spirit. The consequence in a waking state: relating separate things to the general. Second stage: from anxiety arising through fragmentation into separate entities, to permeation by planetary powers. The consequence in a waking state: refreshing of blood circulation and the breathing process. Third stage: experience of the fixed star constellations. Consequence: kindling of the nutritional process. Leading the human being back through the three stages to waking through the moon powers.

pages 1–14

LECTURE 2

STUTTGART, 14 OCTOBER 1922

The Human Spirit and Soul Between Death and a New Birth

Imaginative perception of the spirit and soul. Memory pictures, body-developing wisdom as the spirit and soul's panoramic tableau before birth. Connection of the human being with the universe through Inspiration. Transition from direct experiencing of the spiritual cosmos to its secondary manifestation. The urge for a new incarnation. Moral essence and I after death, moon and sun sphere. The Christ event and its meaning.

pages 15–32

ahrimanic beings under the earth who continually try to make him earthly. Yahweh-moon as regulator of instinctual nature together with the beings of Mercury and Venus in the battle with Ahriman. The influence of Mars, Jupiter and Saturn on the human being; their battle against luciferic beings. Pathological states as safeguard against succumbing to luciferic or ahrimanic beings. The redeeming and reconciling power of Christ.

pages 105–118

LECTURE 9

LONDON, 19 NOVEMBER 1922

Experience Between Death and a New Birth as Consequence of Karma. Creating the
Conditions for our Return to a New Life on Earth

Dissolution of the ether body after death. Moon powers as powers of birth and death; the bearer of karma. Reverse retrospective after-death experience of our past life. Memory of earthly life hindering our passage through the planetary sphere. The urge to embark on a new, compensating earthly life at the moment of cosmic midnight. Assimilation of karma memory. The activity and influence of Christ and Michael: preparing an earthly body for others in future.

pages 119–134

PART FIVE

LECTURE 10

LONDON, 17 NOVEMBER 1922 (semi-public)

Exact Knowledge of Supersensible Worlds Through Anthroposophic Spiritual Science

Spiritual research as an 'exact science'. Living intensively in pure thoughts: experience of the temporal body. Experience of the pictorial world of the ether body after death. Practice of fully aware and voluntarily empty consciousness: continuity of memory in waking life and sleep. Living with after-images of the planetary and star worlds. Experience of the future: life after death. Schooling of the will to attain a higher level of consciousness: ideal magic, to develop the spirit germ for a new earthly life. Direct community of the soul with connected souls after death.

pages 135–152

EDITOR'S PREFACE

The lectures comprising this volume, which Rudolf Steiner gave in Stuttgart, Dornach, The Hague and Berlin, were for members of the Anthroposophical Society, as were those given in London on 12, 16 and 19 November 1922. While in London, Rudolf Steiner also gave three 'semi-public' lectures at Steinway Hall (17, 18 and 19 November 1922) and on 20 November of the same year, by invitation of the 'Educational Union for the Realization of Spiritual Values', a public lecture entitled 'The Art of Education Founded on Insights into the Human Being' at Morley Hall.

INTRODUCTION

The word 'religion' has all kinds of connotation today and has become anathema to many, the source, apparently, of divisiveness and dire conflict. But its meaning, originally, is simply 'to reconnect'. This begs the question, of course, what we might reconnect *with*. Steiner is always at pains, in these lectures and elsewhere, to value and give due regard to what is best in diverse human cultures and beliefs, but he is also clear-sighted about the loss of real vision of many orthodox belief systems, and their increasing reliance on tradition rather than immediacy of experience. One sense therefore in which he would understand reconnection is that of the quest to refresh real and vivid insights into the nature of the world, in his view inseparable from the divine realities continually creating and sustaining it.

It is an illusion to think, says Steiner, that we live only in our own separate skins. Far more than we are often aware of, we live in the whole world, which is at the same time a world order of active love and morality. Life cannot be understood only in physical terms; and while we probably know this subliminally, the great majority of us are still subservient intellectually to the idea of a random and amoral physical world of 'waves', 'atoms' and 'forces'. Such a world seems to have no connection with our consequently rather quaint and impotent moral striving. The opposite of 'religion' therefore might be 'fragmentation'—the fractures between humanity and the universe, between human beings themselves and, last but not least, within ourselves: a sundering of our intellect from feeling, or feeling from will. Reconnecting with the world, and overcoming all these fractures requires us, as Steiner describes here, to move lovingly beyond the narrower confines of ourselves and embrace a reality much greater than us, albeit one in which we are deeply embedded. One name for this reality is Christ, who, in striking contrast to the ways in which his name is used in vain, is the healer of all divisions both within and between us.

Once we begin to acknowledge this greater, redeeming reality, and feel increasingly one with the world and the rest of humanity, we can take the next step—first in felt knowledge than also active deed—of realizing that no individual betterment can happen at the expense of others, but that we are all intrinsically connected for better or worse. Reconnecting with each other, with other human beings of whatever race or creed, is therefore equally a meaning of 'religion'. A fragmented humanity is joined in this greater self, just as the fragmented human soul can be healed by it.

In these lectures there is seemingly no end to the manifold reconnections that start to dawn: between, say, our past, present and future; between our physical actions and limb movements in one life and the forming or sculpting of our head in a future one; between the active, individualizing principle of the 'I' and the physical human body it works upon and shapes; and above all, between the moral actions and insights we develop while alive on earth and our developing 'eye' for spiritual reality in the life after death, with all that this can mean for the future of human evolution.

True religiosity, in Steiner's view, far from being a source of divisiveness, is fundamental not just to moral but also to physical health since spirit and body are profoundly and intimately connected. It is a power in us that, in Steiner's vivid picture, 'strikes a match in our whole being', uniting the fractured soul so that clear insight connects with a warm heart which in turn connects with right actions. In this vein the novelist E. M. Forster once wrote:

> Only connect [...] Only connect the prose and the passion and both will be exalted, and human love will be seen at its height. Live in fragments no longer.

One field of endeavour among many in which reconnection seems urgently needed, and which figures at several key places in these lectures, is that of education. Our view of the human being, and thus also of child development, will inevitably inform the way we shape educational provision and teaching. If we think children differ from adults only in being less cognitively advanced, we may speak only, or predominantly, to their powers of cognition, leaving their soul and sensibility, and capacity for purposeful action undeveloped. We may remain blind to essential qualities that can be nurtured differently in different phases of childhood only by recognizing the subtle yet powerful effect of the teacher and her relationship with each child.

Steiner refers to teaching as the 'highest art'; and the best artists respect and continually learn afresh from their material by staying intuitively alive and responsive to it. Teachers or parents connected to a profoundly creative view of the human being, to their own sources of authenticity and inspiration, and therefore also to the children before them, will in turn give these children a sense of connection to the world as a place in which they can, ultimately, find their own self-engendering morality and meaning. Here again, as everywhere, Steiner's vision of the world is a holistic one, where past and future connect in a creative present in which human potential can come to the fullest possible realization.

Matthew Barton, October 2014

LECTURE 1

STUTTGART, 9 OCTOBER 1922

When people speak of the soul or psyche nowadays, they often use a particular phrase which acknowledges that, in exploring this realm, one must speak of powers that do not enter ordinary awareness. At the same time, though, they admit their powerlessness in trying to do so. The phrase used to point tentatively towards this realm is 'the unconscious'. In speaking today of the intrinsic nature of human knowledge it is commonly suggested that we are initially obliged to seek this in the world around us through observation, experimentation and a synthesis created by our reasoning faculty. But then also, in turning their attention to their own consciousness, people speak of all kinds of inner content there—thoughts, feelings, impulses of will and so on. In doing so they become aware, furthermore, that things stir and surface in the psyche whose deeper nature cannot be fathomed either by using the usual methods of empirical science involving observation and combinative thinking, or through self-observation using the ordinary powers of awareness. Such attempts will not penetrate to the reality of these phenomena of soul life. For this reason they use the term 'the unconscious' and at the same time relinquish any possibility of penetrating this unconscious realm. In fact it is entirely justified to relinquish such efforts if one limits oneself to the faculties of knowledge generally acknowledged today. Such faculties will not fathom the psyche further than to ascertain that during waking life thoughts, feelings and will impulses rise up from our inner depths—expressions of human nature which can easily be seen as connected with our outward corporeal nature. Using ordinary observation, it will not be possible to find any irrefutable way of showing that these phenomena, which seem initially to be so strongly dependent on bodily states, could have any distinct existence above and beyond them.

Now you all know that this, specifically, is the point of departure of our anthroposophical outlook, which is fully cognizant of the fact that commonly accepted modes of knowledge cannot fathom the depths of the psyche. Anthroposophy acknowledges that these ordinary modes of understanding are compelled to refer to an 'unconscious' realm. Basically it is not even necessary to consider the two thresholds of physical life on earth, birth and death—though we will do this in the next lecture[1]—but only the ordinary state of sleep occurring in human beings day after day, and then we will inevitably find that soul experiences, as ordinary modes of knowledge observe them, seem to testify to the following: there appears to be such a great dependency of all ordinary, conscious thinking, feeling and will on bodily states that it is perfectly legitimate to say that soul experiences rise up from these bodily states as if from an unconscious realm, and that during sleep a merely organic life becomes rampant. Thus it does not appear that thoughts, feelings and will impulses have an intrinsic existence, and really there is no more to be said about it. At most, the way dreams play into our awareness makes it seem as if they arose from sleep and are simply recalled when we awake; and this fact might lead us to conclude that the psyche in some way continues to be active during sleep. But all these things are rather nebulous. Basically, a serious, unprejudiced observer drawing on the ordinary modes of knowledge will be able to say only that the soul reveals phenomena that seem very much dependent on bodily states.

It is precisely because anthroposophical enquiry takes these capacities—or incapacities—of ordinary modes of knowledge seriously that it seeks at the same time to find other means of knowledge. And as you know, and as has often been described here, these other faculties of enquiry are those of Imagination, Inspiration and Intuition. These special modes of knowledge that first have to be developed as capacities from ordinary soul life by real effort can serve our endeavour to gain insight into things that are unavailable to ordinary faculties.

And now, without going back over ground I have often covered relating to the nature of the knowledge gained through Imagination, Inspiration and Intuition, I simply wish to draw on these three stages of knowledge to describe a very important aspect of the human sub-conscious or unconscious—that is, the realm of soul experience between falling asleep and waking up again. It is true that I have often described this from various perspectives, but today I'd like to do so again from a specific angle. First of all therefore I want to describe what Imagination, Inspiration and Intuition perceive in the state of sleep. Ordinary consciousness of course knows only that the daily awareness we have while awake, with its diverse contents, is dulled and then extinguished when we fall asleep, giving rise to an unconscious state. In waking life, using only ordinary faculties, we cannot initially say what our psyche does while we are asleep. What occurs then, and in fact what occurs whenever the intrinsic nature of soul reality is experienced, does not enter ordinary consciousness. For ordinary awareness darkness spreads over what the soul experiences in sleep. But you see, sleep begins at the point when the faculty of Imagination starts to brighten: the darkness starts to transform into a luminosity; and with this faculty of Imagination one can already start to gain insight into what the soul experiences in the initial stages of sleep. Drawing further on the faculties of Inspiration and Intuition we can penetrate further into these experiences. You should not picture this as gazing into sleep as if into a peep-box show; rather, through faculties of Imagination, Inspiration and Intuition, we experience states of soul that resemble sleep inasmuch as, within these states, we have a similar relationship to our body as we do during sleep. The difference is that we no longer undergo this experience without awareness but become fully aware of it. By virtue of experiencing things in full awareness while awake, in a way that resembles what happens during sleep, we then become able also to perceive what occurs with the human soul during sleep; and it becomes possible to describe this.

It is a common experience of course that in falling asleep our consciousness, as it grows hazy and dim, can be filled with dreams. This dream world cannot initially offer us much help at all in perceiving the nature of soul life. You see, what we can know about dreams with our ordinary waking faculties remains something very superficial; nor do dreams themselves appear in a way that would allow us to conclude anything specific from them unless we have first gained insight into sleep by other means. Once we have gained real understanding of sleeping states we will see that dreams tend to be misleading rather than offering illuminating guidance. In sleep the soul experiences things unconsciously that, since I am now drawing on faculties of Imagination, Inspiration and Intuition, I will describe to you as if the soul were experiencing them consciously. I will describe to you what the soul experiences between falling asleep and waking up as if they were conscious experiences. They are not consciously experienced; but what I will describe is nevertheless experienced by the soul, albeit without awareness. It exists as reality, working into us not just while we are asleep, but also above all working into our physical organism and acting there primarily while we are awake. When we wake up in the morning, and until we fall asleep again, we bear within us the echoes of our experiences during the night. Whereas all that we accomplish in full awareness is very important for outward civilization, what occurs within us ourselves is scarcely dependent on our conscious awareness, but instead very much dependent on what we unconsciously experience while we are asleep.

Once sensory perceptions have gradually faded and our will impulses cease to be active, we first experience an undifferentiated state of soul. This is a generalized, nebulous experience, informed by a clear sense of time but almost wholly devoid of a sense of space. This kind of experience can truly be compared with a sort of swimming, a moving around in a generalized, nebulous universal substance. Really one would have to coin new words to express what the soul experiences here. You can say that the soul experiences itself as a wave in a great ocean, though a wave that feels itself to be inwardly organized and surrounded everywhere by the rest of the ocean, and feels the effects of this ocean upon it as, during the day, we feel colour or tone impressions or states of warmth in a particular, differentiated way and think about them. Unlike waking experience however, when we feel ourselves to be a person enclosed in our skin and occupying a particular place, just after falling asleep we feel—I'm describing this as if it were conscious; it's a reality but we have no consciousness of it—like a wave in a general ocean, moving hither and thither with no defined sense of spatial conditions. A general sense of time does remain though. But this experience is connected with another, of forsakenness, as if we were sinking into an abyss. It is true in fact that without preparation, if we experienced this first stage of sleep consciously, we would be exposed to much that we would find quite unendurable: to lose our sense of space almost entirely and live only in a generalized feeling of time, and to feel ourselves very undefined and incorporated into the generalized substance of an ocean. If we were conscious of this, we really would feel we were floating above an abyss. And this in turn is connected with something that surfaces in the soul as a huge need for support from the spirit—a huge need to be connected with a spiritual element. In this general ocean in which we swim, we have, you can say, lost all feeling of safety with which the waking world of material things endows us. And for this reason we feel, or rather would do if we were aware of it, a deep longing for connection with divine spirit. Really we experience this generalized sense of moving in an undifferentiated universal substance as being encompassed by divine spirit. Please be aware of the way I have to express this: to repeat myself, I'm describing things as if the soul experienced them consciously. It does not do so; but you can understand that, as you experience things consciously in daily life, certain things are simultaneously occurring in your organism that are simply realities. Let's say you experience joy. Yes, as this joy fills you, your blood pulses differently to how it does when you are sad. You experience the joy or sadness in your awareness but not the pulsing of your blood. And yet this pulse is still a reality. In the same way, what I am describing here as a generalized swimming in an undifferentiated universal substance on the one hand and as an accompanying need for God on the other corresponds to a reality in the life of the soul. And the faculty of Imagination does nothing other than to raise this reality into awareness, just as in ordinary waking life we can raise into our awareness the differentiated way in which our blood pulses in us in states of either joy or sadness. When we wake up in the morning, our organism has in fact been refreshed because our soul had the experience during the night that I have described. The after-effect of what occurs in the soul separated from the body during sleep is of great significance the following day for our waking life. We would not be able to use our body properly the next day if we had not lifted ourselves out of our connection with external, physical things, in order to immerse ourselves in this undefined experience that I described. And in waking life, the fact that something like an inner need arises to relate the differentiated world around us to something general and universal, to relate the sensory world to the divine, is an after-effect of this first stage of sleep. We might ask why human beings are not content, in waking life, to look upon the world's separate and diverse phenomena—why they are not content simply to pass through the world and take plants, animals and so forth as they come. Why do we begin to philosophize—and all do so, the most untutored people as well as the philosophers and, in passing, let's note that the untutored do this far better than the philosophers—about how everything is interrelated? Why do we relate the isolated phenomenon before us to something universal, asking how it is rooted in a universal context and cosmos? We would not do this if we did not immerse ourselves during sleep in this undefined existence; nor would we develop any sense of the divine in our waking life if we did not pass through this sense of the divine during the first stage of our sleep. For our inner human experience we really owe sleep something of great significance.

As sleep continues, we enter other stages that can no longer be perceived by the faculty of Imagination but for which we now need that of Inspiration. The reality of soul experience that arises here is reflected in inspired consciousness in the same way as, say, our pulse is reflected in joy and sorrow; and initially this reveals a certain fragmentation of the soul into a very great number of different aspects, separate entities. The psyche really does fragment its life into separate parts, and this frag-mentation is connected with something which, if it shines up into our awareness, appears as anxiety. After the soul has undergone what we can call a hovering over the abyss or a swimming in generalized, universal substance, accompanied by a longing for divine spirit, it succumbs to a certain anxiety, or rather to something that would be anxiety if we experienced it consciously. This is primarily due to the fact that the soul now not only swims in a general world substance but is as it were immersed in separate soul-spiritual beings who have their own autonomous existence and with whom the soul now forms a kind of affinity. It is now therefore no longer a unity, really, but has become a multiplicity. This multiple state, though, is experienced as anxiety; and is something we have to emerge from in a certain way.

During the era of earth evolution prior to the Mystery of Golgotha, mystery centres where the most diverse religions were practised issued instructions for humanity. Receiving these, individual souls gained experiences and ideas of the divine as befitted the age they lived in, in addition to the feelings arising in them through the outer world of the senses. In these ancient times, human beings still retained some sense during the day of the spiritual world shining into their awareness. The further back we go in humanity's earthly evolution, the more we come to see that people had a kind of clairvoyance in very ancient times and then, later, fading echoes of this clairvoyance. In those times they saw in inner vision that a human being dwelt as a being of soul and spirit in a pre-birth existence before he began his life on earth. This was not just a view they had developed, not something they merely believed in, but instead was something they retained from a pre-birth existence.

Here's a trivial illustration of what I mean: when someone inherits a certain ability—or even just wealth—from his parents, he can recognize how this ability or wealth has a direct effect on his life; he knows that this gift is not something he had to acquire or develop but that it came down to him from his forefathers. In the same way, in an earlier time, people knew that certain experiences in their soul did not originate in what their eyes had seen but were a kind of inheritance from a pre-earthly existence. They recognized this from the very nature of these soul experiences. It is important to keep reiterating that humankind has evolved in a way that has freed it from such experiences of the soul: our modern era is one when ordinary consciousness has no experiences that can be explained as inheritance from a pre-birth existence. Thus people of those ancient times more easily accepted guidance from their spiritual leaders in the mystery centres as to what they should feel about their inner spiritual experiences. The strength that flowed to them as impulses emanating from the mystery centres was one that they carried out of ordinary waking life into their sleep at night, and this enabled them to remain steadfast in face of the anxiety I have described, and to overcome it. This anxiety rises up out of the depths of sleep life; and the strength needed to transform this anxiety so as to bring back to waking life not a general weariness of the organism but a sense of fresh vigour was one that had first to be gathered the previous day during waking life. Our days and nights are interrelated. At a certain stage of sleep the night brings us anxiety; and into this must pour the strength we have acquired from a religious or religious-type experience the day before. When these two things—the remainder of the day before and the night's primordial experience—unite, then a refreshing power streams into our organism during our waking life the next day.

It is no longer tenable for a real science of the spirit to speak only in general, abstract phrases of a universal, divine element governing the world. It is not a viable way forward to describe the superficial appearance of things, and say that universal guidance governs our sensory existence in general terms. Instead, spiritual science has to detail the actual, tangible ways in which this divine governance acts. If we are to be equal to the tasks facing us as humanity evolves, we can no longer just say that we feel refreshed after a good night's sleep, and receive this as a gift from God. We would have to despair of all science itself if we seek a rigorous scientific method in relation to the sensory world but are unable to extend the rigour of this science to the supersensible realm, instead tackling this latter domain with general phrases only, such as that divine powers govern the universe. We can delve ever further into definite realities, showing how the anxiety I have referred to appears at this second stage of sleep, in a sense mingled with the strength drawn from religious feeling cultivated the previous day, which works on into the night, and how from this in turn is drawn a power that refreshes and reinvigorates the physical organism the following day. By such means we increasingly gain insight into how real spirit lives within physical reality; and this is quite different from the modes of knowledge accepted today which have only a physical content and general turns of phrase about some kind of spirit indwelling or overlighting this physical content. Human culture will go on declining, though, if it does not extend the rigour practised in observation of the outer world to the world of spirit too. And now we can see, when we use the faculty of Inspiration to study sleep as it passes from the first to the second stage, that our inner soul experience becomes quite different from what it was during the day.

Now, orthodox science can also show us, as long as we practise it rigorously, how we dwell in a soul element in the breathing process, in blood circulation, and in the nutritional process working through blood circulation. We can feel something occurring when we exert ourselves in movement and so forth. We can feel the soul and spirit's connection with physical processes; and if we describe respiration, say, or blood circulation, we know that this is informed by soul experience during our waking life. Soul experience does not dwell in sensory perception during sleep, but is also a very specific kind of inner life. And in the same way that our inner life during waking hours can be related to respiration and blood circulation, so this nightly inner life is connected, as it turns out, with the inner elaboration of powers comparable to the vigour we acquire from breathing and blood circulation. It is an elaboration of powers that reflect the planetary motions in our solar system. Please note that I am not saying we dwell within planetary motions during sleep or are connected directly with them, but rather that we dwell in a kind of reflection or replica—if you like, a miniature of our planetary cosmos or its movements. As our life of soul inhabits blood circulation during the day, so at night our soul life inhabits a replica of the planetary movements of our solar system. During the day, we can say, the white and red blood corpuscles circulate in us, and we gain vigour from the cycle of respiration through which we breathe in and out. At night by contrast, we have to say that in our life of soul a replica of the movements of Mercury, of Venus and Jupiter circulate in us.

Thus from the moment we fall asleep to when we wake up, our soul life is in a sense a small planetary cosmos. From our personal, human existence during the day we pass into a cosmic existence at night. And the faculty of Inspiration can discover that the powers that kept our blood pulsing during the day can, following our sense of tiredness in the evening, retain their vitality during the night through their own momentum and persistence; but that in order for us to embark on new soul life the following day, we need the impetus received by experiencing a reflection of the planetary cosmos during the night. On awakening, the after-effect of what we experienced in these reflections of planetary movement at night is implanted or instilled in us. And this is what connects the cosmos with our individual life. If this resonance of our nightly experiences was not present in us when we wake up in the morning, the powers we need could not stream into us in the right way to endow us with proper awareness.

From this you can see that it is mistaken of some people to complain about chronic insomnia. Usually, this is major self-deception. But I don't want to discuss this at present, since those subject to this illusion won't believe you. They think they really aren't asleep whereas in fact their sleep is just abnormal; they believe their soul is not outside their body and fails to experience planetary existence. In fact they are in a condition which, while dulled, nevertheless enables them to experience the same as anyone else does who sleeps well. But as I said, I don't want to discuss this right now.

In general it is true to say that we pass through a cosmic life during the second stage of sleep. As I said a moment ago, in ancient times prior to the Mystery of Golgotha, mystery centres disseminated impulses that endowed people with the strength to overcome their anxiety, to resist fragmentation and to undergo what was necessary in a healthy way. This strength was one enabling them to enter into an experience of the planets rather than to go on dwelling in that of fragmentation. Their anxiety originated in the passage through fragmentation; and their experience of being amongst the planets was vouchsafed to them by the strength they brought with them from their experience of the previous day. Since the Mystery of Golgotha, and by directing their attention to the events of this Mystery, people are now able to gain the power that was previously given them through the ancient mysteries. Anyone who experiences the Mystery of Golgotha with the necessary inwardness of soul will find a strong guide in Christ at the moment when his soul enters the realm of anxiety during sleep. Thus in the Christ experience modern humankind has what a more ancient humanity drew from the mysteries.

Passing on from this stage of sleep I have just described, we then enter another, which, since I have dwelled longer on the planetary experience, I will describe to you now in a simpler way, hoping you will not take this amiss. Following an experience of the planets we enter into an experience of the fixed stars. Having dwelt in a reflection of the planetary movements during the second stage of sleep we now live in the constellations of the fixed stars, primarily in a kind of copy of the constellations of the fixed stars in the zodiac. This experience of the fixed star constellations of the zodiac is a very real one during the third stage of sleep. Here we also begin to experience a distinction between the sun as a planet and as a fixed star. Nowadays people do not understand why the sun was regarded in ancient astronomy both as a planet and also as a fixed star. In the second stage of sleep, we really do experience the sun as possessing planetary attributes. Here we become aware of its very distinctive position in relation to human experience on earth. Then we also become aware of the sun as it relates to the other constellations, thus the zodiac. In other words, we immerse ourselves in the cosmos in a still more intensive way than was true of the previous stage of sleep. We have an experience of the fixed stars, and arising from this we gain still deeper, more important impulses for our experiences the following day than is possible from the planetary experience alone. The planetary experience, if I may put it like this, fires our respiratory and circulatory processes. But the after-effect of the fixed star experience is what then, during the day, fires substance processes, ones imbued with the substance they require, so that they become ongoing processes of nutrition for the organism. Nutrients are impelled through the organism at apparently the most material level, though in fact this is reliant on powers higher than the mere movements of blood circulation. As physical human beings our soul and spirit are dependent on the way in which different substances circulate in us, and this is connected, if I may put it like this, with the highest heavens, and with the fact that at this third stage of sleep we feel after-images of the fixed star constellations within our soul-spiritual nature—just as, when awake, we can feel our stomach or lungs within us. Just as, during the day, our body is an inwardly mobile one filled with respiratory movements and circulatory movements, so in the night our soul, the substance of our soul, is something that has inner after-images of the planetary movements. And in the same way that we have the stomach, lungs and heart in us during the day, so at night we have the fixed star constellations which become our interior. In this third stage of sleep, therefore, we really become cosmic beings. This third stage of sleep is the deepest; and from it we gradually return to waking life. Why do we return? We would not do so if powers did not inform our soul and lead us back into our physical organism.

I have described to you in many different ways how we can address these powers, and today I wish to do so from the cosmic perspective. Becoming aware of the fixed star experience through the faculty of Intuition, we also become aware that the powers leading us back into our physical organism are moon powers—that is, the spiritual quality corresponding to what appears to us as the physical image of the moon. Naturally this is irrespective of whether it happens to be full moon or some other quarter, for, in spiritual terms, the moon can also shine through the earth. It does have something to do with the moon's visible metamorphoses, but this would lead us into far more subtle distinctions, beyond the scope of today's considerations. Generally one can say that it is the moon's powers that lead us back again. You see, just as our soul is imbued by the planetary forces during sleep, and by the forces manifesting in the constellations of the fixed stars—is imbued by these powers and remains so since these things go on working in our waking life—so we are also always imbued by the spiritual powers in the cosmos corresponding to the physical moon. These moon forces lead us back. In reality, the process involved is extremely complex. The following is one way to express it. If you stretch a piece of elastic, this can reach a certain point and must then contract again. Similarly, in a sense we stretch the moon powers to a certain point, at which we must return. This is accomplished in the third stage of sleep. The moon forces, which are in general intimately connected with leading the soul and spirit into the physical world, lead us back through the second stage to the first again.

You see, all the powers of initiative we posses in our thinking and feeling during waking life are the after-effect of the fixed star experience during sleep. All the powers of thinking and feeling we bear in us as powers of synthesis, as the powers of wisdom and intelligence, are an after-effect of the planetary experience. But what streams into daily life from our nightly experience of the cosmos has to pass through the body. The fixed star experience quivers into our waking life via the transformation of nutrients. The nutrients in our body would not reach the brain in a way that enabled us to develop powers of initiative if this whole process were not fired by our nightly experience of the fixed stars. And we would be unable to think rationally if our blood circulation and breathing during the day were not informed by the after-effects of our planetary experiences.

Such things are always only drawn in rough outline, and generally true; in the case of people who suffer from severe insomnia, seemingly contradicting what I have described, we have to study and explain the associated abnormalities. If we properly grasp these truths there is no contradiction here. But such general truths allow us to explain fully each individual instance. We can only understand the real nature of the human being if we become fully aware that we do not live only within the skin of our physical body but also in the whole world. It is just that our life within the whole world is hidden from ordinary awareness. In waking life, this is greatly dulled. At most, in our general sensitivity to light, we can experience something of our involvement in all the life of the cosmos; and perhaps in other, albeit very dim feelings, we can sense our rootedness in the cosmos during waking life. Yet all such intimations fall silent so that we can elaborate our individual consciousness during the day, and so that we are not disturbed by what plays into our experience from the cosmos. During the night this is reversed, and then we experience the cosmos, albeit an after-image of cosmic experience. But it is a faithful reflection of it, as I have described—a really cosmic experience. And because we must pass through this cosmic life at night, our waking consciousness is dulled and dimmed in consequence.

As humanity continues to evolve, human beings will increasingly live their way into the cosmos. A time will come when we feel ourselves to dwell in sun, moon and stars in the same way that at present we are aware of being on earth. And then we will look back to earth from the cosmos in the same way that we now look out into the cosmos from the earth during waking life. But the kind of perception we then have will be a very different one.

Anyone who honestly desires to grasp the full scope of evolution must be aware that human consciousness is itself involved in evolution, and that the bodily consciousness that we possess at our current stage of development is a transitionary stage towards another form of consciousness—which in fact is nothing other than the soul reflection of realities we already experience every night. We need these because our waking life can be truly sustained only by their after-effect. Our further evolution will consist in this: the unconscious at work in us today will become our possession as conscious awareness also during normal life. For this to happen, though, people will need to find their way into spiritual science; for just as we have to go in a certain direction when we swim, so our ordinary consciousness today needs a direction in which to go. We cannot simply let ourselves be carried, as is the case when we practise ordinary cognition. We need a direction, and this can only be given by anthroposophic spiritual science since it reveals, to the extent necessary today, things already living in human beings, of which they are as yet unaware. They need to receive this into their awareness, for otherwise they will have no real experience of progressing in the cosmos.

Today I have described part of what is today discarded from ordinary knowledge and relegated to the concept of the 'unconscious'. In my next lecture, similarly progressing from unconscious states we pass through in sleep, I will try to describe the human experiences that underlie birth and death.

LECTURE 2

STUTTGART, 14 OCTOBER 1922

Last time[2] I spoke to you of a realm of unconscious experience—
that is, of things that remain hidden to ordinary consciousness in the
form it exists today. I spoke about sleep, trying to describe to you in
some detail what the human soul experiences between falling asleep and
waking up again. Since what the soul experiences at night involves
experiences in the world of spirit, as you will have seen, it may have been
apparent to you that these human soul experiences are clear manifestations of the soul's eternal, unfading existence. You know of course
that insight into such supersensible experiences can be gained by means
I have often described to you verbally here, as well as in my books
Knowledge of the Higher Worlds, Occult Science and so forth. And you also
know that the kind of knowledge available to ordinary human consciousness can be developed into faculties of Imagination, Inspiration
and Intuition. Unconscious experiences that the soul has during sleep
are in a sense illumined by the power acquired by the perceiving human
soul if it develops these faculties. The same path of development,
however, also enables us, to some degree, to study an aspect of
unconscious human experience of which sleep is only a reflection or
image—that aspect of experience from which the human soul departs
when it enters physical earth existence at birth or, let us say, at conception, and which it enters again when it removes itself from physical
existence on earth at death. Today I will offer some intimations at least
of what underlies the events of birth or conception, and death, as far as
the life of the human spirit and soul is concerned.

When we develop the faculty of imaginative cognition—which I will not describe again here since I have often done this, and also shown how it can be developed—the first thing we encounter is our physical life on earth lying spread out before us in a single great tableau. In ordinary physical consciousness our earthly life only exists in our soul as memory. What is this memory? It consists of pictures, albeit ones which by their very nature point to experiences we have undergone since birth, or since a point in time somewhat after our birth. Yet our ordinary mode of knowledge today cannot regard these pictures as developing an existence independent of the body. Modern scientists are quite correct in saying that these memory pictures are dependent on the physical body's constitution. They are right to suggest that such memory is not present in early infancy but gradually develops along with the physical organism, and fades again too when our human physical organism approaches the evening of its days. Likewise, in post-mortem examinations in the case of certain diseases, they can study how memory loss is caused by certain disorders of the physical organism. Science has no final answers in this field as yet; but if we study the relevant results of physically-based research, we can see that it will eventually be possible to demonstrate that ordinary memory pictures are bound to the physical human organism. These memories of our life however—separate memory pictures we can look back on as we stand within the current of our experience—are not what is meant when we speak of how the faculty of Imagination perceives the great tableau of our life spread out before us, in so far as this life is soul-spiritual in nature. What we perceive here by imaginative cognition is very far from the abstract memory pictures stored in ordinary memory. The faculty of Imagination experiences instead an active, organic life that is not passive like memory pictures but has an inner vigour like the forces of growth at work in our organism when, in assimilating external substances as food, we transform them in a wonderful way into what we need to constitute our organism. What lives and works in us creatively in this process is different from what exists in a more passive way in mere memory pictures. Consider thoughts, which illumine our awareness. Certainly, we owe an infinite amount to the thinking capacity we develop in earthly existence, and only become human, really, and fully aware of our human dignity by virtue of this. Yet these are only fleeting images, bound to our physical organism as the flame is to the candle wax. When, by contrast, we use imaginative cognition to perceive the soul-spiritual life underlying physical existence on earth and see a wondrous tableau unfolding before us, there is nothing passive about this but it is inwardly alive. Spreading before us as qualities of soul and spirit, our direct vision of soul shows it to be, nevertheless, as real as an object of the outer world which our eyes perceive as red. In imaginative cognition we can say that we now not only possess thoughts that flare up in our awareness, but in fact become conscious of the very powers at work within our organism.

I was taken to task severely for once writing what was thought an absurd notion in my little book *The Spiritual Guidance of Mankind and Humanity*. There I stated that all the adult's wisdom accomplishes less than the wisdom of the small child, though this wisdom lives in him unconsciously. Simply look, with the most scholarly and educated human knowledge, at a human brain or the whole human organism in the first years of childhood, and discern how the infant first inwardly configures himself. Even the work of the most brilliant sculptor pales into insignificance compared to the vigorous sculptural activity accomplished by the child's powers of soul and spirit as he shapes and forms his brain. If we reflect on this and understand it we gain real insight into the wisdom that holds sway here: a vigorous wisdom rather than one stored away in the human head for explaining the world—a wisdom that contains an organism of soul-spiritual powers which hour by hour, really, continue to penetrate the child's outer organism so as to make him fully human. Just try for a moment to hold in your mind a fleeting picture of what is at work there (in such majestic wisdom that our reason and intellectual wisdom is left far behind), of what is at work here in the child and must work for long years out of the unconscious. Think, for instance, of the wondrous edifice of human language incorporated into the child. Try to form an image—albeit only an abstract one—of this active wisdom up to the point when we become sufficiently conscious of ourselves to make use of our reason and intellect; at which point, one can say, our reason creates an ephemeral wisdom in imitation of that greater wisdom which has first formed us out of inmost universal potencies. But we must also realize that at the same time as we develop human intellectual reason in what I would call the upper stratum of our being, what worked as a wonderful sculptor in us during childhood and elaborated our organism continues to hold sway in the lower strata of our human nature. And this founding system, this organism of powers, is what imaginative perception surveys in a whole, unified tableau. Our imaginative faculty therefore does not see abstract memory pictures before it, which cannot be said to remain once the organism decays into its constituents since they are bound to the organism, but instead it perceives the system of powers that built up this organism and are therefore not bound to it; they are bound to it as little as the creative brilliance of the sculptor is bound to the material he shapes. For the sculptor's material to become what it does, it must first be shaped by his configuring energy. For us to form the physical organism we possess in earth existence, these extra-telluric, super-sensible powers must underlie our physical life as soul-spiritual organization.

This is the first perception we acquire when we rise to imaginative cognition.

But the moment we are able to perceive what works in us as spirit and soul during our life on earth and is not merely dependent on the physical organism but rather configures and shapes it, we also become able to look away from our earthly existence, to abstract from it, to use a rational expression, in the same way that we can abstract or extrapolate from a thought in ordinary life. Through meditative exercises I have often described, we have to attain the power not just to look away from a thought or image, not just suppress it, but to root out what we have first energetically acquired in our perception of the soul and spirit working upon earthly existence, root out this tableau of thoughts from our consciousness. As soon as we become able, in what I would call a perceiving selflessness, a perceiving altruism, to root out also from our inner vision what we ourselves are as soul and spirit during earthly life, then our truly eternal soul-spiritual nature appears before our awareness; in fact, what we were before we descended from soul-spiritul worlds into physical life appears before our awareness as actual soul-spiritual being. We learn to look upon ourselves as human soul-spiritual entelechy in pre-birth existence—learn to speak of this pre-earthly existence not just in general, abstract phrases but to perceive its development. And some aspects of this development are what I wish to speak of today.

Here, in our earthly life, we feel ourselves connected with our physical body, or at least we do during waking life. However dim a sense of connection it is, this does exist and we become especially aware of it when something in our physical body is not working properly—if we fall ill in some way. In this case we not only feel the physical body as a dim, generalized experience of being alive but also sense its separate parts. Depending on the disorder, we get a stronger sense, say, of our lungs, stomach, heart or head. Ordinarily, this is all submerged in a vague sense of being alive. But if ever our state of health is compromised, we have an opportunity to become more aware of distinct organs. In waking consciousness between birth and death we sense ourselves within our being as belonging to our physical body, to everything enclosed within our skin. But the moment we are not bound up with the physical body in this way, when we experience our soul-spiritual existence *before* we entered upon physical existence on earth, then we no longer have the self-evident sense of an interior composed of our physical body or its limbs. Nevertheless, we still have a sense of interiority. I described in the first lecture how the soul experiences inner pictures during sleep even though it remains unconscious of them. But in the condition in which the soul dwelt before it descended from soul-spiritul existence into physical life on earth, it was aware of a different kind of interior life. This awareness of a different interiority is merely concealed, veiled by the fact that in physical life our body also becomes an organ of perception, obscuring soul perception that can only exist in so far as the soul is free of the body. In this latter condition, what the soul experience as its interior life is now not what is enclosed within our physical skin but instead the configuration of the cosmos. Just as we are bound up in our physical existence with our lungs, stomach, heart and other bodily organs, so in supersensible existence we are bound up with what otherwise appears to us, to our eyes and other sense organs, as the external world of the cosmos. What we perceive as outer world around us during earthly existence becomes our inner world when we dwell in extra-telluric existence. And then, from this supersensible realm between death and a new birth, we look upon earthly life as an external world. In the same way that we dwell in the flesh, if you like, of our lungs, heart and so forth, so we are incorporated, before we descend to physical life on earth, in the planetary movements, the fixed star constellations, the powers that actively infuse the cosmos, all of which later appear to us as outer reflection, as the wide universe around us, when we once more live on earth.

There is no need to be misled by the idea that the external world is anyway a single world for people on earth dwelling in separate bodies. The truly significant thing is that we have one world together when we live in extra-telluric existence, and that the world possessed by one person is the same there as that possessed by another. Here, in life on earth, we are spatially separate because each of us is enclosed within our skin, whereas after death we maintain our distinct existence through inner strength of soul. In extra-telluric existence each person is an individual too, but is then separated not by space but by inner, cohering powers of soul. Yet into these cohering powers flows something that spiritually corresponds to the universe we see surrounding us in the physical reflections of the sun, moon, planets and fixed stars.

Here, in earthly life, we look at another person and see only the form of his face, the light in his eyes, the movements of his body. And yet since we ourselves are also beings of soul and spirit it dawns on us that a soul and spirit are alive in these forms of his face, his gaze, the pink of his skin and his movements. In the same way, someone able to look upon the soul and spirit of the world will see that modern astronomy is incorrect in its view of the sun and moon, the fixed stars, the planets and their movements as being only physical phenomena. Such a view is really the same as saying that the movements of our facial muscles say, or of our eyelashes, are merely external shifts of position and not the expression of sentience and spirit. If we can see the soul and spirit in the world we will recognize that the movements of sun and moon are as much the expression of a physiognomy of soul and spirit as are a person's facial expressions. The movements of the planets are likewise expressions of soul-spiritual occurrences in the same way that impulses of soul and spirit become manifest in our limbs and bodily movements. As supersensible beings, before we descend into earthly existence, we live in these soul-spiritual foundations of what appears to us in the physical reflection of the outer physical sun, the outer physical moon, the stars and their motions; we live in this soul and spirit in the cosmos that corresponds to each individual person's soul and spirit. As a person living on earth I know that lungs and heart are alive inside me; and as a super-telluric human being before I have descended into the physical, sensory world in order to configure my physical body, I know that the sun and moon live within me—although not as a sensory, earthly reflection of sun and moon but rather their underlying reality of spirit and soul. The whole divine, spiritual world works through me and lives within me while my human existence is still in a super-earthly sphere. To understand this gives us a deep reverence for the reality of the whole life of the universe with which we are interwoven, for then we gain insight into the wonderful interconnections between the human being and the cosmos. In considering the human being as we stand here in physical, earthly existence, we come to see that the confines of our skin enclose not only what can be physically discerned, and what the anatomist can dissect and diagnose after death, but also the ultimate goal of all cosmic life. The marvellous saying of primordial religions— that we are made in the image of God himself[3]—acquires a new, infinitely resonant meaning. And knowledge gained through the faculty of Inspiration teaches us to see what we actually experience in pre-earthly existence in relation to the divine spiritual powers on which the whole cosmos is founded.

In considering only earthly human life, we speak first of the human embryo which develops in the womb and then, after birth, into the form of the growing child. Naturally the embryo is seen here as something small that gradually increases in size. In our pre-earthly existence we also live in a kind of embryo, or germinal state, but this embryo involves an experience of the whole cosmos of soul and spirit. Here we have in a sense become one with the soul-spiritual cosmos: divine, spiritual powers indwell us, live and work within us, permeate us and configure in us the grandeur of a spirit germ that contains in itself the powers that must pass through spiritul existence until the time of birth, or con-ception, so that they can emerge again in earthly life when, as its inner sculptor, we need to shape and elaborate our own physical organism. If we grasp this we become aware of the miraculous nature of this physical organism, for, as the goal of the cosmic germ of our inner life, we can experience its immeasurable grandeur through fully conscious soul-spiritual vision. We acquire our physical embryo from the physical world, but our spiritual germ comes to us from the spiritual world. And before we descended to physical earth existence, we were, you can say, a soul-spiritual embryo poured out into the whole world, which subsequently united with the physical embryo that receives us as we come down into earth existence.

Through the faculty of Inspiration we can gain insight into our pre-earthly cosmic existence. Just as we know ourselves to be one with our physical organism here, this further insight shows us to be one with the whole world. Here, in this world, we look upon the external manifestations of spirit within nature and in human life, and have an intimation of the divine spirit behind these sensory phenomena. In pre-earthly existence we are imbued, infused and interwoven with this divine, spiritual existence; and as it lives within us, it implants in us the powers that draw us towards physical existence on earth. Just as we raise our eyes here to the wonderful, star-strewn heavens so, in gazing from extra-telluric existence, we look upon the wondrous edifice of the physical human being living on earth. Let's put it like this: we look up from the earth to the heavens in our physical existence on earth, but gaze from the heavens to the earth in our pre-earthly existence. And then we can grasp the earth as it ought really to live within us—as the work of the gods. All this is immediate experience initially in our pre-earthly life.

But once we have passed through this pre-earthly existence, divine, spiritual beings withdraw from us human beings at a certain point. As yet there is no natural world around us, and in this soul-spiritual existence we do not yet have physical eyes or physical organs and therefore would anyway be unable to see a natural world. Around us still is something like a shimmer of divine spirit. This is a decisive turning point in our pre-earthly life: first we experience ourselves as immediately rooted in divine, spiritual existence, as pervaded by it; and then comes a moment when although our eyes of spirit still gaze on a world of spirit around us we no longer live with divine beings but instead they reveal themselves to us, are apparent to us, through their deeds. This manifestation of spirit and soul is only a reflection of what we ourselves previously experienced. In other words we leave the sphere of direct experience for one of manifestation or appearance. And gradually, as we enter this realm of manifestation, we realize that divine, spiritual beings have withdrawn from our immediate experience and now we can only perceive their appearance. They are still there for us certainly, but only as perceived by our eyes of spirit and soul. At this moment of our pre-earthly soul-spiritual existence there awakens in us something I can only compare with a desire living in our physical organism. We are inwardly infused with a growing desire as the pre-birth world around us becomes appearance rather than direct experience. Only now, really, do we feel a sense of self distinct from our surroundings. We depart from cosmic experience and from an experience of our own human nature which, as cosmic and not just human beings, we possessed for a period of life between death and new birth, during which universal consciousness and a consciousness of humanity were one for us. Now this universal awareness and awareness of our human nature start to sunder so that we no longer experience the world directly but only manifesting at one remove as a separate interior life emerges in us. Previously our inner life was one with the world but now an interior experience forms that is separate from our surroundings, and this first manifests as an inner desire, a wish, a will. A wishing, a will, a desire always has a focus or object. This wishing, will and desire homes in on our future life on earth, which we will descend to again after a while. We are filled by visions of our future life on earth, and with this we absorb powers that then become unconscious when we pass through foetal development in the womb. First we possess these visions consciously, but this consciousness is increasingly dulled; and a point arrives when our desire grows strong and when even the manifestation of the divine, spiritual world in which we were previously alive and active grows ever darker. The world of spirit around us becomes ever more shadowy. What previously shone brightly as effulgence of divine revelation grows darker and more shadowy. As these outer spiritual surroundings grow obscured the inner powers of desire become all the stronger and more insistent; the surroundings of our spiritual existence darken while our interior world becomes more vigorous. And after some time, this vigorous inner world of ours deprives us completely of an awareness of our future life on earth. For a period not long preceding earthly conception, our view of earthly existence is darkened and obscured, whereas before we were able to gaze upon it as the vivid goal, the majestic cosmic tableau within which we were living. Now, though, our view of the earth vanishes and is replaced instead by a different sight. Not long before we descend to the earth we lose our vision of the earth and instead gain vision of the etheric world. Our gaze opens to etheric phenomena that conceal light within them, and life forces: everything spread out in space but working not centrifugally from the earth up into space but as it were centripetally from the world's periphery to the earth, the etheric pouring into the earth. An etheric world becomes spiritually visible around us as if in a great cosmic mist within which the most diverse forms can be seen. And from this etheric world, with the power we still possess, that of desire, we can draw our own ether body from the universal etheric, the cosmic mist; we can form it and, in doing so, we configure with this etheric body a reflection of what we once were previously in the soul-spiritual world. We incorporate this ether body into what we meet coming towards us as genetic inheritance, the physical substantiality with which our forefathers endow us; and we descend to earthly existence.

I have only briefly outlined what we perceive by the faculties of Imagination and Inspiration when we enlarge our awareness beyond the confines of ordinary, earthly consciousness. During earth evolution, as we progressed to the state of consciousness we possess today, which is strictly bound up with physical corporeality, we lost our original state of awareness as I have often stated. I have pointed out that history really only describes the outward aspects of humanity's life on earth, and that we also need a soul history which would show that we have not always had our modern state of consciousness. Today people use the rational mind alone to create a synthesis of what their sensory organs perceive, and can only raise to their awareness what rises from their physical nature. The further back we trace past eras of humanity, the more we see that people once had a kind of primordial clairvoyance, albeit dreamlike in nature. What we can today acquire by the faculties of Imagination and Inspiration is a fully conscious perception, really just as conscious as mathematical thinking. In a former time people had only a dull, dreamlike awareness, although it was one imbued with wisdom. These people of a former era not only sensed what modern human beings experience when they reflect upon themselves but also had a clairvoyant feeling of what I described to you yesterday. If we return to the most ancient Egyptian era, and still further back to times of which no historical records are extant—of which only the kind of history I presented in my *Occult Science* can tell us—we discover human beings who could gaze upon their pre-earthly existence without the need for exercises such as I have often described to you. They could do so because something like a memory of this pre-earthly existence still lived in their souls. Today people have acquired their freedom at the expense of having only a faculty of memory in the form of abstract thoughts, of events and experiences during their earthly life. In primordial times, human beings could gaze into their souls and draw from within not only such memories of their current physical life but also soul pictures of what I have described. Today we can recall by our ordinary faculties what we experienced 20 or 30 years ago; and in the same way a person of more ancient times could in a sense recall what he had experienced in pre-earthly existence, and what I have presented to you today as the findings of spiritual science. In those ancient times a person was as certain of his pre-earthly existence as you are certain that you were not born yesterday, and had this certainty by virtue of what he experienced within his soul. This gave him the assurance that the intrinsic nature of his soul experience already existed in a soul-spiritual world before he descended to physical earthly existence and that this entelechy passes through the portal of death and is independent of the physical organism, both building up the physical organism for earthly existence and entering a continued existence after passing over the threshold of death.

But what is it exactly that continues on after physical existence on earth? The thoughts we experience here on earth are bound up with the physical organism. By contrast the expressions of will that spring up so wonderfully from within us in a way we can only grasp in thoughts and ideas are all deeply unconscious for the soul, like the events of sleep themselves. We know we wish to lift a hand or an arm but have no idea what actually occurs between the motivating thought and the actual lifting of an arm, in this whole intermediate miracle leading to the tensing of a muscle. The will that rises in us remains largely unconscious, or in other words is only reflected in our conscious mind. But if we study this life of will through the faculties of Inspiration and Intuition, we can make huge discoveries.

In physical earthly existence as considered only from an external perspective, we perform actions which a materialistic age sees fit to believe are fully contained within this physical realm and have no further significance beyond it. But if we can look down into the true will nature of the human being, which remains unconscious to the ordinary waking mind, we find as we progress through our earthly existence something taking shape that is composed of an evaluation of our actions, and this does not arise from thinking but from will. In the physical realm we say that an action is good or bad, that we are satisfied or dissatisfied with it. We might believe that this is only an abstract judgement which we add to the action. When we use true faculties of Inspiration and Intuition to gaze into the nature of the human will, we see that what is here only a thought there becomes an actual being; we see how our evaluation of satisfaction or dissatisfaction with an action inwardly becomes a reality of the will, and how a whole being takes shape in the depths of our human nature. The countenance of this being, if I may put it like this, depends on the nature of our actions here in earthly existence. If we have done bad deeds which a fully developed human conscience cannot be happy with, a being ugly in countenance develops within us, whereas if we have done deeds we can be satisfied with, a being with a sympathetic countenance emerges. So you see, the evaluation of our actions gives rise to an inner being in us. When we are children our thoughts are still working to shape our physical organism, after which they become abstract. And as our thoughts increasingly become dependent on the physical organism, become if you like a kind of corpse in our physical organism—for they are not alive, they are dead thoughts—so at the same time our moral nature stirs below in the unconscious, and we elaborate this ourselves during our lifetime. This moral being exists and unites with our I being, and it is this moral being that we then bear with us over the threshold of death when we enter the world of spirit. As we cross the threshold of death and emerge into the world of spirit—you will find an account of this in my book *Theosophy*—we have laid aside our physical body and dwell in our etheric body, still retaining there an awareness of our earthly deeds. But this awareness starts to be infused with cosmic, universal awareness. The etheric body resolves into the general world ether. Just as we gather it together before birth, so now it dissolves in the world ether. What I call the astral body in my book *Theosophy* is what we gradually live our way back into the cosmos with, at the same time united with our newly formed moral and spiritual organism. It is this we initially bear out with us as we find our way back into the cosmos.

And now a task arises for us, connected with what I said about human sleep in our last lecture. I spoke of how we have the strength during sleep to re-enter our physical organism by virtue of what we can call moon forces. These moon forces are what bring us back into physical earth existence—and do so each and every morning. We find ourselves within this sphere of moon forces after we have laid aside our physical and etheric bodies; but that encompassing universal consciousness I described to you cannot be acquired within these moon forces since here, through this moral earth organism, we have something that still ties us to the earth. We have to detach ourselves from the moon forces, leaving behind in the moon sphere what we ourselves have woven into being from the moral quality of our actions, from all that we ourselves accomplished as moral or immoral actions. We have to leave this behind in the moon sphere and penetrate further into the sun sphere, the world of stars. Now we must not only enter the reflection of it, as I described in relation to sleep, but the real world of sun and stars as we detach ourselves from the moon sphere.

Primordial humankind also had a clairvoyant awareness of this, and could speak of things we can only discover today by developing our powers of soul and spirit. Primordial human beings could speak of these things through the natural, elemental powers innate in them. But they were at the same time always guided by the teachings that issued from the mysteries, as we are guided today by science, by various educational establishments—which of course did not exist in more ancient times. The perception of life before birth and after death was in a sense governed by the higher knowledge of initiates of the mysteries. The latter knew by inner experience that the human being cannot release himself from the moon sphere after death by his own powers, and they passed this insight on to the rest of primordial humanity. The initiates knew that a spiritual being must come from the cosmos to meet the human soul, and that the sun is the outward, physical reflection of this being. This being had to come to meet them, had to draw them away from the moon sphere. They had to leave behind what they bore with them as guilt from their sojourn on earth, and were then led up into the guilt-free sphere of the cosmos by what all ancient initiates called the great sun being, which was marvellously described in all the ancient mysteries. In those days people were told that they needed the strength that came towards them from the heavens. But at that time people had a very different organization, as I have said, and possessed inner clairvoyant powers. While on earth they still knew from inner vision that there was a supersensible world. They really had no fear of death, for what was death? An experience in life, and part of it. And they saw that they possessed something within them that was untouched by death, something in their body; and because it dwelt in their body they could see how the sun being came towards them, whose help they could welcome after death.

Implicit in the earthly advance of humanity is the fact that human beings have lost perception of their eternal nature. Humankind has acquired an intellectual mind completely bound up with the physical body and dependent on it. Our earthly consciousness depends on the way our physical body is organized; and this earthly consciousness obscures our vision of the world of spirit, even before we are born and also after we die. Unlike primordial humankind, or even people in ancient Egypt, it is not the case today that we bring a certain light with us when we cross the threshold of death to illumine the surrounding space—if I can put this metaphorically—of the supersensible world, or rush headlong towards the lofty sun being who comes to lead us away from the moon sphere. Back in those times they possessed something within them between birth and death that enabled them to perceive this sublime sun being.

There is no need to feel awkward about this expression: based on their insights, the ancient initiates inevitably called this being the sublime sun being. But a time came in humanity's evolution when people would have lost the capacity to penetrate worlds after death that they must penetrate if they do not wish to lose themselves. On the other hand, humanity had to advance towards the only kind of consciousness in which one can acquire human freedom. This would have meant humanity falling into a terrible condition at a certain point, a complete separation from the supersensible world. The perfection they acquire here on earth, that predestines them for freedom, would have led to their loss of the world of spirit: they would have been unable to find a connection with the spiritual being who draws them away and releases them from what connects them with the earth in their life after death.

What therefore came to sustain humanity's further true evolution? No abstract knowledge or theoretical doctrine could help here, but only that same being who had formerly dwelt in supersensible worlds and came to meet human beings in the supersensible realm between death and a birth. The only thing that could help was for this being to descend to the earth so that human beings can find a connection with him while still on earth. And this descent is the event of Golgotha. The Christ being descended and took earthly existence upon himself in Jesus of Nazareth.

In our earthly life we gain a connection with Christ Jesus. Enhancing our earthly consciousness by looking towards Christ Jesus, and feeling sympathy and compassion in relation to the Mystery of Golgotha, awareness flows into our earthly consciousness that we are not just an I that can be free. We can fill ourselves with the Pauline saying 'Not I but Christ in me',[4] and make this a truth here in earthly life. The I we acquire here would otherwise constrict us and separate us from the supersensible world; but when this earthly consciousness connects us with what entered earth existence through the Christ being's sacrifice, we can bear this I through death. The capacity we formerly had only by virtue of possessing elementary powers is something we are now endowed with, since the Mystery of Golgotha, by the connection of our mind and soul as earthly human beings with the Christ, with the Mystery of Golgotha, which safeguards our life as we pass through the portal of death. You see, the consciousness we acquire through the physical body would inevitably be lost again when we relinquish this body and we would not find our way through worlds of spirit. But if on earth we find our guide—the Christ—who passed through the Mystery of Golgotha, and if we have joined our earthly humanity with his spiritual strength in accordance with the Pauline saying 'Not I but Christ in me', then we come living through the portal of death. We can therefore give full seriousness to another Pauline saying—that if Christ had not come to earth,[5] or in other words overcome death, human beings would gain no help from all their faith.

The ancient initiates told people that a super-earthly being would connect with the consciousness that they possessed here by virtue of their whole human nature, and would lead them away from moon existence into the pure, universal existence of the cosmos. Modern initiates must say instead: Consider what occurred through Christ at the Mystery of Golgotha, and take up into your consciousness the substantiality of Christ with all its power! This will pass with you through death and lead you towards the worlds that you must traverse between death and a new birth. In the moon sphere you will leave behind your moral being and only rediscover it when you return there. And your earthly destiny will be a reflection of what you left behind in the moon sphere and then rediscover there.

The things I am telling you have only been available to naturally endowed human enquiry through powers that humanity developed since the last third of the nineteenth century. Previously these powers were more or less obscured. They existed in the ancient times I described, but then in a dreamlike way. In the early Christian centuries people did not possess what we can achieve today through Imagination, Inspiration and Intuition, but they had a natural, atavistic clairvoyance, and there were still old initiates living at the time of the Mystery of Golgotha. They told the people who trusted in them that Christ, who was present in the world they recalled as the period of their pre-earthly existence, and formerly dwelt only in spheres beyond the earth, had descended to earth through the Cross of Golgotha.

This is why, in the first four centuries of the Christian era, in the West also, people very largely focused on the Christ who descended to earth. Everywhere you find that accounts from the early Christian centuries—almost all of which were destroyed—described how the

Christ came down to earth from cosmic worlds of spirit and took on earthly life in the body of Jesus of Nazareth. Very great emphasis was placed in those days on this descent to the earth. But when the old initiates started to die out in the fourth century AD, before the advent of a new initiation science that would appear only in the last third of the nineteenth century, the lack of any direct perception obliged religious authors to set down what they received by way of tradition, and to pass it on. To acquire freedom in their consciousness, humankind needed to forget the old initiation science for a period. As the nineteenth century approached, therefore, humanity increasingly forgot about the descent to earthly existence of the super-earthly Christ being, and his encompassing of this existence in the body of Jesus of Nazareth. In the end, the historical events were all that remained, so that Jesus increasingly came to overshadow Christ in people's awareness. Christ was no longer seen as a supersensible being. Today we must learn anew to speak of the Christ as a supersensible being, understanding what it means that Christ sustains the life of the human soul. The body, you see, has altered during humanity's evolution. Why did ancient people possess a clairvoyant faculty? Because their body was softer and the glands at work in it were more active than ours. Our glands in particular have become harder; and as this hardening progresses, as the human body grows harder and glandular activity grows more sluggish, intellectualism is supported by this, and increasingly develops. Glandular activity in the human body grows more sluggish, and at the same time this body itself becomes extremely useful to the rational mind. And we must acquire our connection with the world of spirit all the more through our soul instead. Initiates in the early Christian centuries still knew all this, but expressed it with a courage nowadays lacking from people's words. They described how people would gradually have become increasingly sick and ailing in body if Christ had not come and endowed them with soul health. In these early Christian centuries, therefore, Christ was revered not in abstractions, as is our practice nowadays, but above all as healer, as the great universal physician, the Redeemer.

We must relearn and re-acquire all these things, but this will only be possible if human beings can gain insight again into the secrets of birth and death. The ability to do so can only be gained on a path of knowledge we develop through faculties of Imagination, Inspiration and Intuition. Gradually we must learn of these secrets, for then we will also already acquire perception of them in our souls.[6]

LECTURE 3

DORNACH, 20 OCTOBER 1922

In observations we began here a short while ago[7] we considered the great events of history, and of human evolution itself on the one hand, and on the other the individual human being. And basically, each can only be properly understood in the light of the other. Today, therefore, I want to add a study of the human being himself to the broad historical perspectives we surveyed, so that these two aspects can in a sense be combined again in the following days. Let us once again describe the human being as anthroposophy sees him, as we have often done in the past. First we distinguish the physical human organism, which is permeated in turn by the etheric organism; then, into this system formed of a physical and etheric organism, the astral organism and the I are incorporated. From the way we enter the state of sleep and return from it to waking life, we can tell that the physical and etheric organisms have a closer mutual affinity, and the astral and I are likewise more closely connected. In the waking state these four aspects of human nature are joined together but separate during sleep so that the mutual connection is stronger between I and astral organism on the one hand and between the physical and etheric organism on the other. In other words, the astral and etheric organisms are not as close-knit, if you like, as the I and the astral bodies, or the physical and etheric bodies.

In studying these things, we will need to picture the way they work and interact. And here I'd like to start from some very specific observations. We look at the world around us—but what does this actually mean? Let's be very factual for a moment. Looking at the world around us means that something impinges on us or affects us. But in considering the whole human being we have to ask what in us the surrounding world is actually affecting.

Though it might appear superficially as if what we see is impinging on our physical organism, this is not the case.

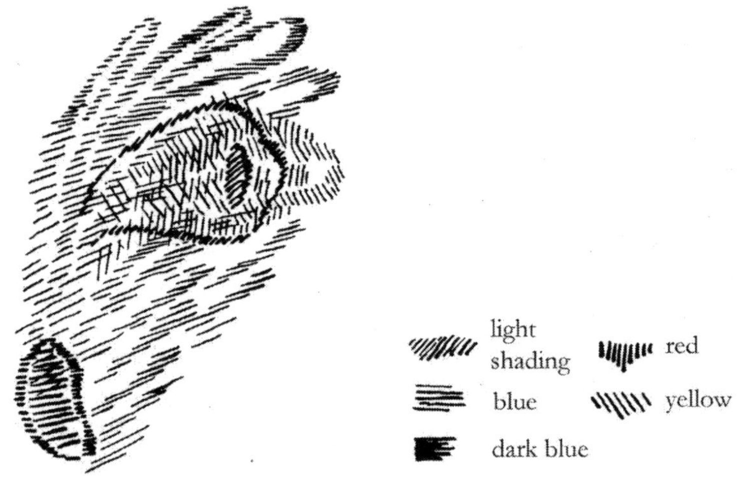

Our physical eye, it is true, is involved when we see something in the world around us [drawing, light shading]. Yes, we have physical eyes, and yet everything that occurs in the physical eye is secondary, whereas the primary occurrence is really an interplay of processes in the I and the astral organism. I'll indicate this here by showing the activity of the I penetrating the eye as yellow—naturally this I also works further into the organism—and the astral organism as red. We have to be clear that the primary occurrence when we see something involves processes in the I and the astral organism. You can recognize this if you consider your own power of vision in a somewhat more intimate, less superficial way. You need only reflect, when you look at the colour red for instance, whether you are able to distinguish between your own self, your I, and this red. You cannot. You are not able to make a distinction between yourself and the red because you *are* this red. It fills your awareness entirely, and you are nothing other than it. It is easier to recognize this is so if you imagine that this red is the only thing you can perceive.

Imagine seeing a big, red surface. In doing so you have to first recall that you are an I, must first detach the I from this experience. But while you're looking at this big, red surface, the red and your I have merged. And the same is true of our astral organism.

Processes in the I and the astral organism must therefore be considered first of all in relation to how we see things. In studying the eye we must consider—and here you see how complex this is—that we have a kidney system, which I'll draw here schematically [dark blue]. This kidney system belongs to our physical organism firstly, and possesses solid parts. As you know, I have often said that there is not so very much solidity in us, not so much that is mineral in nature, for we are 90 per cent water, a column of water if you like. But we do have some solid constituents, which are continually afloat in fluid, in a watery element. Thus we must see the kidney system at the same time as a point of departure for the watery element present not only in the eliminatory function of the kidney system but pervading the whole organism and, among other things, also rising into the eyes.

But this watery element which in a sense radiates outwards from the kidney system, and even streams into the eyes, is not dead but living fluid. You would form a very mistaken idea of the fluid, the watery element in us [drawing, blue] if you were to imagine that this water within the living human organism is the same as the water in a brook. This is not so. The brook contains dead water while the fluid in the human organism is alive. Not only the blood plasma but all fluid within us is alive. And finely dissolved in the waves, if you like, of this fluid element are also the solid constituents I mentioned earlier, which are borne everywhere through the organism, also as far as the eyes. On these waves of the inner, fluid element the human being's etheric organism also shines into the eyes. Two different things now meet in the eye: our etheric organism [blue] pervades it, and then there is the optic nerve. And now the astral picture arising in the human astral body [red] streams into the fluid filled by the etheric organism. And this aspect here [yellow] arises through the I. It streams into it, and then also streams onwards.

This means that in the human eye, and also in the human optic nerve, we have a meeting of the external impression, really first present in the I and the astral body, with the physical body and etheric body from within: the physical body borne on our mineral constituents and the etheric body borne on our fluid constituents.

Now this does not remain with the eye. What the eye mediates shines into the rest of the organism. Vision, we can say, really involves an encounter between the extraordinary complex process at work in the I and astral body on the one hand, and the physical and etheric body confronting them from within the organism—the former in its mineral constituents, and the latter in the waves or currents of living fluid.

What I have here described in relation to vision in fact continually occurs throughout the human organism. On waves of living fluid driven by the physical body the etheric body continually encounters the I-impelled astral body with all its external impressions. And our whole human constitution, our whole very interior situation is dependent on the way in which these two streams encounter each other within us, for they need to encounter each other in the right way. What does 'right' mean in this context? Here, once again, we meet some extremely complex factors. In our head organization [see drawing, p. 37] the head is really a modelled reflection of the powers which we possessed in our pre-earthly existence as being of soul and spirit. The head has been modelled, and develops very early on in the embryo, really only retaining a sculpting capacity. If the human head did not have this modelling or sculpting capacity it would be a dead entity. The human head is a wonderful structure, a faithful image or imprint of the physical, etheric and even the astral body and the I; it models and reflects how these forces enter earthly existence from a super-earthly realm. The head does indeed form itself as an image of cosmic experiences which we undergo in pre-earthly existence, retaining only the power to sculpt and shape. In studying the child we can see that all shaping and modelling power emanates really from his head, shining down into the rest of the organism and giving appropriate plastic shape to his organs as he grows.

What emanates from the head is nothing other than a plastic, shaping power. And when processes such as those involved in vision penetrate the head, they encounter an incipient power which seeks to shape and configure them. What enters through the eyes seeks to assume form inwardly in us. Above all it seeks to shape the nerves, the nervous system so that in a sense a kind of reflection arises within us of the outer impression. So we can put it like this: in this direction [drawing, downward arrows] passing inward from the senses, a shaping power enters. This power seeks in a sense, and subtly, to make us into a sculpted column. This is really how it is: everything we see is trying to make us into a column, in a certain, subtle sense.

Coming to meet this is another power, in this instance from the kidney system, acting in everything I have described [arrows rising from below]. This power continually dissolves what is seeking to assume shape. Reflect on this for a moment. If I try to illustrate this for you, I would have to say: a very subtle image enters from the eye and tries to form a shape, even to the extent of trying to make this a physical configuration. The kind of influence exerted here involves salts that are otherwise dissolved forming conglomerations, trying to become solid salt in a continuing tendency to shape and form. But now, likewise continually, there rises from below a tendency to dissolve this again. Thus we have in the human organism an ongoing inward-penetrating tendency seeking to form a column and something from within that continually dissolves it again.

This process occurring in the encounter of the astral with the etheric, in which the latter is borne towards the astral on waves of fluidity, is immensely important for human life; in fact, it encompasses the whole of it. Imagine for a moment that someone tells you something this evening—for this too is an impression albeit one that arises differently, involves different senses from when you see a red surface. What is communicated to you seeks to assume form or shape within you. If it succeeds in doing so you retain a memory of it. And if your head is of the type that is very keen to salt away every impression, then you'll have a wonderful memory, and can rattle off whatever anyone has told you like a robot. But this is not true of most people since they largely tend to dissolve everything again; and what does this dissolving is the stream of fluid bearing the etheric body and meeting and confronting the plastic, shaping forces. This continual, dissolving current is a warm one in fact. As we study this we become aware of something extremely interesting.

If we wish to possess human rather than robot-type memories that we rattle off mechanically, we ought not to form a solid salt structure whenever someone tells us something. There are people who do this, but they lose their autonomy in the process. Rather than being the person who remembers things, they can start to be driven by them and become mechanical. If one wishes to be an autonomous person, the following process has to unfold.

What another person tells you, or what you read, remains initially in the I and the astral body and now seeks to penetrate through the brain organization, the head organization into the fluid system first of all, and can then consolidate and call forth a kind of mineral-type structure. But it is good that the inner stream arrives and initially extinguishes this so that at most the impression itself penetrates the fluid—though it grows vague and blurred there—and no solid structure is created. Since no solid structure arises, the process remains in the astral body only. Now, when night comes, one falls asleep and the astral body and I depart, taking the impression with them, which gains in strength during sleep [see drawing, right].

Then it enters again when we wake up [left] and is possibly extinguished again; and usually this process is repeated three or four times. Only after the fourth night is the extinguishing power no longer strong enough; and then this impression settles in us as this plastic structure, that is no longer dissolved, and become the basis for memory pictures.

You will say, though, that you remember things you heard yesterday,

 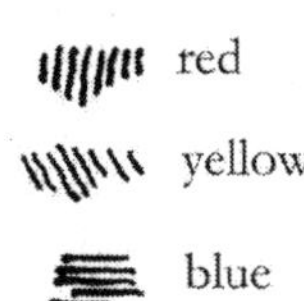

when you haven't yet slept on them a few times. That's quite correct; but that is a different matter. Remembering things you only heard yesterday is due to them still remaining in your astral body, or possibly making an impression in the etheric body. But one does not forget things after just a day, or even after two or three. When something is truly forgotten, the inner, dissolving power is so vigorous after the fourth day that the impression is entirely extinguished—then it really *is* gone. We irretrievably forget something if the strength available can still dissolve it as it recurs in us a fourth time.

This is very interesting, and can be observed by the faculty of Imagination so that we learn how things are retained or not. And this leads us to something else: to understanding that the human head is a much slower customer than the rest of us. In speaking of the threefold human being, with the rhythmic organism in the centre between the neurosensory organism—that is, the head organism—on the one hand, and the system of limbs and metabolism on the other, we can say that the head organism works at a much slower tempo in its whole development and existence than the organism of metabolism and limbs. And while this inner conglomeration [left], this shaping and forming resulting from some impression or other takes, let us say just as an example, a second, the kidney system has in the same amount of time already given four extinguishing impulses—four extinguishing attacks if you like [see drawing, p. 37].

It is interesting that in this encounter I have described, the upward impetus from the kidney system and the downward impetus from external influences relate to each other in the same rhythm as that between breathing and pulse—and that, in fact, there are four dissolving attacks to every entering impression. And it is also due to this that we must sleep on something four times before it becomes solidly enough inscribed in us.

These things cohere in a wonderful way if we can really study the inner configuration of the human organism. But this also relates to something else.

As we rise upwards towards the head in our consideration of the human being, we enter a tempo of life that is four times slower than the one we meet when we look at the digestive organs, say, or the kidney system. The kidney system works speedily, bringing what it inwardly processes through into the etheric realm that floats upon the waves of living water. When we shut our eyes and consciously dull our brain, and then study what streams from the kidneys, we arrive at imaginations that float upon the living water. In other words, we see our own interior in imaginations. This reveals an extremely interesting structure. If you imagine this to be the kidney system [see drawing] you can say that what we're calling the living water streams out from it towards the whole organism.

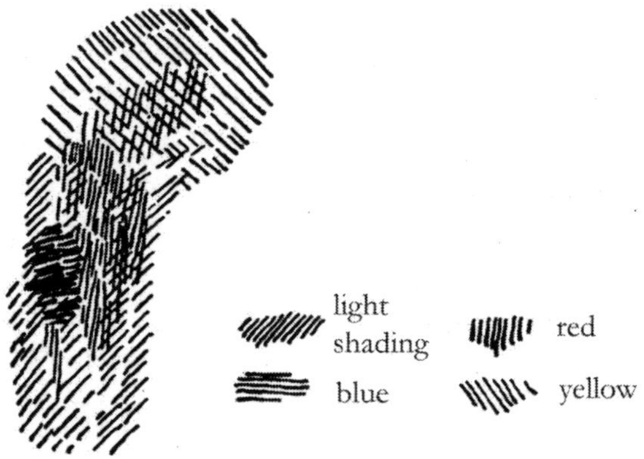

What is eliminated here is only the relatively exhausted excess, which passes outwards. But at the same time this enlivened water, imbued with the etheric organism, goes towards the whole of the rest of the organism. This etheric organization contains plentiful imaginations [red]—is entirely pervaded with them. We can perceive these imaginations as an image of our own organism if we subdue our brain consciousness and all sensory perceptions. This is a healthy process. But if the kidney is diseased, and this leads to a strong irradiation of the life water, all kinds of forms arise in it, giving rise, as we know, to subjective apparitions that can affect people with kidney disease.

The impetus working as I have described—basically an impetus in inner images, through which inner body warmth continually pulses, meeting impressions from without that seek to become sculptural—works four times faster than the influx working inwards from without. And we find this expressed once more in a certain periodicity occurring in our life in so far as we see such periods as issuing from the etheric organism—in other words issuing precisely from what I have drawn here. We speak of seven-year periods in our life: up to second dentition, then sexual maturity and so forth. For instance, at the end of the sixth year of life, when the second teeth are emerging, the physical body approaches the end of its intrinsic action, and then the etheric organism comes more fully into its own, up to the time of sexual maturity. But something issues from the head and opposes what unfolds in these periodic and rhythmic processes from one seven-year period to the next, continually seeking to slow down these processes, since the head proceeds in a far slower way. By the time someone is nearing the end of his 28th year, the head has really only arrived at the point that the rest of the human being achieved at the end of his seventh year. This is a very important secret of the development of a human individual.

Outwardly this comes to expression in the fact that we cannot really think of ourselves as fully grown, both inwardly and outwardly, until our late twenties. Everything issuing from the head only comes to completion then. At the age of 28, the head is really only 7 years old; and so this is something we have in our whole being. In the same way that we have breathing and blood circulation, and the relationship between them, so, as a correlation throughout our life, head processes relate to the processes that emanate from the digestive system and from our whole system of metabolism and limbs. This too has a one-to-four relationship, and is of great significance for life. For instance, it means that everything we teach a child between 7 and 14 only gradually comes to expression in the head; and really not until the age of 35 has everything come to expression in the head, so that the head has caught up and everything has achieved its full resonance there. This takes four times seven years, the first period being that between 7 and 14, the second from 14 to 21, the third from 21 to 28 and the fourth from 28 to 35.

This casts a really vital light on the right way of teaching and educating children. You can see that education must be arranged in a way that takes proper cognizance of these things. If you consider only what the child finds interesting and can absorb between the age of 7 and 14, what catches his attention, then you can teach him what he wishes to take notice of at present. But the processes at work in the system of limbs and metabolism, which initially physically sustain what is absorbed, fade after seven years. And now something must remain, even if the substance sustaining it is gone; it must be accessible to the head and must be adequate to last until the age of 21, when substance has again been replaced. Once more it must last until the age of 28, when the substance has again disappeared, and it must have the capacity to last through until the age of 35. Then finally it will have settled entirely in the ether body, and will not so easily be dispelled from it since this body is not replaced in the same way as physical substance.

So you see how things are interrelated in human life, and we therefore need to know that if we were nothing but a head we would really only be 7 years old by the time we were 28; and only 14 years old by the time we were 35. As far as the intrinsic aim of the human head is concerned, our tranquil development is continually exposed to attack from the system of metabolism and limbs. So if we want to understand human nature we cannot regard the substance of the head as being homogenous with that of the rest of the organism, but must instead see the interplay between the metabolism-limb system and the head organism as a rhythmic relationship that works right into individual organs.

Consider the eye. Here we have the optic nerve on the one hand, and the blood vessels on the other [see drawing, red].

The system of metabolism and limbs is found in the eye in the form of blood vessels, whereas the neurosensory organism is represented by the optic nerve. Now let's take a closer look at the eye, where we find a one-to-four relationship between processes at work in the optic nerve, in the retina, and the tempo of the pulse. In the eye there is a continual intervibration between two different rhythms in a one-to-four ratio, and visual processes depend on this. What occurs in the eye's choroid membrane seeks to dissolve what is trying to consolidate in the nerves. The optic nerve keeps trying to create contoured forms, whereas the choroid membrane, with the blood flowing there, keeps trying to dissolve this.

Things are not as simple as people usually picture them; the eye's arterial vessels have their own network, and the venous capillaries incorporate themselves into this in turn [see drawing, red] so that the one does not connect directly with the other. Specifically in the eye, we can say that the arterial blood streams out in a sense and only then is absorbed by the venous system, giving rise to a gentle outflow and reabsorption in the eye. It is quite mistaken, a great over-simplification, to think that the arterial blood passes directly into the venous blood here. That is not the case. Instead we see a fine outflow followed by absorption. The circulatory rhythm vibrates in this outflow and the breathing rhythm vibrates in the adjoining nerve, and these enter into interplay in the eye. Thus vision really consists of the encounter of these two rhythms in the eye. It is worthwhile reflecting that if these two rhythms were identical we would be unable to see anything.

Imagine you're running alongside a cart. If you run as fast as it is going you will not feel its motion, but if you walk four times slower but still keep holding onto it, you will feel a pull. The cart will carry on, and you will have to hold it back if you wish to slow it down. The same is true in the eye. The function of the optic nerve tries to hold back the rhythm that is four times faster; and in doing so visual perception arises in the same way that you'll feel the cart if you're walking four times slower than it is going. If you walk or run at the same speed, you won't feel anything pulling you.

And how do you experience yourself as an I? By virtue of the fact that your head runs four times more slowly than the rest of your organism.

Here you sense yourself, perceive yourself inwardly because your head functions are slower and out of step with the tempo of the system of limbs and metabolism.

And now there are countless human illnesses and disorders which result from the following. Every organism has a certain measure of equilibrium in this four-to-one rhythm. A certain measure of equilibrium obtains depending on the precise nature of our organism. The relationship is never exactly one to four, you see, but there are all kinds of possible permutations depending on the diverse nature of individuals. A certain ratio holds sway in each human individual, and if this is disrupted—if, say, one to four is the normal relationship for a particular person at a certain time of life but circumstances arise where, instead, it becomes one to four and one-seventh—then the dissolving force grows too vigorous and the person in question cannot develop a sufficient columnar quality. You need only think of conditions involving excessive deliquescence.

The opposite can occur equally, giving rise to conditions that manifest as cramp-type disorders. If the astral vibrates too quickly through the etheric and physical bodies, flickering through them and not grasping them slowly enough, cramps appear.

Consider ordinary cramps or seizures in childhood for instance. These are caused by nothing other than the astral organism and the I not yet properly descending into the physical and etheric organism. The right interplay and relationship still needs to be established. You see, the astral organism and the I at first vibrate too quickly into the organism of limbs and metabolism, and the latter cannot yet properly cope with this. When the vibration occurs in the right way, the astral organism and the I slowly penetrate a piece of the physical and etheric organism. We can say that every astral current always properly grasps a tiny drop of the life water through which the etheric streams. They adjust to one another if the right tempo is present. But if the entering vibration is too rapid [drawing, red, light shading] then the astral gives a jolt to the etheric, and thus also to the life water, giving rise to cramplike conditions—especially in childhood since the proper rhythm for this influx has not yet been established [drawing, red, blue].

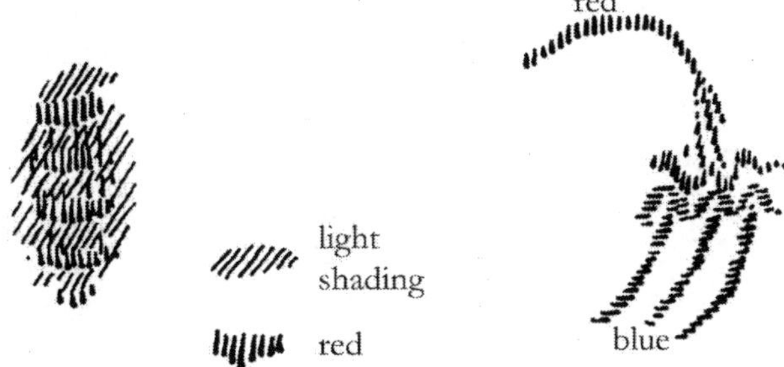

This has far-reaching implications—for instance, we can at least explain a severe disorder, seen as a great problem today, in terms of a particular disruption to the proper harmony of this relationship. I am thinking of the grave condition of polio or infantile paralysis. We thus find an explanation for this disease, although not its cure immediately, since the discord of tempo here is caused by less accessible conditions.

In general we can only gain real insight into the human organism if we can take account of such conditions—knowing that it is not an abstract truth to say we sleep when our I and astral body withdraw from the physical and etheric body, and that what exists outside the physical and etheric body at night contains impulses for a much slower kind of life activity than do the levels of our being that remain behind. In sleep we are almost entirely a being of limbs and metabolism, through into the brain, since then everything that occurs is subject to the sway of the organism of limbs and metabolism.

Now inwardly, in relation to everything subject to the slower rhythm, we are greatly exposed to ahrimanic powers, while all that corresponds to the quicker rhythm has an affinity with luciferic powers. If you take a look at the Group statue[8] you can see that everything ahrimanic in nature there is oriented to the slow rhythm, and therefore the corresponding forms are hardened into stiff, angular ones. Everything of a luciferic nature in this wooden sculpture relates to a fast rhythm, which, because of this rapidity, rounds all the forms—giving them a wavelike rather than sharp, spiky or stiffened appearance. Just by observing the forms themselves you can see the tempo of relationship depicted there between three or four and one.

These things are important for understanding both the healthy and the sick human organism. Science will need this enlargement of view, which can only be provided by what I here call anthroposophical spiritual science. I will continue these reflections and subsequently reconcile them so that we can start to see history arising from human nature and, on the other hand, the human being arising from history.

LECTURE 4

DORNACH, 22 OCTOBER 1922

TODAY I want to show how a certain understanding of the human being can also serve as a foundation for considering broader historical contexts. Tomorrow, from this perspective, we may then be able to gain insight into some contemporary phenomena. The day before yesterday I spoke about the human constitution itself; and today I want to embark on this again from another angle.

If we consider the human being in his mundane daily life, initially from the most ordinary, everyday aspect, we see that he has to eat to live. He has to ingest the substances of nature, derived from the animal, vegetable and, to some extent, also the mineral kingdoms. What he thus absorbs, however, undergoes a huge transformation within the human organism. The foods we eat ordinarily, prepared at most by cooking, enter our organism initially in a form more or less as they exist in the surrounding world, although perhaps a little modified. The air we breathe in enters us, likewise, in the condition in which it exists in our surroundings. This is true too of more important things still, such as light, but we will leave this aside for the time being. Now food and air have to undergo a huge transformation within us in order to fill our organism and in a sense become human within it.

An outward account of the process involved here is very familiar to us nowadays. We ingest food as I have said in more or less its original form, although it may have been prepared a little for eating. We work on it initially, especially through secretions from glands and the rest of the digestive tract: we take it into us, fluidize it, saturate it with a substance called ptyalin which is secreted by the salivary glands. Then we draw the food further into our digestive tract. I do not need to describe the whole tract to you, but I must describe the process involved. As we absorb and ingest foods and process them within us, they are changed from what they were originally. What they become within us could never have come about through external processes. In the chemical laboratory we can subject foods to all kinds of processes but this will not mirror what happens to food when it enters our stomach, and from there the digestive tract. There food becomes something quite different from what it was to begin with.

The first thing that occurs is the eradication from the food of every trace of outer life. People eat meat, drawn from their external sur-roundings, from the animal kingdom. But in doing so, mastication and the further process of digestion drive out everything that this food represents within animal bodies; and likewise all life that vegetables possess in the plant kingdom. All the life they possess by virtue of being plants has to be driven out of them. The only things we absorb as they exist in the outer world are mineral constituents as such. If we add salt—already mineral in nature—to a meal, or sugar which has been prepared in a way that renders it dead, even if it may originally have been drawn from the organic realm, we have in fact ingested something dead and this undergoes the least transformation within us—merely one that could be induced externally in a lab. But everything that enters our organism from the animal and plant kingdom has to be first thoroughly killed off if I may put it like that.

Our cooking also involves a kind of preparatory killing when we expose foods to heat and so on. Our digestion takes this further, thoroughly accomplishes it so that by the time our food has undergone a certain inner development and arrives in the lower digestive organs, the intestines, basically everything has been expelled to which they were originally subject—all that was governed by the animal's astral and etheric body, and all that was subject to the plant's etheric body and so forth. On its journey from mouth to intestines, all food has to be ren-dered dead.

As food is conveyed to the glandular organs which lead it onwards from the intestines into the lymph vessels and blood vessels, it is then re-enlivened again. Our food must first become dead inside us and then re-enlivened. We could not endure a perpetuation within us of life as it exists in an animal whose meat we eat, or of the plant we eat. At most inorganic nature can be absorbed without offending the laws at work within us. We could not, say, eat cabbage and let it approach the villi in our intestine with the same etheric forces the cabbage possesses when still a living plant. The etheric and astral attributes possessed by our food first have to be got rid of. And then our own etheric body must be able to absorb and re-enliven what we ingest. The life in our food has to come from us, and this occurs as food passes from the intestines through the blood vessels to the heart. You can picture it like this: food reaches our blood, and as this blood fills the heart, our etheric body absorbs the initially dead food we ingested. When food arrives in the intestines, the last traces of the external world are divested from it but here [drawing, red] they are re-enlivened as they pass towards the heart.

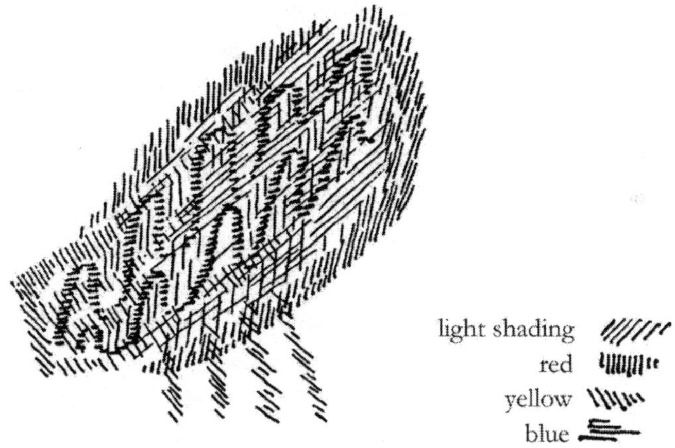

This re-enlivening means, in fact, that the foodstuffs have been absorbed by our own etheric body. But if this were all that happened, they would possess too little of an earthly character. And then we would be beings who possessed nothing but a mouth and digestive organs through to the heart, and we would start to be angels since our etheric body could absorb the food and completely dissolve it. We could not be earthly. We would have to be just mouths flying around with attached gullets, with stomach and intestines and heart; and then, you see, our etheric body would absorb everything. We would have nothing but an etheric body, and the food would just evaporate in the ether body. We could not be earthly human beings if this were so. That we can be is due to us absorbing oxygen from the air. The oxygen in the air is introduced into the food permeated by the etheric body, and this means we can go on being human beings of flesh and blood here on earth between birth and death [drawing, light shading].

You can say that the oxygen makes everything that would otherwise be dispersed in our etheric body into something alive in an earthly sense. Oxygen is the substance that transposes into earthly nature what would otherwise only form etherically. Now we have arrived at the connection between heart and lungs. The heart would not yet render us earthly as human beings but would only bring us to the point of connecting our ether body to the heart and flying around as angels on earth as it were: angels, though, who might have attributes some would think rather unlovely, such as a mouth, intestines and blood vessels through to a heart. But because the heart is in connection with the lungs and takes in oxygen, the food we ingest is not just etherized but also rendered earthly.

And now it becomes necessary to incorporate into the astral body what our etheric body has absorbed so that we can be earthly human beings, and what has been pervaded by oxygen. Everything that has developed to the extent of becoming an activity of heart and lungs must now be taken up by the whole organism, and this must happen in a way which involves the astral body too. The human kidney system mediates this activity, eliminating unuseable parts of the substances that are absorbed, but conveying everything else into the whole organism in ways which are not described anywhere in modern physiology, yet which do exist.

Here the whole mush, if I can call it that, or chyme—which remains alive, after first being killed off entirely in the intestines and then re-enlivened and pervaded by oxygen—is conveyed into the astral body by the activity of the kidney system whose influence extends throughout the organism and radiates everywhere. The astral body can now help in the further forming of what food brings about in us [drawing, p. 49, yellow].

This astral organism, in so far as it gains impetus from the kidney system, is now in turn connected with the head and neurosensory system, which in a sense is like a covering over it. And together the kidney and head system continually work in a way that forms into specific organs what heart activity basically renders fluid and formless. If only our mouth, stomach, intestines, heart and lungs existed, we wouldn't have any solid organs. The stomach itself would have to be a fluid, inwardly mobile organ, and so would our lungs and heart. None of this would be solid. These organs are shaped by the influence of the kidneys, and the latter are aided in this by what emanates from the head.

You see, organs not only have to be formed during childhood but on a continuing basis, for they are continually being destroyed. Over the course of seven to eight years an organ such as the stomach is entirely destroyed. Its substance disappears and is continually renewed. This means that formative forces must always be available to renew these organs. During childhood a great deal more work of this kind has to be done, but these form-giving forces are still there later on.

It happens like this [drawing, below]. The kidney system streaming out these forces in one direction would only create organs in a one-sided way. For instance, it would shape a lung in a way that was nicely delimited behind but fluid in front here, flowing away. It must encounter a power emanating from the head so that the front of the organ is shaped by this influence. Individual organs are formed in the

encounter between the forces streaming from the kidneys and those emanating from the head, which inhibit the former. This endows the organs with shaped and rounded contours. The influence from the head forms surfaces from without while the kidneys supply a kind of streaming or radiation into the organism.

It is a bit like what happens if I try to sculpt a form. I take plaster or some kind of soft substance in one hand, and then learn to build up the plaster with one hand {drawing, yellow, red} while the other smoothes it down.

The first, upbuilding movement represents the kidneys. I could do this by having some kind of tub and taking the substance from it {see drawing}. I sling it up, smooth it off at the top, and in this way obtain these organs, formed really from an out-streaming and rounding off. Thus our organs are formed in connection with the kidney system and the head system, and inside them the forces of the astral body are at work. This is something therefore that involves an extremely vigorous change to the nitrogen—which here is already a long way from having the properties it does outside us. The nitrogen that still resembles external nitrogen becomes uric acid and urine, and is eliminated. But what streams out from the kidneys and is assimilated is really a nitrogen that has been inwardly altered in correspondence with the active powers of the astral body. And this is something quite different from external nitrogen.

What we take in as food is driven to the point where it is incorporated into astrality, into the astral body of the human organism. These pro-cesses I have described here occur in animals too, in a somewhat modified way. The animal has these processes too, and in fact in higher animals they proceed still further. In the lower animals, though, one finds at most just hints of what I will now describe. The higher animals possess it by virtue of branching off from the human race. They still have it, although in a deformed and degenerate state.

Something else shines into all that develops here. So first we have this driving of foodstuffs into a dead state. At the end of this process we have the pancreas as one of the last glands that advance the whole process so that, driven towards the lymph, food is enlivened and can be absorbed by the etheric body. Then, through the communication between heart and kidneys everything is driven into the astral body. But now the I must also be engaged. The I has to lay claim to everything existing in our organism.

Now I have already described to you how the etheric and astral organism must lay claim to whatever becomes part of us, how the kidney system absorbs it and radiates it into the astral, and how it becomes earthly in nature with the aid of nitrogen. Otherwise—if nitrogen did not work within us—we would inevitably be angel-like, for, emanating from the kidney system, nitrogen sustains the astral body within the realm of earth. But if the liver system were not also present the whole thing would not configure us to allow the I to participate too [drawing, p. 49, blue]. The liver system drives the whole thing into the I. This, you see, is a continuation of the heart influence, which works right into the intestines.

Absorption through the lymph vessels also belongs to the heart. By and large the heart is the organ which, together with the lungs, drives external substances into our etheric body. Then, proceeding further from there, the kidney system drives them into our astral body. And the liver system with its bile secretions is what drives all of this into our actual I. Only the higher animals possess a gall bladder and liver system. Lower animals do not—not even bile is found in their bodily substances. So the liver with its unique structure, with the portal vein and so on— and all this can be demonstrated anatomically—conducts everything so that the I can take hold of it. If all we had were what the kidneys radiate into the body, only the astral body would absorb it. Because we have the liver, which secretes bile that mixes with the chyme in our intestine, so imbuing it with liver secretions [drawing, p. 49, blue], it can then be driven into our I organism. In other words, our I organism, through the liver—the latter largely represented in physical substance by hydrogen—participates in the whole composition of the human organism. We do not in fact need to take in anything of a living astral nature from outside us. What we take in from outside us we first have to reconfigure within our own organ system so that it can be incorporated into our own astral, etheric and I systems.

Here we have what I would call our whole normal organization. Just reflect on how this all has to be in accord and work together. For instance, the activity of the kidneys cannot be interrupted—and if it is, because of kidney stone or cirrhosis, the astral body cannot act. Or rather, the reverse is true: when the astral body does not work properly, this leads to kidney stones or cirrhosis. When such a condition arises this gives us a tangible picture or reflection of what is really happening in the astral body, just as heart disease shows us precisely and pictorially what is happening in the human etheric body. Last time I said that there is even a rhythmic accord. The upstreaming from the kidney [drawing, p. 49, yellow] always involves four pulses compared to the single rounding impetus that emanates from above, from the head. And this is the same relationship of one to four as we find expressed in the breath and the pulse. If I may use this comparison once again, I would have to round things off with one hand four times more slowly than the pulse coming from the other. This in fact is what the organism does [drawing, p. 52, bottom].

All this must be in the subtlest accord, otherwise things go wrong. Being ill means, in fact, that this accord is disrupted. Let us assume that the etheric body is working fine but the astral body is not powerful enough to absorb all that streams over from the heart to the kidneys and assimilate it in the right way. This can be because the etheric body is working too strongly. I said that it was working fine, but let us assume for a moment that its action is too vigorous. If the etheric body works too strongly and the astral body is normal, kidney stones (blockages) can develop, with their distinct consequences. If the etheric body is fine but the astral body works too strongly, the kidney is not engaged sufficiently. Because the astral body is working too strongly, it engages with what streams across without the kidney playing its proper and necessary part in regulation. Thus the kidney is overlooked, not involved properly, leading to kidney cirrhosis which at the same time has follow-on effects that lead to heart dysfunction and deterioration.

In this way, you see, things occurring in the human organism are interrelated. The deterioration of organs can show us how different levels of the human organism—physical body, etheric body, astral body and I—are not working together in the right way.

We just need to realize that all these things have to be in accord with each other and work together properly. Let us assume that a certain supersensible aspect—say the astral body—does not properly inform a particular organ system in us. There are two ways in which this can happen: either the impulses emanating from the kidney system— remembering that a rounding impetus comes from the head and a radiating one from the kidney system—are stimulated too strongly, so that in fact everything working from the heart towards the kidney system gives rise to excessive stimulus of the kidney system. In this hyper-stimulus we actually find the original cause of all inflammatory conditions—of all inflammatory and ulcerative conditions in the human organism. We just have to discern how an inflammation arises in the organism and then try to remedy things medicinally so as to curtail this excessive stimulus of kidney activity.

The simplest means to achieve this is to try in some way to inhibit too strong a radiation of inner bodily warmth—always a concomitant of this—by administering the specific substances that develop in the flowering organs of plants. This can bring about an inner cooling. The peculiarity of substances that develop in the blossoms of plants is that they can be used to combat inflammations since they engender an inner cooling in the organism. On the other hand it may be that there is an excessive sculpting activity from the head, which counteracts kidney activity. This gives rise to tumour-type formations. Here the plastic, rounding, or one might say crystallizing activity is too strong. By means of an external warmth application—though this must be done in the right way—we try to envelop the swelling or turgescence in warmth applied externally to bring about a gradual healing from without [drawing, p. 56, yellow, red]. All such swellings are really healed from without. We have to ensure that the swelling is enveloped and irradiated by certain substances that are injected into the organism and diffused through it [red].

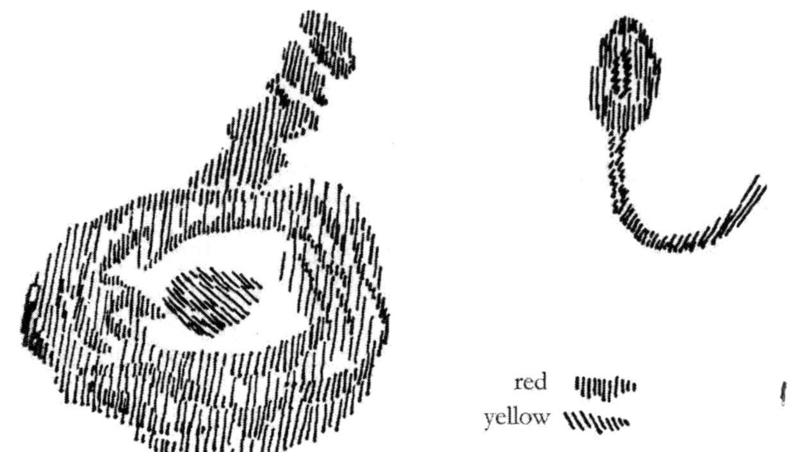

When you succeed in doing this, in irradiating the swelling from without, it can dissolve and cease. If you have an inflammation, by contrast, you have to introduce a medicine via the digestive tract into the organ where the inflammation is located, introducing a cooling effect via the digestion. An inflammation has to be treated from within {right-hand drawing}.

One just has to find ways to do this. Every substance is disseminated in the human organism in a specific way. For instance, there are substances which, when administered orally, take no notice of the oesophagus. It is irrelevant to them—pepsin, ptyalin and so forth, only take notice of the heart. Other substances disregard the heart: they are conducted to the kidneys through the stomach and heart, and only begin to act when they reach the kidneys. Thus every substance has its own inner affinity with an organ, and one has to find the right substance to use medicinally. For instance there are substances which, if you inject them, would completely disregard a stomach carcinoma, having no affinity with it, but would take notice of, say, a breast carcinoma.

So we have to find a means to inwardly combat a tumour or an inflammation, or to tackle something from without, to besiege it if you like. Tumorous growths must be surrounded and besieged. Things within the organism must be studied in this way, and must all accord and cohere, naturally by understanding how these higher aspects of the human being work and act. It is quite impossible to gain insight into the kidney simply by a post-mortem examination. All you see then is the kidney lying next to the liver, and can say only that they are both composed of cells in diverse ways. In fact, the kidney has an intimate connection with the astral body, and the liver with the I, and this is what endows them with their specific character. Without knowing this it is quite pointless to consider or define these organs.

If you take an organ such as the spleen, you will find that ordinary physiology and medicine don't have much to say about it. In the relevant textbooks you will find very little about the spleen—a note perhaps to say that little is known about its function. You can find this in all the textbooks—just have a look. Nor is this at all surprising. The genius of language is in fact a great deal wiser in this instance—and in many others too—than science. The word 'spleen' is very accurate, for it is connected with all human activities that go above and beyond the I and approach the Spirit Self. The spleen in fact is the organ of the Spirit Self, and takes us a long way into the realm of spirit. But approaching the Spirit Self requires persistence and endurance. Most people cannot endure a really spiritual realm, and this means that spleen activity in them does not stimulate them to spiritual activity but they become 'full of spleen' instead. They become downcast and irritable. 'Spleen' is nothing other than spirit which devours itself in the intestines; and the word 'spleen' is therefore an excellent name, pointing as it does to a spiritual quality for which the spleen is the corresponding organ.

This is why the spleen has a balancing effect as you can read in the pamphlet written by Frau Dr Kolisko[9] and published by our Institute of Physiology in Stuttgart. She presents spleen activity in relation to blood platelet formation and all digestive activity. This is an excellent first systematic and scientific account of spleen activity. If such a study were published by any other research institute, it would soon come to be regarded as very innovative. But whenever something inspired by our Society emerges, it fails to make headway in the world. No mention is made of it anywhere. It is not about praising something; but it would be good to be mentioned, because such things could have a beneficial effect in the world as it is today. However, to make things known in the world, they first have to be spoken about in our Anthroposophical Society. I wonder how many of our members have taken full advantage of the fact that these very important things are available to them! If the Anthroposophical Society itself does not take any notice of work we accomplish, it is hardly surprising that it attracts no public attention either. We not only have to dispense with interest in our findings from the public but, in the most important matters, from the Anthroposophical Society as well! But I say this only in passing—today at least. It really is important that we come to understand the human organism, and we can only do so if we gain insight into its higher aspects.

So you can see how subtly these things need to accord with each other. Something will immediately go awry in the organism if the slightest disorder affects the astral organism; at this moment the kidneys will cease to function properly, and then we get all the repercussions of a kidney malfunction.

But this is not true simply for the human being as such or in general, but changes as we develop through the ages. Our organization is extremely subtle but does not always remain constant. If we look back only a few centuries—not much of course in the overall span of evolution—we come to a period when our modern age, that of the consciousness soul epoch, began. Tracing things back through the fifteenth, fourteenth and thirteenth centuries we return to an earlier Christian period. And however grotesque this sounds to people nowadays we find that roughly from the fourth through to the fourteenth centuries kidney function was the most important aspect of the human organism, especially for the civilized world, whereas liver function superseded it in importance thereafter.

Over the centuries, and still more over millennia, human anatomy and physiology does alter; and we cannot study history if we do not attend to the subtle structures of the human organism and discern how changes in the prevailing culture, such as the transition from the medieval period to the modern era, are also connected with transformation of the whole of our human organization.

We have to develop a sense for these things once more, for otherwise we will never bridge the gulf that opens up between science on the one hand, which grows ever more irreligious and ends up relying on its scalpels, probes and sensors, and religious life on the other, which has nothing left to say about the world but merely addresses human beings' instinctual egotistic desires for a life after death. These things stand in crass juxtaposition. All our religious life today has forgotten that God created the world. It speaks of the divine but forgets that God created the world, and that we can find everywhere in the world's phenomena the traces of divine Creation. Rather than just uttering vacuous and abstract generalities about cultural developments throughout history, we need to know that, via our delicate human organism, divine, creative powers transform the human being by fine-tuning this infinitely subtle mechanism of our human organism, and that by first plucking more strongly on the string of kidney function and then on that of liver function a quite different cultural music emerges.

Only when we do not restrict ourselves to a view of God as separate from the world itself but instead trace God's workings in detail, in each type of bodily function, can we find what we will need in future. Otherwise we will cultivate nothing but abstraction in the end, and end up with an utterly materialistic science. Only when we can penetrate right through to specific details of how divine creation configures substance and works within it will we be able to imbue religion with science and lead science, in turn, back to religion.

And so we discover that at the transition arising in the twelfth, thirteenth and fourteenth centuries an outlook develops that I have previously described from the most diverse angles, which comes to expression in the Grail legend, in the legend of Parzival and in all that was conceived by poets of the age such as Wolfram von Eschenbach, Hartmann von Aue and Gottfried of Strassburg.[10] You can find these motifs in their writing. In the Parzival poem, the authentic version, one finds a motif, especially, that expresses the human being's need to develop towards what was called *saelde* in those days. This is a certain inner sense of joy—*saelde*—close to what we might call bliss or blessedness, but not quite the same. *Saelde* means to be imbued with a sense of inner joy of a certain kind. This motif surfaces in, and in fact dominates European culture in the thirteenth and fourteenth centuries. All poetic themes, and all prose ones too—especially the Parzival theme—are pervaded by this idea, and everything strives towards it. People strive for this *saelde*, this inner sense of joy or bliss. It is not irreligious nor simply comfortable inner happiness but is really a state in which they are ensouled by the Creator's divine powers.

Why does this arise? It is caused by the change in emphasis from kidney to liver activity in the human being. Physiology can help us understand this. Earlier physiologists were of course better physiologists in a sense than modern materialistic physiologists. I am thinking, really, when I say this, of the writers of the Old Testament[11] who said the following about bad dreams for example: 'The Lord punished me last night through my kidneys.' This knowledge of certain connections between abnormal kidney activity and bad dreams persisted; and in the eighth, ninth and tenth centuries, for instance, people were still deeply convinced that kidney activity renders you heavy. People felt that the kidney had gradually acquired something of a heavy quality. Naturally, to say something is weighing on you is just a metaphor suggesting there's something you can't get the better of. They felt bound to the earthly realm. Physical permeation of the organism with bile, by contrast, was connected with *saelde* quality, a sense of being imbued with this as an experience of deliverance, inner deliverance. It was experienced as an inner yet divinely filled sense of bliss, a striving away from the dullness of the kidney. You see, the kidney also develops thinking activity, a dull thinking activity mediated by the system of ganglia which is then connected in turn to the spinal cord and the brain system. It develops in particular the kind of thinking that also played a particular and major role in the Middle Ages. At that time it was called mental 'dullness' or *tumpheit*. And this development from *tumpheit* to *saelde*—to illumined bliss—became the theme of Parzival. Parzival develops from *tumpheit* to *saelde*, from dullness to inner joy.

We should not think of this only in abstract terms but also regard it with some feeling and sensitivity. To begin with Parzival is a man of his time, emerging from a culture that has grown ponderous. He is sluggish. Only later does *saelde* enter him after he has passed through a state of doubt. Doubt inhabits him, causing turmoil in his cardiovascular system. Only after passing through this condition does he find access to inner joy, to *saelde*.

It is indeed possible to trace in the human organism the moods at work in the broader history and evolution of the world. Leading individuals such as those who fashioned the Parzival motif were pioneers in a sense, precursors of this new organization we possess in the modern era, who experienced the transition from an older kidney activity to a new liver activity.

We should not dismiss such things. We should not say that these things are just part of our lower physical and sensory nature. After all, God did not consider it beneath him to create 'lower' matter but went ahead and did so. And our task, equally, is to trace the divine activity of Creation right into the furthest reaches of the material world—rather than keeping aloof from such things as dainty historians, rather than just commenting on the Parzival motif while refraining from lower matters such as physiological functions.

The world is a unity, and to understand the great contexts of history we must at the same time be able to shine a light upon specific human circumstances and conditions. In former times, and in the Middle Ages still, people retained traces of such knowledge. You can discover this in accounts such as that of 'Poor Henry'[12] which show how moral healings occur, and suchlike.

These things should give you some sense, initially, that all human knowledge is a great whole, and that the highest religious ideas relate to what people often regard as so lowly that they fail to pay it any attention. Modern science in its present form is to blame for this outlook, for it ignores the fact that we must trace the spirit through into matter's furthest reaches, and only then will learn to understand the world. Only then will we also raise ourselves to a truly religious view of the world, rather than one which is commonly egotistical because it addresses people's egotistic speculations without informing our actual knowledge of things. And this in turn leads to the decline of civilization rather than to its renewal.

The renewal of civilization is after all connected with people's capacity to become illumined and to use this light within to observe the world in light rather than in darkness. Modern physiology and anatomy, whose insights are gained by a post-mortem scalpel and merely study symptoms of illness observed by material means, will not succeed in grasping the inner nature of the human being.

We really only understand ptyalin and pepsin in the food we

assimilate and break down if we see it like this: we ingest food, break it down, enliven and astralize it, and transform it into the I. Conveyed into the lymph glands, conveyed to the heart which energizes it, irradiated by the kidneys and rendered entirely astral, it is then absorbed by liver function and led over into the I. Then all this can be absorbed by pancreatic activity, and through this activity we can either become enthusiastic, as someone who receives strength from the world of spirit, or instead a person of spleen, a pessimist who just wants to sit there on his chair and not let the spirit take hold of him, who prefers not to think much. There are plenty of such people around today and they drive you to desperation by sitting there like a heavy lump as if they had no head at all. Pancreatic activity, which could be something lofty in us, in fact has a crushing effect on such people. They have spleen rather than enthusiasm, and today this manifests in the most diverse ways.

What we need nowadays is a kind of work that transforms spleen into enthusiasm, into fire, so that people wake up and create a civilization that is awake and not somnolent. Anthroposophy ought to engender this: being awake, being enthusiastic, transforming knowledge into real activity, into actions and deeds, so that we not only know something but something emerges and *develops* through anthroposophy. Only then does anthroposophy have its goal and purpose and can also really achieve this goal. But if anthroposophy makes you somnolent this means you accord much too much respect to the physical quality of the pancreas rather than making the pancreas's high, spiritual qualities fruitful in you. And this points to something that modern humanity greatly needs: fire, enthusiasm, the capacity to be fired by something. Until this is possible, we will keep on thinking only of ourselves, which means placing too much importance on the uric acid secreted in us, urine, whose real task is not to just circulate in cell and protein, but to be transformed into the fluctuating protein that in fact entirely constitutes us. Basically we are a large, living cell continually involved in lively motion: we have carbon in us, then acquire oxygen as food is etherized, acquire nitrogen as food is irradiated by kidney activity, acquire hydrogen as liver function plays into everything in relation to sense activity—and by this means also already acquire sulphur, either of the inappropriate kind of which people mostly speak today or of the proper kind. But we also acquire what is needed to ensure we are a living being consisting of protein, carbon, oxygen, nitrogen and also of sulphur; but as I said, this must be the right kind of sulphur. Today too much of the other type is present—the type referred to by students in speaking of their professor of philosophy in Wuerzburg. He had become so dull and boring that in the end there were only two students still attending his classes. And then even they had had enough and gave up on him. And then someone wrote 'sulphur den' on his door. That is not the kind of sulphur we need, which is far too prevalent today. Today, instead, people must be fully alive, thoroughly so, must be ensouled, imbued with spirit. And that's something we can learn, too, especially if we trace the spirit through into the furthest reaches of the world of substance. And only then we will develop a physiology worthy of the name, which can really give therapeutic support to human nature.

Lecture 5

DORNACH, 23 OCTOBER 1922

From many of our previous studies you will have seen that I am not too keen to refer to our era as one of 'transition' since every age is a transitional period from the past to the future, and so the only question really is what the nature of this transition is.

But in our times a very important transition is occurring and can be recognized by those who perceive the world of spirit. It is a transition repeatedly mentioned in the wisdom of very ancient times, in eras when people still meant something real when they spoke of a world of spirit, although their knowledge was dreamlike in nature. In ancient times it was always said that the so-called dark age would end at a certain point, giving way to an age of light. If one carefully studies the words of these wise people of ancient times one finds that they were indeed referring to the transition occurring between the nineteenth and twentieth centuries, the time we are living in now. But there is no need for us to embrace old, dreamlike forms of wisdom through anthroposophy. This is not the case at all, as I have often said. In anthroposophy, instead, we are concerned with what spiritual research can discover today. In other words, anthroposophy does not aim to renew some form of ancient wisdom but is a modern form of knowledge. Yet in this matter of a transition from an age of darkness to one of light, our modern knowledge concurs with ancient wisdom.

If we go by current external events it does not appear as if humanity, civilized Europe in particular, is progressing from worse to better conditions; yet it is true nevertheless that we are entering an age of light as ancient wisdom tells us. We just have to see things in the right way. I would like to offer an example, firstly, to show the difference between an age of light and an age of darkness.

Those who spoke in these terms, around the fifth millennium BC, describing an age of darkness and one of light, saw this dark age as the consequence of a former age of light, and expressed the view that, once the dark age had taken its course, it would be followed by another age of light. It will therefore be instructive to look back and discover how the earlier age of light existing around the seventh or eighth millennium BC affected human affairs, and how it differed from the subsequent age of darkness from which we are now set to emerge.

To study this I want to use an example as I said—that of healing or medicine. We can learn a great deal from this domain in particular. In the ancient light or lucid era, healing did not take the physical human body into account. No one even thought of doing so. In that ancient epoch of light, no one even spoke of illness as we do today; and in future we will once again cease to speak of it as such. Naturally in those times human organs could degenerate and give rise to some kind of loss of health, but instead of regarding this as illness, people spoke of death taking possession of a person. Whereas we say that someone is ill, in those days people saw a kind of battle between life and death. They said that death was battling within someone where we would say that he has fallen ill. And recovery or healing was seen as a combating of death, a driving out of death from the human being. Thus life and death, not health and illness, were seen to be at work, and what we regard as illness was just a special instance of death, a little death if you like, whereas health was seen as life.

Why was this? It was because in those days healing was accomplished entirely through the etheric body. The physical body was ignored in healing, and instead only the etheric body was considered.

How was this accomplished? Well let's assume that someone was suffering from a condition we would call pneumonia today. We'll use this word although an inflammation of the lungs was of a different kind then. In those days such a person would be seen as too dependent on the region of the earth where he lived. This was during an era when human migrations were less common than today, when people rarely left the place where they lived. Mostly people stayed their whole lives in one place. But in such a case a person would be thought too dependent on the region where he was born. In those ancient times, you see, people were very aware of their pre-earthly existence and knew that, during this existence, they had themselves decided where they must live on earth in fulfilment of their destiny. They would therefore say that someone who succumbed to pneumonia before the age of 40 had not made the right choice when deciding where he would dwell on earth. They would say that he was not living in the place that suited him best. In other words, they saw the cause of the disorder in the relationship between a person's organism and the region where he lived.

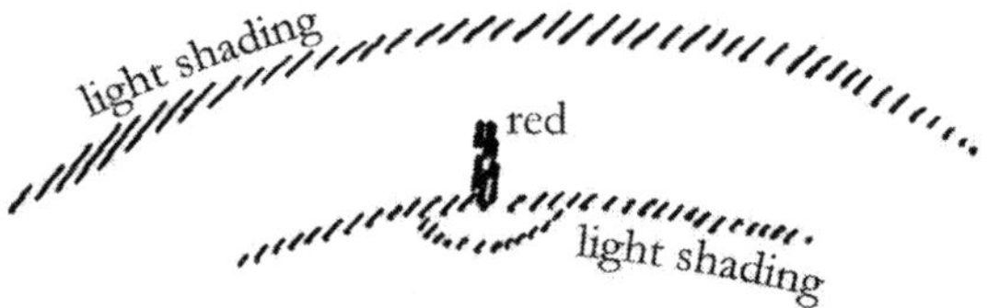

I could draw it roughly like this [drawing, above]. In picturing the earth like this people said that someone living in this spot is too dependent on a particular region, and must be healed by inwardly liberating him from his outer dependency on this region; and this could be done by bringing him into relationship with the surrounding cosmos, with the encompassing heavens. People regarded the heavens as the home in which the person concerned had been dwelling before he came to live on the earth. He was thought to be at odds with his dwelling on earth, and was to be healed by establishing his proper relationship to the cosmos. To do this they proceeded as follows. Because they regarded him as suffering from excessive earthly influences, too much gravity and all that is connected with it, they believed they must alleviate this condition by introducing supersensible forces into him. Perceiving that super-earthly powers were at work in one type of plant flower or another, they obtained the juice from such flowers. They saw that a particular plant flowers at a certain time of year and does so due to the influences of the cosmos; and they studied the extent to which a human being is influenced by this season of the year. In long-gone times people sought to discover the human being's dependency on heavenly phenomena by means of horoscopes and suchlike; and then medicines were administered that would cause a certain general resonance in a person's ether body. They saw it like this: here is a human being [drawing below, red] and here is his ether body [light shading]; he has contracted pneumonia because his ether body is too strongly attracted to the earth in the region of his lungs [blue], and because the earth forces exert too strong an influence on him. Now he was given the juice of certain flowers which acted upon him to overcome these forces [yellow]. In other words they sought to reconnect such a person with the cosmos by administering the right substances and their powers. Efforts were made to induce the proper resonance in a person's whole ether body in order to balance certain incorrect resonances. And so the question was always what the ether body needed, and what should be done to help it.

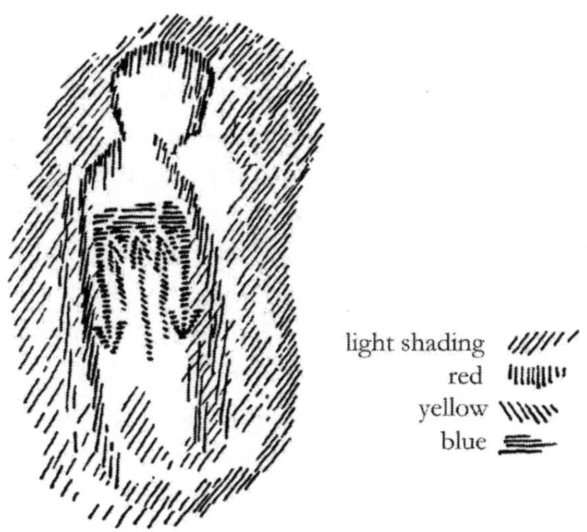

But what enabled them to proceed in this way in the first place? They were only able to do this because they had a clear idea of the human etheric body. In those former times people not only perceived the physical body but they saw it shine too, they saw the ether body. The human being was a being of light; and in the same way that we can tell by looking at someone nowadays if he is feeling 'off-colour', if he is pale and therefore ill, so in those days people's state of health was apparent in the ether body, its colouring—in its red, blue or green appearance for instance. At that time human knowledge was founded on light, on the light indwelling people. So we can take the phrase quite literally: this was an age of light, when the light living in people could really be perceived.

If you consider human health and illness you will find that today light still has a huge effect. We have to ensure that the right amounts of light enter our organism. As we know, children who are deprived of light at a delicate age can get rickets or other disorders that are likewise connected with lack of light—though also of course with other factors since illness never originates in a *single* cause. But conditions such as rickets are certainly connected with receiving too little sunlight. Children living in the city in blocks of flats where not much light penetrates are on average far more likely to get rickets than those exposed to adequate daylight. So we can still say today that we absorb light.

Yet the light we assimilate today, if I may put it like this, is mineral light. We absorb the light that has shone down upon the earth, on its minerals, and is reflected back to us. Even the light that falls on meadows and trees is conveyed to us minerally. It is dead light, which we imbibe through our skin, through the whole of us. In those ancient days of light preceding the age of darkness people were aware that this dead light really had no significance for them.

Modern historians and cultural historians know nothing about such things. The light we value so much today was of scarcely any worth to those people in olden times. The distinction they made between the light they valued and the light we value so much today could roughly be described as one we make between a plate, fork and spoon when we eat, and the cake or other food on our plate. We eat the cake. The knife and fork are useful of course, but we don't eat them. So for those ancient people the light we value was present too, but the light they esteemed came from the realm of plants. And this is something we no longer assimilate at all in the way people did once, in those old eras of light. Nowadays we enjoy going out into the sunshine. In ancient times a person enjoyed walking over a meadow or through a wood because he absorbed through his skin the light that the wood had first assimilated, that was enlivened in the wood and on the meadow. And the other light, the dead light, was an added flavouring, like salt. For us the salt has become the chief thing. In olden times people lived in the light which the flowers and the trees gave them. They experienced this light as a source of inner enlivening, feeling themselves imbued with inwardly living rather than dead light. We have no conception at all of this with our abstract pleasure in the woods, in the flowers, in everything which, one can say, is philistine in cosmic terms. Of course it is still beautiful but it is philistine when compared to the inner rejoicing experienced by ancient people when they walked in the woods or over the fields, when they encountered everything living under the heavens. A person of these ancient times felt connected with his trees and with a particular plant that suited him well. Ancient people felt the most vital sympathy and antipathy with this plant or that—whereas when we walk over the fields surrounding the Goetheanum, say in autumn, we have only a philistine sense of the meadow saffron, the *Colchicum autumnale*, perhaps just admiring its beauty. When a person in ancient times walked past such a plant he would grow sad, his head even grew a little dry, his hair limp. But if he passed a flower with a red blossom, plants like our poppy, his hair would fluff up, grow soft or silken. Thus these people of olden times had a full, immediate experience of light in the world of plants. It was the age of light, and their whole culture was oriented to healing ability, or in other words to fighting death by observing and treating the ether body.

This only very slowly faded; and even if we study medicine in ancient Greece, if we read about Hippocrates,[13] we see insight there into fluids in the human organism, black and yellow bile, blood and phlegm. In Greece memories still survived of the ancient age of light. Phlegm really referred to the ether body, and blood to the resonances which the astral body caused in the ether body and so forth. Memories of an older vision remained, and really not until the time of Galen, when the merely physical world had begun to be a factor in human culture, did people's view of the human being in relation to healing processes acquire a physical character. Then people started to focus on the human being's physical body.

But really this did not come into its own until the great transitional era in the fifteenth century, the first half of that century, when people no longer knew anything about the human etheric body, not even how it manifests in the temperaments; and at that point the human physical body became ever more central. An older kind of physical medicine was somewhat different from what it became in the eighteenth and nineteenth centuries, and possessed traditions, at least, of earlier ways of healing through the etheric body. One can gain a sense from this older medicine, also in Europe, that old principles were retained and simply transferred to the physical realm. One can say that the physical organism was continually regarded as subject to the influence of the etheric organism. Only in more modern times, in the Copernican era and that of Galileo, did people begin to consider the physical body alone, losing a knowledge that had been very highly developed in former times. Nowadays people think that if they eat a particular food that exists outside in nature it will basically remain the same substance in the human body. But this is not so. Salts remain close to their original form but everything originating in the plant or animal kingdoms is transformed completely in the human organism. The human organism converts these substances completely. In former times it was known that the inner constitution of the physical human organism is 'not of this world', and that basically falling ill is nothing other than a continuation of what occurs when we eat. At one time, in fact, especially among Arab physicians, digestion was regarded to some degree as a pathological process, a view that is indeed justified. When we eat something we ingest something alien to us and are, in a sense, ill. Our inner organism and inner organ functions first have to overcome this 'disorder'. Really, as we do this, we are 'a little bit ill' and must overcome this slight disorder a little, cure it a little. We eat ourselves into a sick state and digest ourselves to recovery again. For a while Arab physicians subscribed to this outlook, and indeed it does have much truth for actually there is no clear boundary between what we call healthy eating and eating that makes you ill. Just think how easy it is to do yourself harm by eating—when what we can overcome as a matter of course passes over immediately into our failure to do so. Then we become ill. But there is no clear boundary between the two.

Likewise there is no clear demarcation between contusions or bruises that heal naturally and those requiring medical attention. It was therefore quite justified to see internal complaints as a continuation of the process of eating, of an eating that was not quite in order. And so these physicians studied the daily process of digestion to learn how it makes us healthy again.

It is therefore also a very good habit for some people who do not care for certain unsalted food to go on adding salt to it. Some like to add pepper, or paprika too. They do so because this makes the food more palatable to them. Again there is no clear boundary if someone needs pepper or paprika as a remedy—no clear boundary as to whether one gives a person pepper or paprika so that he can regain his health via digestion or, if things get worse, something from the mineral realm. It doesn't matter whether one gives this as spice with a meal or as medicine—the two things run into each other without a clear distinction.

So people possessed the clear knowledge in those times that whenever someone ingests something from the external world this impairs his inner organism and he has to overcome it. It is only a matter of finer distinctions whether I get a rusty splinter in my thumb which my organism has to get rid of by forming a boil, or whether I introduce something into my stomach that cannot remain there in that form so that my organism has to undergo all these processes in order to assimilate it. But this insight existed: that the human organism is not of this earth and can only be sustained on earth if continually stimulated to overcome the earth's forces. You see, we do not eat to put some food or other inside us, but to inwardly develop the powers to overcome the ingested food. We eat in order to offer resistance to earthly forces; and we live on this earth by offering resistance.

But this was slowly forgotten. People started to see things in wholly materialistic ways, and ended up just investigating whether this or that substance is useful in this or that plant. Yes indeed, this is what was once meant—and what we must again understand today—by the 'age of darkness'. Everything has been darkened and obscured. In former times people could perceive the bright ether body as the human being himself. Now people no longer perceive it at all, instead only determining where in the organism substances are found, and adhering to dead light. But this dead light is something initially which people see only in abstract, intellectual concepts. Today we stand at a point of transition where a need arises for us to perceive and recognize light again in a new way. In former times people knew that they possessed this light-filled ether body. Now we must increasingly develop a form of etheric perception in the external world, in particular the world of plants.

Goethe made a beginning here with his ideas on metamorphosis, although he still formulated them in an abstract, intellectual way. This must increasingly become pictorial, and we must realize that we should get to the point of seeing the plant world in luminous images. In the ancient age of light, the human form shone; and in future the world of plants in nature around us must shimmer and shine in the most varied imaginations of plant forms. Through this luminosity of plant forms we will once again discover remedies in them. This needs to happen in future. Whereas people of a former age of light perceived an inner light, nowadays we must gain vision of the surrounding world and find light there, this light of the outer world.

And in fact this light can be kindled as one increasingly fathoms spiritual science. You might say that you find only concepts when you read spiritual science, anthroposophy, that in reading, say, *Occult Science* you also meet concepts there and have no need to really gain vision of anything. But my dear friends, this *Occult Science* has a dual aim: firstly for you to familiarize yourself with its content. But that is not all. Once you have read my *Occult Science* as you would read any other book, then all you have for the time being is the match. If you want fire there is no point in saying, 'This match is not fire!' Of course a match does not look in the least like fire. *Occult Science* does not look like clairvoyance! But the match will look like fire if you strike it. And if it doesn't catch at the first strike, you strike again, and keep trying. It is the same with *Occult Science*. Having read it like any other book, you just have the match in your hands; but strike it properly in your whole being, and you'll find it flares up. It will do so, my dear friends, even if so far it shows scarcely a flicker. And those who say that this is still far removed from the clairvoyance they seek are just looking at the match and not striking it. You have to first know the nature of the match for otherwise you might delude yourself into thinking that a pin could strike a flame. A pin—in other words modern science—cannot do this. Only a match will burst into flame. A real match can and will.

Today the human race faces the need to do this; and it may be that something like medical knowledge and skill will most vividly show whether people find a transition or not from merely looking on at the obscurities of substance—observing a flower outwardly, say as people do today—to an imaginative, pictorial vision gained by striking the match and using insights acquired in this way to perceive how a particular substance affects the human organism. This is where humanity stands today: it needs to pass from darkness into light, and learn to use light-filled judgement.

Let me clarify this with an example. Let's assume a modern physician diagnoses dilation of the heart in a patient. There's not a lot you can do with such a diagnosis. Perhaps one sees if something or other will help, but there is no insight into the whole context, no connected understanding. True insight will show us the following, however. I have often explained that we renew our organism entirely every seven years, and last time I told you how this renewal is accomplished. Starting from the kidney system, unprocessed substances are in a sense continually dispatched upwards or forwards or downwards. The head system accomplishes a rounding-off action [see drawing]: from the head system continual waves emanate [blue] which create form; and from the kidney

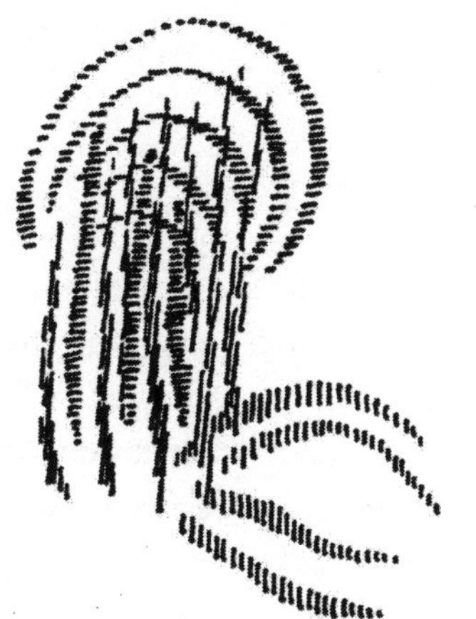

system come effects which these waves interrupt and shape [red], doing so four times faster, as I said.

Now consider an organ like the heart [drawing, below, light shading]. Here too a renewal occurs in all of us after seven or eight years. The heart is made new. You can observe that when you cut your fingernails they grow again, keep growing; and the same is true of the whole human being. His substance is renewed from within outwards. Now consider what happens, though, if the rhythmic system is not working properly, specifically in a case where these radiations from the kidney system shoot out far too quickly for the rhythmic organism, giving rise to the wrong ratio rather than four to one. This varies from person to person, for we are all individual, but basically this is the ratio that applies in the organism we possess. Let's assume this is not functioning properly, that the radiation coming from the kidney system is too rapid. What would result?

This can result in the following. The process of renewal is happening all the time of course—and now let us assume that before the old substance has been entirely expelled [drawing, light shading] the new has been inserted there [red]

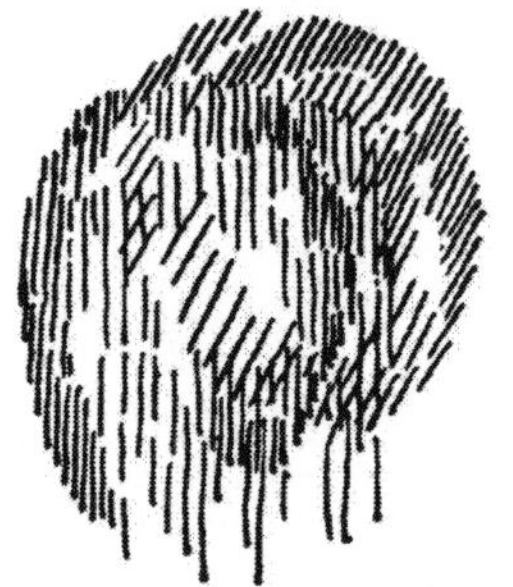

Things are happening too rapidly. If renewal is happening too fast, we get conditions such as dilation of the heart. Incipient heart dilation will tell you immediately that kidney function is not in order. If you give serious credence to the fact that our bodies are renewed in seven or eight years you can discover this: that a renewal has been accomplished after seven years without enough of the old substance being expelled, so that the organ stretches or at least seeks to do so. We need to learn to look at things in such terms, to see them in living movement. This is a development we must embark on. Above all we must learn to look beyond narrow confines—for how do physicians make their diagnoses today?

A modern physician diagnoses such a condition by recording the shape of the heart, in other words by examining its current, finished form. But in fact doing so is not of great importance for the heart is an organ that continually flows away and is reconfigured: an inner mobility is at work here; and if I just record its given shape at any moment, it's rather like drawing a flash of lightning which is also in continual motion. I have to grasp the living nature of the human being if I wish to understand him. And I only find this living quality if I understand the whole world, and draw my insight into the human being from the whole world.

This enlivened way of working and seeing is one we must embark on. Above all, we ought to start developing such inner mobility in children in school. It is a terrible thing to keep children immobile in school. I always feel pained, for instance, to see children using a fixed triangle for all kinds of things. Such stasis is of little worth. Really the children should have a triangle that can alter its shape and position so that they gain a sense that everything should be grasped as moving and changing.

Of course it is terribly difficult to discuss such things with those who want an easy life and have no desire whatsoever to engage in real activity. It is hard to discuss this with people who get fed up even when children themselves dance about, let alone being asked to embrace learning aids that dance about as well. Naturally it is hard work to enter a living realm—but that is what we need to do. And summarizing all this we arrive at a prompting to raise ourselves into a new age of light—to pass from a dark age into a light age.

And since people are unable to do this—or rather, they persuade themselves that they can't—or because they don't want to, because they cling to what they are accustomed to and refuse to enter a new domain, we are witnessing terrible catastrophes in our time, for the old is no longer adequate. And such catastrophes will increase if people continue to drag their heels when it's time for a new departure.

The catastrophes that occur are a reaction by the age of darkness which no longer belongs in the modern era. Yet it is of course incredibly hard to meet with understanding since any inkling of the new age of light arises, at most, in the conflict between the older and younger generation. Young people will think that the older generation are philistines, and this has its precedents. The great German philosopher Johann Gottlieb Fichte sensed this when he made the classic state-ment[14] that all 30-year-olds ought really to be killed, since people are only decent human beings until that age. Fichte famously said this; and since Goethe was already a good deal older than 30 when he did, he was extremely annoyed and made this notion the subject of mockery in Part II of his *Faust*.[15] In fact of course one finds that young people happily regard older ones as philistines but then, after a certain age, often become still greater philistines themselves.

Well, it seems to me that we have two choices: either to become adherents of Spenglerism,[16] which will spell the downfall of the West, or to get used to the idea that a new era of light is emerging, to affirm this new era as opposed to one of darkness when people were like earthworms in relation to the cosmos. Historically we needed to be earthworms for a while to avoid being entirely subsumed by light. We could only develop our freedom in this age of darkness, and then really only at the conclusion of the dark age in modern times. We could only achieve freedom because light left us to our own devices to lead an earthworm life.

I told you that people in the ancient era of light primarily received light from the world of plants. Plants imbibed the cosmic light, if you like, and human beings drank this light in turn from the vessel offered them by plants.

Today we have only dead light; but on the rays of this dead light Christ once entered and fulfilled the Mystery of Golgotha. This is the great cosmic secret of modern times. It is true that we have dead light and this cannot fill us with bliss. But Christ entered the realm of earth on the rays of dead light and fulfilled the Mystery of Golgotha. And it is because we have the dead light outside and surrounding us today that we can enliven Christ within us. And then, with Christ living within us in the right way, we enliven all light around us on earth, bearing life into the dead light, ourselves having an enlivening effect on the light. In other words, we must enter the new age of light with the right Christ impulse; and repudiation of the Christ impulse is really what is preventing people today from perceiving how a dark age is passing over into an age of light.

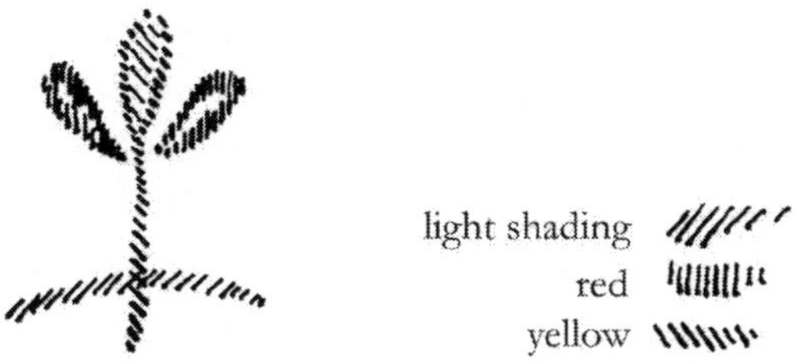

As the plant grows out of the soil [drawing, above], as I described, it develops the ovary by using powers originating the previous year. Only the petals of the flower grow forth from this year's light. What the plant draws from the soil really originates the previous year. And thus what plants gave human beings in the ancient era of light was in fact a preserved light. And now we must become able to grasp the dead light around us with a sensibility engendered in us as we absorb the power of Christ in a living vision of the Mystery of Golgotha. In doing so we enliven light, as I have said. But we can only do so if we learn to regard all things in the way I have tried to demonstrate in the course of these lectures.[17]

LECTURE 6

THE HAGUE, 5 NOVEMBER 1922

I am always pleased to speak here in our branch meeting in The Hague after giving public lectures[18] and attending public events, and this evening I will try to offer a somewhat more intimate addition to what I was speaking about in the public lectures. When seeking knowledge of the world of spirit and attempting to live inwardly with this spiritual world, we must always try to see the hidden side of human existence in the right light. Hidden aspects of human existence are what count, after all, when evaluating and judging human life in general. People who think in superficial, materialistic ways may not readily admit this, and yet it is so. No one can gain insight into human existence without being able to consider its hidden aspects.

One might feel like calling the gods to task, if you like, for concealing what is most valuable in human life behind hidden veils rather than offering it to us as an open book. If they did so, however, humankind would remain powerless in a higher sense. Only by first wrestling our way through to true human dignity, by having to work hard to become truly human through our own activity of spirit and soul can we acquire the soul-spiritual powers that can permeate our whole existence. In this self-conquering, this need to do something ourselves to become human, lies what strengthens us, and what can fill our inmost being with the necessary powers.

In order to explore this overriding theme I wish today to speak from a certain angle about the hidden side of human existence that is veiled in sleep's loss of consciousness. And I will then tell you of something concealed and unconscious during earthly life that occurs in our pre-earthly life and life after death.

Falling into the unconsciousness of sleep, after the transitional state of dreaming—a highly dubious kind of existence with a very dubious significance for human life if one only considers it as it seems to be—we emerge again from this condition when our I and astral body sink down again into our etheric and physical body, thus using these two organizations as a tool to perceive our physical surroundings and working with our will within these surroundings. But what lies beyond birth and death veils itself in the intrinsic human nature that becomes unconscious as we fall asleep. And now I'd like to describe, as if they were conscious, the states a person passes through in this process. We can only become aware of them through faculties of Imagination, Inspiration and Intuition, although all pass through the conditions I will describe. A modern initiate who studies sleep discovers its true nature but this does not mean his own sleep is different from that of anyone else who enters it quite unconsciously. We can give an accurate account if we describe conditions that remain unconscious as if we passed through them consciously—and that is what I will now do.

After the transition of dreams—as I indicated already—we pass over into loss of consciousness as far as ordinary awareness is concerned. But the reality of this loss of awareness appears to supersensible perception as if, directly after falling asleep, we enter a kind of blurred state. If we grasped this condition consciously we would feel ourselves to be poured out, as it were, into an etheric world. We would feel ourselves to be outside our body, not narrowly confined but poured far abroad. We would perceive our body as an object outside us. If we became aware of this condition, our psyche would be pervaded by a certain anxiety or trepidation: one feels that one has lost the firm support of one's body, and is standing before an abyss.

What we call the threshold of the world of spirit has to exist because we first have to prepare ourselves for the sense of having lost the anchor, the purchase which our physical body gives us, and for enduring the anxiety that arises because we face something initially entirely unknown and undefined.

This feeling of anxiety, as I said, is not present ordinarily when people sleep. It is not a conscious awareness, but we pass through this state nevertheless. And the way that fear manifests in daily physical existence comes to expression here too, albeit only in subtle processes in our physical body: certain vascular activities are different in the body when we are afraid than when we are not. In other words, there is an objective occurrence, quite apart from what we experience in our awareness as agitation and so forth. The objective nature of this soul-spiritual anxiety is something we undergo when we pass through into sleep. But this sense of anxiety is connected with something else: with a feeling of deep yearning for a divine-spiritual reality that pervades and imbues the world.

If we experienced in full consciousness the first moments—or even perhaps for some the first hours—after we fall asleep, we would initially dwell in this anxiety and yearning for the divine. Any religious mood that we feel during waking life in fact originates primarily in our unconscious experience of anxiety and longing that we pass through during the night, which works through into our waking mood. You can say that spiritual experiences are here projected into physical life, filling us with the echo or after-effect of the fear that in general drives us to wish to perceive what is real in the world, filling us too with the echo of the yearning we experience in sleep and express in our religious feelings in waking life.

But this is only true of the initial phases of sleep. As sleep progresses, something remarkable occurs: the soul is as if split, fragmented into many souls. If we consciously experienced this state, which only a modern initiate can perceive nowadays in its entirety, we would seem to ourselves to be many souls, and this would make us feel we had lost ourselves. All the separate souls—which are really only shadow images of souls—present themselves as something in which we have lost our-selves. In relation to this phase of sleep, the human being appears differently depending on whether we consider him prior to or after the Mystery of Golgotha. You see, we need the external aid of the cosmos when encountering what I would call fragmentation into many soul reflections.

In ancient times before the Mystery of Golgotha, the ancient initiates gave humankind certain religious instruction, doing so via their pupils—the teachers they sent out into the world to help human beings—and such instruction, enacted in rituals, evoked feelings in people's waking life and strengthened their souls. Thus they could take back into sleep something like an echo or after-effect of this religious mood.

In the interplay between sleep and waking therefore, we experience in our yearning for the divine during the first phase of sleep something that, on awakening, inclines us to develop religious feelings. If this religiosity is developed in waking life, on the other hand—as it was in ancient times by initiates—then it works back in turn on the second phase of sleep: through the echo of this religious mood the soul then feels itself strong enough to endure its fragmentation, and to survive, at least, amidst such multiplicity.

That is the difficulty for non-religious people—that they have no such nightly aid to confront their sense of fragmentation into many souls; and that they then bear back with them into waking life what they experience there without religious strengthening. Everything we pass through at night, you see, is brought back with us into waking life as an after-effect. Irreligious and anti-religious attitudes do not yet have a very long tradition in humanity, since they largely originated in the nineteenth century. So far people have retained some echo of what they were endowed with in earlier, more honestly religious times. But as an irreligious age continues, this will have significant repercussions: people will bring back with them from sleep the after-effect of this fragmentation of the soul, and this will mean, quite particularly, that they will no longer possess the cohering powers during their waking life to distribute the effects of their food in the right way through their organism. The consequences of an irreligious outlook will, in not so very distant times, come to expression in significant illnesses.

No one should think that the spirit and soul have no relationship with the physical. This relationship is not such that an irreligious attitude will directly meet with retribution, in the form of illness, meted out by some kind of demonic divinity. Life does not work in this superficial way. Yet there is an inward connection between what we undergo in soul and spirit and our physical nature. To be healthy during waking life we need to feel during sleep that we belong to divine, spiritual beings in whose activity we immerse the core of our own eternal being between falling asleep and awakening again. Only when we stand within the world of soul and spirit in the right way during sleep can we draw forth the right, healthy powers of soul and spirit during our waking life.

During this second phase of sleep we enter a state where we possess, instead of our ordinary consciousness, not exactly cosmic consciousness but a cosmic mode of experience. As stated, only the initiate can become aware of this condition, but everyone experiences it while asleep during the night. And during this second phase of sleep we enact within us reflections of the planetary movements of our solar system. During the day we experience ourselves within our physical body. In speaking of ourselves as physical beings we feel that we contain lungs, heart, stomach, brain and so forth, as physical interiority. By contrast, during this second stage of sleep our spirit-soul interiority is the movement of Venus, of Mercury, the sun, the moon. We do not carry into us this whole interplay of planetary movements themselves but instead the reflections, astral replicas of them, which then compose our inner organization. It is not that we are spread out through the whole planetary cosmos, but we are of huge dimensions compared to our physical dimensions in waking life. We do not incorporate the actual movements of Venus into us during sleep but a reflection or replica of its movements. And between falling asleep and waking up again, during the second phase of sleep, planetary movements circulate in astral substance in our spirit and soul, in the same way that—stimulated by the motions of our breathing—the blood circulates through our physical organism during the day. In other words, during the night we have a kind of replica of our cosmos circulating in us as our interior life.

We first have to pass through a fragmentation of the soul and then we can experience this replica of planetary circulation. As I have said, in ancient times before the Mystery of Golgotha, initiates gave their people instructions for enduring this splitting of the soul, enabling the soul to find its way into these movements which then constituted their inner life. After the Mystery of Golgotha, these ancient teachings were replaced by what we can acquire as feeling, perception, soul life and soul mood by forming a true inner connection with what Christ did for humanity on earth through the Mystery of Golgotha. If we feel ourselves strongly enough connected with Christ to the degree of fulfilling within us the Pauline phrase 'Not I but Christ in me',[19] then through this deep connection with Christ and the Mystery of Golgotha we develop in our sensibility something that works on into sleep; and this gives us the strength to overcome the soul's fragmentation and find our way within the labyrinth of the planetary movements, which have now become our interiority. You see, this is also necessary: to find our bearings, even if we only unconsciously bear these planetary circulations within us as replacement for the blood circulation of waking life, which continues of course in the body we have left behind.

Having passed through this condition, we enter the third phase of sleep. Here—and what we experienced during the first phase still remains, while the experiences of the following stage are added—we enter into what I will call an experience of the fixed stars. After experiencing the circulation of planetary replicas, we do actually experience the configurations of the fixed stars, the zodiac as older eras regarded it, for example. And what we experience here is needed by our soul, because we have to bear this experience of the fixed stars back into our waking life if our soul is to have the power of mastering and enlivening our physical organism.

It is true to say, therefore, that during the night every person first passes through an etheric prelude in cosmic fear and divine yearning, then a planetary stage in which his astral body feels after-images of the planetary movements, and then an experience of the fixed stars during which he feels—or would do if he was conscious—that his own inner soul and spirit are a replica of the starry heavens.

Someone who understands these stages of sleep will find that a significant question arises for him each night. The human soul, the astral organism, the I being detach themselves from the physical body and their inner life is filled by a replica of the planetary movements and the configurations of fixed stars. And the question is this: why do we return to physical existence again every morning after sleep?

In fact it becomes evident to initiation science that we would not do so if, as we enter the planetary movements and fixed star forms, we did not also find our way into the moon forces as we grow out into the replicas of cosmic existence.

We enter into the spiritual moon forces, those powers of the cosmos reflected in the physical moon and its fluctuations. Whereas all other planetary and fixed star powers really draw us out of our physical body, the moon forces bring us back time and again into our physical body. The moon is connected generally with everything that brings us down from spiritual existence into physical existence. The moon is always present in the spiritual world, and the physical constellation plays no part here—whether it is new moon, full moon or waning moon—although this does have a certain significance. Moon forces are always there and guide the human being back into the physical world, into his physical body.

You see, the description, albeit only schematic, of what we pass through between falling asleep and waking up again is a picture of our sojourn in the world of spirit altogether. Each night, basically, we experience a reflection of what we pass through between death and a new birth. If we use the faculties of Imagination, Inspiration and Intuition to look back into our pre-earthly existence then we first glimpse ourselves as human spirit-soul being at a very early stage of this existence. There we see ourselves possessing cosmic consciousness, no longer dwelling in a life that carries in it mere replicas of the cosmos, as in sleep, but instead actually poured out through the real cosmos. And roughly around the middle of life between death and a new birth we feel ourselves fully conscious as spirit-soul beings—with a much clearer and more intense awareness than we can have on earth—and surrounded by divine, spiritual beings, by the divine, spiritual hierarchies. In the same way that we work with natural forces here on earth so work unfolds between us and the beings of the higher spiritual hierarchies.

What is the nature of this work? In union with a huge number of sublime spiritual beings in the universe, our being of soul and spirit weaves the cosmic spirit germ of our future physical body. However strange this may sound to you, the very greatest, most significant work that can be conceived of is to weave the spirit germ of the human physical body out of the cosmos. The human soul undertakes this in the condition I have described, in collaboration with hosts of divine, spiritual beings. If you picture the most complex thing that can be created here on earth, this is primitive and simple compared to the mighty weft of cosmic grandeur and glory that is created there, later to be reduced and compressed through conception and birth, filled with earthly matter to become a physical body.

If we speak of a seed here on earth, this is a small germ that later grows relatively large. But in speaking of the human body as an outcome of spirit, of a spiritual seed, this seed is of huge dimensions. As we move on from the time I have described, towards our next birth, this human germ of soul-spiritual grandeur increasingly shrinks; and we work further on it, elaborate it with a view to weaving, reducing and condensing it into the physical human body.

It is really with good reason that the initiates of older eras spoke of the human body as a 'temple of the gods'—through clairvoyance we no longer possess, though initiation science teaches the same thing. It is indeed a temple, woven each time anew out of the universe by the human soul in union with divine beings between death and a new birth. And then we are endowed with our physical form in a way that I will describe. In weaving the spirit germ of our physical body at the indicated stage of our sojourn in worlds of spirit, we are in a state of soul, a soul mood, that can only be compared with what a modern initiate calls Intuition. Our soul lives amidst the deeds of gods, flowing out entirely into the gods' divine existence. In this middle stage between death and a new birth it experiences the life of divine beings, shares in this life.

But as we progress further, moving towards conception and birth, this alters. In a sense we become aware that the divine beings of the higher hierarchies withdraw from us. And then what we receive is more like a manifestation, a reflection of glory, as if the gods have withdrawn and only their mistier reflections still stood before us—as if a kind of veil has been woven as misty replica of what was previously there as reality. The Intuition consciousness we possessed before now passes into cosmic Inspiration consciousness. We no longer live with the divine, spiritual beings but with their revelation; but at the same time, instead, an inward I increasingly develops in our soul consciousness. At what I would call the high point of our life between death and a new birth, we live entirely with beings of soul and spirit of the higher hierarchies and our I has no inner strength. It only starts to become aware of itself again as the gods withdraw, leaving only their manifestation. The glory or radiance of the gods enters us now in a kind of Inspiration consciousness; this loss in immediate reality is balanced by our sense of ourselves as an autonomous being. And what awakens in us initially here is something I would call desire, a strong wish.

At the mid-point between death and a new birth we work on the spirit germ of our physical body out of a deep inner fulfilment. Though we anticipate the goal of our new physical body in our next life, this is not pervaded by desire but only, if you like, by wonder at the nature of this physical human body in universal terms. The moment we no longer dwell in divine worlds themselves but in the revelation or manifestation of these worlds, desire awakens in us to be re-embodied on earth. As our I consciousness becomes ever stronger, this desire awakens to be incarnated again on earth. We distance ourselves from divine worlds and start to approach what we will subsequently become as earthly human beings. This desire grows ever stronger, and what we perceive outside us also changes. Previously we dwelt entirely amongst beings in the divine, spiritual hierarchies, and knew ourselves to be one with them. The cosmos was our interior life, but this cosmos itself consisted of beings at lofty levels of consciousness with whom we lived. Now, instead, we see external appearance within which gradually emerge the first pictures of divine, spiritual beings as physical reflections. From the sun being we encountered in further realms there emanates a shimmer within which the sun now appears, as seen externally from the world. Here on earth we look up towards the sun. As we descend before birth we first see the sun from the other side. But the sun and the fixed stars dawn for us, and behind them the planetary movements. And as these planetary movements surface, quite specific forces emerge too: the spiritual moon forces which now take possession of us, and gradually bear us back into earthly life.

This is in fact the view we have as we descend from cosmic worlds to earthly existence: we pass from an experience of divine, spiritual hierarchies to pictures of them. But these images of their being gradually become star constellations, which we enter as if from behind initially: we enter into what appears to us on earth as the cosmos. Modern initiation science can to a large degree penetrate with understanding the details of what a human soul accomplishes here.

Only by concerning ourselves with the specific details of these things do we come to a fuller understanding of life. You see, no one really grasps life if he sees the human being only in terms of earth existence. He won't be able to make much of life in this case. In the huge spans of time between death and a new birth the earth is of no importance to us to begin with; and the external light that shines upon us here is there transformed into whole worlds of the divine, in which we then dwell, and which only reveal their outer aspect to us again as stars when we approach the earth again to embark on a new life on earth.

What we first weave as the spirit germ of our physical body we know initially to be one with the whole spiritual universe. But as we come to see only the reflected manifestation of the divine-spiritual world, this spirit germ increasingly becomes our body, which is now also a reflection of the cosmos. And from this body of ours arises the desire for an earthly existence, for I consciousness in our body.

This body is still a spirit body as yet and therefore much about it is still untouched by earthly existence. At a certain stage, for instance, no decision has as yet been made as to whether the person concerned will be a man or woman in their next life. You see, there is no sense at all in considering this distinction during much of the period between death and a new birth. Not until a very late stage in the process of approaching earthly birth does this question become meaningful. The soul is dwelling in quite different conditions than those in which man and woman come to expression on earth. There are conditions that unfold in spiritual existence and are reflected in earthly realities; but what appears as male and female gender on earth only acquires meaning at a relatively late stage before one descends to earth again. And we can trace the specifics of how—if certain former karmic conditions suggest to the soul that it will best undergo the forthcoming life as a woman— the human being descends towards earthly existence and, connecting with the human physical germ, chooses the time which on earth we perceive as that of full moon.

If we look up at the full moon from any region of the earth, this is the time during which beings descending to earth choose to become women. Only then is this decision made. And those who wish to become men choose the time of new moon. In other words we enter into earthly existence through the gateway of the moon. But the strength the man needs to embark on earthly life shines out into the universe at that time, and he comes towards it as he enters from the universe: it streams out from the moon at the time of new moon on the earth. The strength the woman needs, by contrast, shines out from the moon at the time of full moon. Then its illumined face is turned towards the earth and its dark aspect sends out into the universe the strength the human entelechy needs if it is to become a woman.

What I have described to you will show you that ancient astrology was well founded even if it has become entirely decadent today in its prevalent forms. It is only a question of perceiving things inwardly, and seeing interrelationships. It is not enough merely to calculate the position of a physical constellation but we also have to grasp the spirit corresponding to this. It really is possible to enter into specific details here.

At a certain stage we descend again from the cosmos, passing from the spiritual cosmos into the etheric cosmos. At the moment I'm still speaking only of the etheric cosmos: the physical stars play a lesser role here, and the physical moon is still less significant. The key moment when a person chooses to descend to earth is connected as I have said with the phase of the moon, with moon conditions; but as the soul descends it is frequently exposed to the full moon or new moon. And therefore after the decisive new moon or full moon influence, when a soul has decided to become male or female, since this descent occurs only gradually the soul choosing to become a man can still decide to expose itself to the full moon influence. In other words, the soul has decided to become a man and has used the new moon forces for this, but in descending can still draw upon the moon's further phases. The soul is then filled with moon forces in a way that no longer affects gender but chiefly the head organization instead, all that originates in the cosmos and is externally connected with the head organization, when the particular constellation occurs as I have described. And so if the human soul has decided to become a man through the influence of the new moon period, and then continues to dwell in the cosmos and is exposed to the following full moon period, the influences of these moon forces will, for instance, give him brown eyes and black hair. The way the human soul passes the moon not only determines gender but also the colour of hair and eyes. If someone, say, has passed the full moon as a woman and is subsequently exposed to the influence of the new moon, this can endow her with blue eyes and fair hair.

This may sound grotesque, but certainly how we experience the cosmos predestines the way in which our soul and spirit work into our physical and etheric organism. Whether we have black hair or blonde is not determined before this point, but is decided by moon forces as we descend from the cosmos and pass the moon.

In the same way that we pass the moon, which really guides us into earthly existence, so we also pass the other planets. It is not an indifferent matter whether we pass Saturn in one way or another. For example, we may pass Saturn at a time when, due to a particular constellation, the power of Saturn works together with that of the constellation Leo. Because Saturn is here strengthened by Leo in the zodiac, as we pass this region—although our previous karma determines this—we acquire the strength that enables us to meet external events in life with prudence so that they do not always disconcert us. If Saturn is, say, more subject to the influence of Capricorn, then we become weaker people who can collapse under the pressure of circumstances.

We bear all this within us as, entering from the cosmos, we prepare our life on earth. Naturally education can overcome such weaknesses, but not by saying, along with materialists, that all this is nonsense and there is no need to consider it. Not in that way, but by developing the powers intrinsic to us, really developing them. And in future, humanity will learn once more not merely to ensure that a child receives good milk and good sustenance but to perceive also whether Saturn forces or Jupiter forces are at work in someone under a particular influence.

Let us say that, in a particular case, a person's karma means that he bears Saturn forces within him under the most unfavourable influence— for instance under the influence of Capricorn or Aquarius, and he is therefore exposed to all life's greatest difficulties. Then we can carefully seek for other powers within him and try to strengthen these. We might ask, for instance, whether he passed through the Jupiter sphere, the

Mars sphere or through some other sphere, and it will always be possible to set one thing against the other to supply a remedy.

We will have to learn to think of human beings not just in terms of diet and earthly concerns but in connection with their passage through cosmic worlds between death and a new birth.

As a human soul draws close to his earthly life, in a sense he loses some of his intrinsic being. As you saw from my description, he has been connected with the spirit germ of the physical body he has been weaving. He has also interwoven this spirit germ with his experiences of descending through the fixed stars and the planets. At a certain stage, very close to conception and birth, the spirit germ is no longer present, but has in the meantime descended to the earth, taking its powers down with it as energy system. It has lapsed from us, and independently merged with inherited physical substance passed on through ancestors and the future child's mother and father. What is woven into the organism precedes us to the earth, ahead of our intrinsic being of soul and spirit. And when a soul feels that he has passed to his parents what he himself really wove in the cosmos, he is able, at this last stage before earthly life begins—since he no longer needs to weave his physical body, which is largely ready and has been given up to the stream of inheritance and incorporated into it—to draw what he needs as ether organism from the world ether and mantle himself in it. He draws his etheric organism together. And along with this etheric organism he now connects with what he himself has prepared through his parents. He takes on his physical body, into which this whole cosmic weft of the spirit germ has contracted, inscribed with what the person himself experienced as, in descending, he passed through this or that region of the stars. He does not arbitrarily pass through the gate of new moon or full moon, or randomly become a man or woman, with black or blonde hair, or blue or brown eyes, but all this is intimately connected with the outcomes of his former karma.

You can see from all this that whereas in sleep we only pass through replicas of the planetary world, of the world of fixed stars, between death and a new birth we traverse these worlds in reality. As we pass through them they become our inner life. The moon forces are always what bring us back to the earth, and as such they are different from all other star powers. In sleep they return us to the earth, and likewise they return us to the earth after we have traversed all the regions I described and approach a new life on earth.

But now let us consider once again the astral and I organization that are outside the physical body when we sleep. Rather than a fabric of physical bones and physical blood, our whole moral worth is interwoven with our spirit and soul. Here on earth we are composed of bones, blood and nerves, but what rises out of us as we fall asleep and enters us again when we wake up is composed of a reality that has coalesced from judgements about our own moral actions.

If I did a good deed during the day, the effect of this is inscribed into my spirit-soul sleep body that rises out of me at night. My moral quality dwells in it. And when we pass through the gate of death, we bear with us the whole, realized estimation of our moral being. You see, we create a second human being within us, in fact, in our life on earth between birth and death. This second human being who emerges from us every night during sleep is the outcome of our moral or immoral life, and this passes with us through the gate of death.

This outcome, incorporated into the eternal core of our being, is not the only thing we possess in our soul and spirit as it rises out of us at night. But particularly after death, when we dwell first in the etheric body and then in the astral body, we discern almost nothing other than this moral entelechy of ours. We can then perceive clearly whether we did good or ill: we *are* this. Just as we are a person with skin, nerves, blood or bones on earth, there we perceive ourselves in terms of our morality or immorality.

And now, after death, we make our way outwards, first through the moon sphere then through the fixed star sphere, until we arrive at the time when we can begin to work with the beings of the higher hierarchies upon the spirit germ of our future physical body. But if we bore this moral element right up into the highest worlds where we must weave the spirit germ of our future physical organism, the latter would become a real monstrosity. For a period between death and a new birth, we must be lifted beyond our moral quality. In fact, we leave it behind in the moon sphere.

You see, as we pass beyond the moon sphere, we leave behind there our moral or immoral aspect and enter into the pure sphere of the gods where we can weave our new physical body.

But now, once again, I have to highlight the difference between older eras before the Mystery of Golgotha and those following it, through to modern times. Ancient initiates told their pupils, who passed this on to all humankind, that to find a transition from the world I described as the world of souls in my book *Theosophy*, which we pass through entirely, really, in the moon sphere—to make this transition and gain entry to what I called spirit land—we must acquire feelings on earth which allow the spiritual sun beings to guide us upwards after we have left this whole baggage of moral effects behind us in the moon sphere.

Everything that history tells us about the first three Christian centuries, about the fourth century AD too, is really false. Christianity was quite different from how it is described during these centuries. It was different because a view prevailed during this time which still originated in an understanding of ancient initiation. This initiation wisdom gave people the knowledge that the great, sublime sun being led the human soul, once it had left its moral baggage behind it, out of the moon sphere after death and then led the soul back again as it returned to the moon sphere. This was known to endow people with the strength— which they could not acquire by themselves—to incorporate this moral aspect at a certain period before birth so that, in their souls, they could fulfil their destiny on earth. This moral quality was not to enter the body, for otherwise a person would be deformed at birth and suffer great physical disease or disorder. It has instead to be taken on again by the soul as we enter the moon sphere so that it does not enter our future body.

The initiates living at the time of the Mystery of Golgotha, and three to four centuries afterwards too, told their pupils that the lofty sun being used only to dwell above in worlds of spirit. But as humanity progressed, I consciousness became so bright on earth that it became correspondingly darkened or obscured in the world of spirit. You see, the brighter our I consciousness is here on earth, by virtue of the physical body alone, the darker it is up above. If Christ had not descended and undergone the Mystery of Golgotha, human beings could no longer have approached the sun being or, by their own strength, found the transition from the moon sphere into higher spheres. The being whom we used to encounter after death only in the spiritual world descended and since the Mystery of Golgotha lives here upon earth. We can gain a relationship to him by holding to the Pauline saying, 'Not I, but Christ in me.' By this means we take with us from this earth the strength given us by Christ here on earth to leave behind our moral being—which we ourselves individually engender—in the moon sphere, and to pass on into the higher spheres to weave the spirit germ of our future physical body. And this means in turn that we find the strength as we descend again through the moon sphere to take our karma upon us by our free choice, to shoulder the consequences of our good and bad deeds. During the course of evolution we have become free human beings; but this is only because the power of Christ, which we acquire here on earth, enables us to take on our karma by our own free strength as we descend to the moon sphere. Quite irrespective of whether this thought pleases or displeases us while on earth, at this stage of life between death and a new birth we do this if we become true Christians.

I have tried to describe some of what modern initiation science can perceive of the worlds we may call the hidden aspects of human existence; and really human nature can only be explained by considering these hidden aspects. At the same time I sought to show you the related importance of the Christ impulse for modern human beings, for this is something we must keep coming back to. We cannot be full human beings in the time after the Mystery of Golgotha if we do not find our way to the Christ impulse, and therefore anthroposophic spiritual science has to increasingly illumine the Christ impulse in the right way. The obscured way in which Christianity was seen in the past, with dulled consciousness, would deprive most of humanity of the opportunity to embrace Christianity. Think of people in the Orient, and the inhabitants of other regions of the earth. But a Christianity deepened by anthroposophic insights is something which, if the living core of it is understood in the way I intended here, will be embraced by people in the East particularly, who possess an ancient, albeit now decadent spirituality—embraced by them with full hearts.

Only in this way can peace come to the earth. It must arise from the human soul and spirit. Every open-minded person knows at heart how important peace is to the earth. People will increasingly come to see how worthless is all superficial tinkering with outward forms and institutions, and how important it is, by contrast, to address souls directly. But we cannot address them if we have nothing to tell them about the soul's true home, and about what we experience beyond physical existence in states of consciousness I have described today. While these states of awareness may not be present during earthly life, their effects and consequences exist. Oh, anyone who understands life will see in every human face an image of the cosmic destinies a person has passed through between death and a new birth!

I described to you today how the destiny of being either a man or a woman can be understood through insight into the cosmos—how even the colour of our eyes or hair can only be understood if we can perceive cosmic existence. Nothing is comprehensible in this world if we do not see it in connection with the cosmos. People will only feel their full humanity if we draw on real spiritual insight to show them their deep connection with all that underlies physical sense existence. Even if people are unaware of this today, unconsciously they thirst for such insight. And the convulsions we are experiencing in all areas of life—in our culture, in the field of human rights, in economic life—all of this can ultimately be traced back to the spirit. And all of it can only be lifted out of decline, and rejuvenated, if people learn again to understand something of their connection with an existence beyond the physical world. This physical existence is nothing if it is not seen in connection with a life beyond physical reality. Our physical human body only acquires its meaning if we see it as the confluence of all the majestic powers that are woven into it between death and a new birth. The tragedy of the materialistic world-view is that ultimately it does not even understand material reality. We place the human corpse on the dissecting table, and conscientiously study its tissues and various physical attributes. We do so because we wish to understand matter. But we do not come to know it by these means, for it is an outcome of the spirit; we only come to know it if we can trace it back to the realms where it is woven from the spirit. Physical and material existence itself will only become comprehensible to people when their soul is guided towards cosmic realities of soul and spirit.

If we fill ourselves with an awareness that we need to increasingly understand how we are connected with the spirit and soul of the cosmos, we become true anthroposophists. Here at least I will not be ridiculed, I'm sure, if I say that the world needs true anthroposophists who further humanity's ascent with a form of awareness that arises when we experience the spirit, even if to begin with we only grasp it as an image or reflection and do not ourselves perceive it clairvoyantly. We do not need to be clairvoyant ourselves to possess knowledge of the spirit and work charitably and beneficially. When we eat meat we do not have to know exactly what constitutes it—it will still nourish us. In the same way we do not need to be clairvoyant to bring about, through the way we work, our whole connection with the life of higher worlds. Assuming the spirit exists before we become clairvoyant is like consuming spirit. Clairvoyance does not really add anything to what we can become through a spiritual knowledge of the world. It only satisfies our need for knowledge, which we inevitably have. Of course there must be people who study the precise composition of meat, but we do not have to stop eating until we know this. Likewise, we need people with clairvoyance nowadays to study how human beings are connected with the world of spirit. But for humanity to work in the right way, we need only be healthy human souls, who will sense their power of soul digestion when they hear someone speaking of the science of the spirit. They will absorb this spiritual element, assimilate it and incorporate it into their work. And this is what we need today throughout the civilized world: outward human work which is rightly and truly filled with spirit.

Lecture 7

LAST time I was here,[21] you may remember that I spoke to you about the human soul's experiences during sleep; and today I wish to develop this theme further.

If we consider only our waking life, half of human life remains hidden from us. The most important things occur during sleep. I have spoken to you here in London before about the method of enquiry based on exact clairvoyance,[22] and so there is no need for me to explain again today that what I will describe is based on this. I will assume that you understand that insights presented here draw on an exact science of clairvoyance.

When we pass from a waking state of consciousness to that of sleep, which is basically a state of unconsciousness for people today, we are no longer in our physical or etheric body. During sleep we are a being of pure spirit. And while we are asleep, as a being of spirit and soul we experience the things I described to you last time from a particular angle.

You will recall that during sleep we first experience our being penetrating the cosmic ether, which causes a certain anxiety to rise up in us—a fear of the unknown, nebulous and undifferentiated. And you will also remember that something awakens in the soul at this moment which we can name with an expression drawn from our conscious life: a yearning for the divine. Then you will also recall that in a second stage of sleep we pass through replicas or images of the planetary movements, and that for a person who has a relationship to the Mystery of Golgotha

Christ appears as a guide through these otherwise chaotic experiences, these images of the life of planets we pass through during sleep. Then comes an experience of the world of fixed stars; we have now passed beyond the planetary sphere, though only in image or reflection, and experience the fixed star constellations. From the moment we fall asleep to the moment of awakening, therefore, we experience all of extra-telluric, cosmic existence. And I also said to you that the moon forces, the spiritual counterpart of moon phenomena, always lead us back in the morning or whenever we wake up into our physical and etheric body.

Today I would like to describe these experiences during sleep from another perspective. In our waking consciousness during the day we possess, if we are not entangled in modern humanity's materialistic ideas, a moral and religious foundation for our life. Besides our sense-based knowledge we need to feel that we also have moral obligations and responsibilities, and furthermore that our whole being rests and is rooted in a world of spirit. We can call the latter a religious awareness. This moral and religious consciousness is something we possess while awake, and yet we only do so by virtue of inhabiting our physical body. In fact we are not alone in our physical body but spirits of higher hierarchies are also present with us, dwelling with us in our body. In our etheric body, too, we live alongside the moral intentions of these spirits of the higher hierarchies.

In other words, our religious consciousness is dependent on living in the physical body, while moral life is dependent on our life in the etheric body. This can make us aware that the world ether from which our etheric body is drawn has two aspects, one of which is warmth, light, chemical ether and life ether. But underlying all these etheric qualities of warmth, light, chemical processes and life is the other aspect: the moral essence of the cosmic ether. This moral essence only exists however in proximity to the stars and planets. In living upon earth, you see, even though you are unaware of this during the day, you are also contained in the cosmic ether as moral essence. And when you wander through the starry worlds you are also within the moral essence of the world ether in the neighbourhood of a celestial body. Between the stars, sunlight drives out the moral element from the ether. The light the sun shines—but not the sun itself, a celestial body which for us human beings contains the primordial source of the moral ether—dispels the ether's moral essence. And therefore when our eyes look out into the world we see flowers, see springs, see everything without imbuing what we see with a moral quality; and this is because sunlight dispels and deadens the moral element.

And when, in falling asleep, we emerge from our physical and etheric body, as beings of spirit and soul we initially have nothing other than what we acquired during earthly life by perceiving the natural world around us. However paradoxical this sounds, we leave behind in bed our religious feeling and moral sensibility with the physical and etheric body, and live as an amoral being during sleep. During this time we live in a world otherwise illumined by sunlight. And because the moral world order is dispelled from the ether, the being of Ahriman gains entry to this ether into which we come as we fall asleep. As we sleep, this ahrimanic being speaks to us; and basically this is a dire business, since Ahriman is rightly called the spirit of untruth. This is because he presents good as ill, and evil as good, to sleeping human beings .

Recently there was a piece published in the newspaper about something scientists have also been studying—the question as to why criminals sleep so well whereas moral people with a good conscience often sleep badly. This can be explained by what I have said. Someone with a strong conscience, a person of inward and moral sensibility, possesses a soul that goes so deeply into moral feelings that he takes this with him into sleep and sleeps badly if he believes he has done much ill. But a person without a strongly developed moral conscience takes no pangs of conscience with him into sleep, and then his ears of spirit are wide open to the whisperings of Ahriman, who presents evil to him as good. This is why a criminal sleeps so soundly.

People think this is unjust: why should criminals sleep soundly while decent folk toss and turn? As I said, scientists have found this to be so. But it is caused by what I have described. The temptation to evil during sleep is huge, and as a person wakes up in the morning he can easily bring the most demonic powers of temptation with him. Only as he comes back into his physical and etheric body do the pangs of conscience reawaken in someone who is not such a good human being. During sleep an earthly human being very easily succumbs to the temptations of Ahriman.

This has only gradually come to be so, however, over the course of time. Only in our modern era are people exposed to such a great degree to the demonic powers that present evil to them as good while they sleep. This was not so in earlier periods of human evolution, when, as I have often said, people did not have such a strong I consciousness. During their waking life they had a weaker sense of I, and this meant that during sleep they did not sail so blithely into the realm of evil as they now do. Human evolution is at a crisis point, a decisive era. People must arm themselves against the power of evil that approaches them. In former times human beings were protected, for as they fell asleep they merged more with the group soul, lived in the group soul during sleep. This group-soul life is something we still develop to a certain degree in waking life, feeling ourselves part of a nation, often even of a 'tribe' or— sometimes with aristocratic airs and graces—as members of a family. But nowadays sleep deprives us entirely of this group-soul feeling. It is no longer possible nowadays to be easily aristocratic in sleep. Indeed, sleep educates us far more than you imagine, on the one hand makes us more evil and on the other more democratic. Sleep is certainly a great teacher. In olden times people entered the group soul when they fell asleep; and when they woke up again, returning to their physical and etheric body, they brought with them a strong sense of being part of a group. That is one aspect of the human being—what he is during sleep.

But what occurs in sleep and is so greatly subject to evil as I have described is something we also possess within us today. We just have to immerse it during waking life in our moral and religious awareness, let it flow into this. Religiosity is given us by the powers that live with the physical body and morality by those that live with the etheric body.

All this changed for humanity's evolution with the Mystery of Golgotha. In ancient times people lived strongly in their group-soul consciousness during sleep and when they awoke, sinking back down into their physical and etheric body, they lived more individually. But here we find another difference between people in olden times and nowadays. When a person of former eras began waking up, as he was immersing himself again in his physical and ether body he had a clear awareness of his pre-earthly life before he woke up fully. And the same was true as he was just falling asleep. Thus in those times people had both a stronger group-soul consciousness and a strong awareness of their participation in a life removed from the earth. They knew how they had descended from the world of spirit, passing through the world of stars and choosing a physical body here on earth. Later, this consciousness became dulled and obscured. Instead humankind became clever, as we call it. People were imbued with faculties of judgement, discrimination and such things. This only slowly evolved; and this is also why we can judge things so well in the morning—because our physical body gives us the power of judgement. We penetrate our physical and etheric body more strongly than people once did, and this was why they were aware of their previous existence while we have a stronger sense of earthly existence. We settle down solidly in our physical and etheric body, something that was not the case in olden times. In older eras people wore the physical and ether body more as something external to them, having the same sense of them that we have of our clothes. We no longer have this feeling. We no longer say, as was said in olden times when someone went in through a doorway: 'I carry myself through the door'. He meant his physical body—this was a common, natural figure of speech in old languages. Nowadays we say: '*I'm* going through the door,' because we push our I very solidly down into the physical body. And we consider this way of putting it self-evident and natural.

As these developments continued, people lost an awareness of their connection with the world of spirit and the stars. In older times a person knew that he was connected with the world of stars and, behind it, with a world of spirit, and had descended from these worlds to earthly existence. In the modern era we say: 'I need food to live—meat, vegetables and eggs.' All these are products of the physical world, with which we are so involved from birth to death. Please don't think I mean to express any disregard for such things; they are all very good, and part and parcel of life, and their full importance absolutely has to be acknowledged. All I wish to say is that people of olden times knew that to live they not only needed the strength of the earth that lies in cattle and cabbage and eggs, but also the strength of Jupiter, Venus and Saturn. They knew that just as they needed to eat on earth so, as they descended from the world of spirit, they needed to have imbibed the power of Jupiter and Venus to be a human being at all. A key concern of people today is what they should eat in order to be healthy; and similarly, people of ancient times felt it essential to have a relationship with the world of stars. They knew that if they were in some way deficient on earth, incapable of doing something, then they had not conducted themselves properly as they descended from the stars, and would need to correct this the next time they sojourned between death and a new birth. In olden times people developed what can be called a spiritual diet. In the ancient mysteries there were guides and leaders who resembled something like the modern physician, though the latter gives recommendations only about the body. This is quite natural and fitting. But the ancient guides in the mysteries, who in this respect were also physicians, gave suggestions about how, say, if someone was suffering from one complaint or another he should improve his relationship to Venus or Saturn. And this was accomplished by giving people certain instructions for their soul conduct. Let us imagine that an ancient physician of this kind found that the person seeking healing from him was too strongly connected with his physical body, and that, more than a kind of clothing, he lived in too strong a connection with it—a little like someone going to bed in his clothes perhaps. Such a physician would say to this patient suffering from a disorder involving excessive involvement in the physical body, 'Try to wander a little under the full moon when it rises in the evening, and as you do so, speak this or that mantra.'

Why would he recommend this? Because he knew that when someone goes walking in moonlight and speaks a mantra, this counteracts the power of Saturn. Saturn gains less power over such a person. And this ancient physician in the mysteries knew that excessive clinging to the physical body, this full immersion in it, arose from a person adhering too strongly to Saturn as he descended from the world of spirit through the world of stars into earthly existence. His disorder was traced back to this excessive sympathy with Saturnian life. Moon and Saturn are celestial bodies that counteract each other. And thus an ancient physician would use moon forces to cure the negative influence of Saturn forces. Thus he gave a spiritual diet, and this was an ancient method of healing.

We have a physical diet that we choose as appropriate for us. But in ancient times one needed a spiritual diet; and this is something we need to learn to add to our physical diet. The task of our modern era is to help people acquire a spiritual diet to enhance their physical diet, and this will enable us to meet the challenges of our times. That is what I wished to say in this first part of the lecture.

I am very pleased to be able to give two lectures to you here, and so I am not in such a hurry today as I often am. I can therefore speak to you at leisure of what I had in mind.

In ancient times, through an elementary clairvoyance, people were able to look back to their life in the world of spirit before their earthly life began, and before they united with their physical and etheric body on earth. Today we can only achieve this through real spiritual science as anthroposophy endeavours to develop it.

Then, by looking back through a faculty of Inspiration to the time preceding our descent to earth, we can realize that we live for a period in a world of pure spirit, a world without the natural kingdoms of minerals, plants or animals, not even containing stars as we see them in the earth's enfolding heavens, but instead seeing that we were surrounded by beings of the higher hierarchies. For a period between death and rebirth we live amongst spiritual beings, and only then do we descend to the earth, passing the starry heavens as we do so with greater or lesser sympathy for different celestial spheres. Here we do really prepare our earthly life. Depending on the way in which we relate to the starry spheres as we pass through them, this forms our future earthly existence. And now I would like to illustrate this with an example.

When we emerge from a world of pure spirit, we first pass through the sphere of fixed stars, and next time I will speak of this in more detail. Then we pass through the sphere of Saturn, Jupiter and Mars, the sun sphere, the spheres of Mercury, Venus and moon, gradually descending to the earth. As we emerge from a world of pure spirit, in a sense we approach the stars from their far side. Here on earth we look up to Jupiter from our earthly perspective. But as human beings emerging from the world of spirit and descending through the starry spheres towards earth, we see Saturn, and all the stars, from the other side. Our being in a sense approaches a celestial body from behind, seeing always the opposite of what human beings see on earth. But the human entelechy approaching the earth from the world of spirit does not perceive in the same way as we do here. We have no eyes then of course, which we only acquire through the physical body. And so we see the spiritual aspect of Saturn, Jupiter, Mars, the sun; the spiritual aspect of Venus, Mercury and moon. Accordingly, as our being descends, and depending on the sympathy or antipathy experienced in one sphere or the other, it must assimilate the qualities of each sphere—of Saturn, Jupiter and so forth.

Now something like this can happen. A human entelechy who lived in a particular way in a former life gains the impression as it descends towards a new life that it would be good to become a woman the next time it is born, to incarnate in a female body. This is very much a consideration for the descending human soul—whether to become a man or woman. Of course the soul's whole destiny will greatly depend on this, for it is not a matter of indifference whether one spends one's life on earth as a man or a woman. But this isn't a simple, quick decision for the soul. It has to be prepared. And this preparation involves the human soul who desires to become a woman approaching the earth at a time that we below see as full moon. When we see the full moon in the sky above us, the human soul, as it enters from the spiritual sphere, perceives the spiritual aspect of the moon, perceiving it in fact as dark, or in other words filled wih particular beings. Yes, the soul sees the moon spiritually. And these beings prepare the soul so that it attracts towards it an earthly female body.

But when it is new moon from our earthly perspective, the descending soul sees the illumined moon from its other aspect; sees light shining out into cosmic space, or rather the spiritual aspect of this. And then it can become a man.

It therefore depends on how the soul is passing through the starry spheres whether it acquires the power to be male or female. But in the same way that the soul passes through the moon sphere, it also passes through the Mercury or Venus sphere for example. Whereas the soul becomes a man or woman in the moon sphere, it is endowed with sympathy for a particular family in the sphere of Venus, for it could become a man or woman in any number of families.

The human soul descending to the earth can either descend at a time when Venus is on the opposite side of the earth, so that it does not even need to pass through this sphere at all. Then the person will become someone who is not much concerned about his family. Or instead the soul will pass through the Venus sphere, and this leads him to a particular family. It is therefore possible for the soul to prepare itself for a particular family, by choosing the ray, if you like, that shines towards it from Venus. The soul will approach the earth from the far side, the dark side of Venus, and in this way comes to a particular family. Likewise it passes through the sphere of Mercury, which leads it to a particular nation. So again this is true: when this nation's region is illumined by the rays of Mercury, as the soul approaches from the far or dark side of Mercury, it will find the way to this particular people.

Thus the moon prepares human souls for birth, and, in spiritual terms, for the decision about becoming a man or a woman. Venus shows us the way to a particular family, and Mercury to a particular people or nation.

Our whole human life on earth is therefore dependent on how we shape things as we descend. This is something we need to come to understand once more, feeling ourselves as creatures of the world of stars in the same way that on earth we feel ourselves to be creatures of hydrogen, oxygen, nitrogen, carbon, sulphur and so on. We are not merely physical human beings composed of protein and a few other substances, but have been formed by all the powers of the universe that work upon us as we descend towards birth, which we then contain within us and of which in a sense we have a memory in sleep.

But memory is, as you know, always weaker than the original experience. If someone close to you dies, the grief gradually wanes. In the same way, in sleep, our intimate involvement in the world of spirit and of the stars is weaker than it originally was; and this is why we are exposed in sleep to everything I described at the beginning today. In sleep we have only a weak reflection, a cosmic memory if you like, of our spiritual and star experiences between death and this latest birth.[23]

LECTURE 8

LONDON, 16 NOVEMBER 1922

TODAY I will need to speak to you about the spiritual powers and beings who live supersensibly in our proximity and have a share in our earthly life. You will understand that everything occurring between spiritual beings in the supersensible world and the way such spiritual beings relate to one another is different in nature from what human beings customarily do during their life on earth, and that it is therefore difficult to express in human language—which is of course intended for human circumstances—the nature and activities of what we may call supersensible intelligences. Since this needs to be done nowadays, however, we must do it pictorially. And you will understand that some expressions I use appear to be coined in relation to human conditions. In fact they are accurate, but inevitably drawn from human circumstances and offered as a picture.

Nature surrounds us with her diverse realms, the mineral, plant and animal kingdoms and, we can also say, with the physical human kingdom. The natural world surrounding us has, you can say, a second nature behind it, a spiritual, supersensible one. We perceive the natural world with our senses. Supersensible nature which lies behind it is not ordinarily perceived but nevertheless has a great effect upon our earthly existence.

The second thing to be considered is that we have a physical nature and, when we look inside ourselves, perceive this physical nature as our instincts and passions. Naturally this is all astral, but it streams up out of our physical nature. Underlying what we perceive in this way within us as instincts, drives and passions is a kind of kingdom of beings with an intimate relationship to us, yet they are subhuman in nature. On the one hand, therefore, we look around us with our senses and see as it were the surface of nature, its exterior countenance under which we must intuit supersensible nature; and on the other, looking into ourselves and perceiving our own drives, instincts and passions, we have to intuit a subsensible nature underlying these and coming to expression in them, and through us. We can only gain insight into the supersensible nature around us by spiritual vision, looking beyond the strictly natural laws on which scientists focus their gaze. The results of scientific research will never be able to reveal supersensible nature underlying the natural world, but it does become apparent if we sharpen our spiritual perception not of what is strictly lawful but of what people usually refer to as chance or random occurrence.

Chance governs everything in the world around us that comes to expression in the weather, in the irregularities of the atmosphere through the seasons. You can attribute, say, a London fog to certain general causes, but you cannot identify the precise detail of every factor involved. Wind and weather are considered to be fairly random in nature. And weather forecasts do not offer a prediction as certain as that the sun will rise tomorrow. In other words, natural laws seem to be something quite different from what manifests in wind and weather, which people think of initially as fairly random occurrences. It is possible to develop a certain prophetic gift for predicting the weather, but this is something intuitive or inspired and cannot be formulated in strict laws.

Well, there are beings living in everything that comes to expression in wind and weather, and they are not perceived because they have no body visible to the senses that earthly beings possess. These beings living in the wind and the weather do exist nevertheless and have a body composed only of air and warmth, without any water, fluid or solidity. Their body is one of air and warmth alone.

This body of theirs dissolves and undergoes rapid transformations. The cloud formations we see, the sensations we have of wind, are only an outward expression of the deeds, if you like, of these beings, behind which is their body of air and warmth. Looking out into our atmosphere as it encircles the earth where we live, we have a world of beings composed of air and warmth, and their nature is one I have often described in my writings and lectures as luciferic.

These luciferic beings have a very special endeavour in relation to humankind. Although they often live in weather we find unpleasant, they are beings who have an extraordinary interest in the moral element at work in the human social order. They adhere so strongly to the moral element that they consider we ought not to have a real, physical body— or at least we ought not to have a body containing earthly and watery nature. They wish they could have shaped humankind like themselves, making us into entirely moral beings, though without freedom. We would be better off, in their view, if we did not have a physical nature at all and were moral beings alone. And during the year these beings battle furiously to draw the human being away from the earth and pull him into their own sphere—to alienate him from the earth and make him earthless. These beings are especially dangerous for anything in us that is quixotic or ungrounded, any kind of foggy mysticism. People with a tendency to foggy mysticism and ungrounded enthusiasms succumb very easily to these beings who seek to draw us away from the earth, to make us a kind of angel so that we cannot possibly fall prey to immoral temptations.

This probably sounds very strange and paradoxical. These powers expressed in the wind and weather, pulsing in the atmosphere, hate human freedom above all else, and wish to have nothing to do with it. They want to destroy it if possible and yet at the same time make us into moral automata, into nothing but angelic goodness. And, if I may use an earthly expression to describe this, they 'fight tooth and nail' to achieve this.

In contrast to these beings which, if you like, build their fortresses in the air—though please understand I am speaking metaphorically— there are others I mentioned last time in a particular context. These have to do with what expresses itself in us in instincts, drives, desires and passions. But they do not dwell inside us—only their effects are to be found there. These beings live directly upon the earth, yet in a way that is invisible to people because they never acquire a body formed in a way we could ordinarily see. They possess only a body that lives in the elements of earth and water. And their deeds manifest in the ebb and flow of tides, in volcanic eruptions, earthquakes and tremors. Behind these phenomena which, as you know, leave scientists helpless and perplexed, the spiritually honed gaze perceives a world of subhuman entities. And these subhuman entities are subject to the rule of powers I always refer to as ahrimanic. These ahrimanic powers with their diverse sub-spirits—including sprite- and goblin-like beings who dwell in the elements of earth and water—have set themselves a different task. We really can't hold it against all these beings that they do what they do. There is no point in being annoyed with luciferic beings, for they have the very best motivations: they want to make us intrinsically moral, albeit without any freedom at all, moral automata. Yet they do want the best for us. The other beings, who have their fortresses directly under the earth's surface, exert influences that rise into our metabolism. The ebb and flow of the tides, and the volcanic eruptions or earthquakes we witness too, though less regularly, are something that comes to expression also in a continual ebb and flow of human metabolism and is always present there. These are the ahrimanic effects.

Whereas the luciferic spirits build their castles in the air to battle against the earth on behalf of morality, these other beings battle to harden us and make us resemble them. By succumbing to them we would become endlessly clever in the material realm, endlessly ingenious, incredibly intelligent. These beings cannot achieve this directly and therefore seek to do so indirectly. Their millennia-old exertions have indeed succeeded in shaping and developing a whole race of subhuman entities that take possession of human instinctual nature—if this is especially rampant—so that such people fall prey to these ahrimanic powers during their lifetime.

If someone has fallen prey during his lifetime to the ahrimanic powers, is given up entirely to his passions, instincts and drives, becoming rampant in his desires, these beings can 'harvest' this after his death to create a whole population, a subhuman populace of the earth, which does indeed already exist. This does really exist in the elements of water and earth.

And if we ask what such ahrimanic beings intend with this subhuman populace, it is this: to draw this kind of instinctual nature from a human being and make it into a being of earth and water. And beings of earth and water do now actually populate the strata directly below the earth's surface. There they dwell. People who can use spiritual vision to observe mines know such entities very well: they exist there, having been torn from a human being at the moment of his death. And there waits Ahriman, there wait the ahrimanic powers for a person's karma, caused by instincts, drives and passions, to lead him down into an incarnation where he takes special pleasure in such a being, and therefore finds in a particular life on earth that he does not wish to return to the world of spirit. Having left his physical body—from which, after all, we depart again for a supersensible life—he will seek instead to be embodied in a subsensible being of this kind, to remain united with the earth: no longer to die but choosing to remain united with the earth as a sub-sensible entity.

One has to be astonished since ahrimanic beings, after all, are extraordinarily intelligent. As paradoxical as it sounds, they always think—and this is a quite accurate finding—that by this means they will be able to entice so many people into their race that eventually the earth will be populated entirely by subhuman ahrimanic entities of this kind. And their intention is to make the earth immortal as a result so that it does not atomize in universal space.

In our earthly human environs, therefore, we have two hosts: one of beings in the atmosphere, who want to make us moral but by lifting us away from the earth; and of ahrimanic beings directly below the earth's surface who seek to draw us down and bind us irrevocably to the earth.

These two types of being exist in the mineral, plant and animal kingdoms, and also in the ordinary physical domain of human nature. In so far as we do not dwell excessively in drives, passions and desires, they are compelled to endure each other's presence within us.

In primordial times the God who is called God the Father in the Christian religion maintained peace in the mineral, plant and animal kingdoms, and also in the external, animal and physical nature of humankind. God the Father kept the peace in these kingdoms, and also in the animal nature of human beings in so far as it is not raised into the soul domain and so cannot be contaminated by our drives, desires and passions.

If you pick up a crystal, a stone or a plant, you won't notice any discord there between these two types of being. But the moment you consider how our soul penetrates the body, you will find the luciferic beings relating in a particular way to the ahrimanic ones, as it were saying to them: 'We promised God the Father that we will not dispute about minerals, plants or animals, nor about the human being as long as he remained, in olden times, an unconscious being who did not reflect, who lived like an animal. But we will fight tooth and nail over the human being who has achieved self-awareness.' Indeed, a terrible war is waged between beings of air and fire and those of earth and water to possess the human being. We have to realize this. Nowadays humanity has developed great knowledge of external nature. Within this natural world luciferic and ahrimanic beings live side-by-side and endure each other. But human beings are unaware of what lives beyond the sensory world, of supersensible nature and subhuman nature. These two realms conceal beings who fight this terrible war to possess the human being as I have described.

The being called Yahweh or Jehovah in the Old Testament dwells— if I may use this expression, and remembering what I said about how I'm using such words—in the moon. In other words, this entelechy in the cosmos belongs to what comes to expression in physical moon phenomena. This moon being, Yahweh, has the following task in the world order. The primary task of this intelligence is to lead to earth the human being as he descends from the world of spirit and soul and mantles himself in a body. But this Yahweh being also, if you like, retains the right to be involved with the human being on earth as well, and to regulate everything that relates to the powers of reproduction. So this Yahweh being, dwelling as it were in the moon, leads us down to earth and seeks to rule in us everything connected with the drives and instincts of reproduction. Yet reproduction cannot be ruled in isolation, since it connects with other human instincts and drives; and therefore the Yahweh being needs helpers to maintain harmony between the instincts relating, for instance, to eating and drinking, and those involved in the instincts of reproduction, and to ensure that drives and instincts are ruled in general. And Yahweh, the moon god, if I may call him that, finds these helpers in Mercury and Venus.

In the spiritual cosmos, therefore, we find a kind of alliance between the moon, the Yahweh being there and everything populating the moon alongside Yahweh, and the beings in Venus and Mercury. The beings in this alliance seek to maintain dominion over our flesh and blood from the moon, Mercury and Venus. We are not just earthly beings, but effects play into us from the universe.

If we now consider the beings I referred to earlier as ahrimanic, who, as beings of earth and water build their fortress below the earth's surface, we find that they have not grown mature enough to approach these celestial bodies in the same way that Yahweh inhabits the moon or his helpers inhabit Mercury and Venus. In the world order they are condemned to reside below the earth's surface rather than dwelling in the moon, Venus or Mercury. As you can imagine, therefore, these entirely immoral beings not only wage war against the beings of air and fire, but primarily against Yahweh and the powers of Venus and Mercury, trying to dispossess Yahweh of his rightful dominion. Yahweh regulates the instinctive aspects of our nature; because he does so from beyond the earth, they remain subject also to a power other than moral ones, and yet they do not necessarily become immoral. Yahweh's proper dominion means that the human race has developed on the earth in the way we know, and for this to happen the powers of the moon, Mercury and Venus were necessary.

To oppose the human race subject to Yahweh, these ahrimanic beings try to establish the other race I described. And a primary means for them to do so is what I characterized last time. While a human being sleeps, they approach him and tell him that good is bad and bad is good. It is so terribly easy for a person to accept this while asleep and then to bring it back into his physical and ether body on awakening. And these ahrimanic entities believe they will achieve their goal by whispering into our sleep like this, inspiring us to heinous evil. In other words, we ought really to depend entirely on the higher powers of the moon, Venus and Mercury as far as our lower nature is concerned. Our lower nature is not intrinsically evil or base, only becoming so in so far as the powers in enmity with Yahweh enter people as I have described. Yahweh wants these entities to come to expression only in the ebb and flow of tides, in volcanic eruptions and earthquakes; but they make strenuous efforts to assert themselves within us as well, not only initiating attacks from their earthly fortress against beings of air and fire but also, primarily, against Yahweh and his helpers on Venus and Mercury.

Thus human beings are caught up in a battle waged on the one hand by Yahweh and his hosts who fight for justice in the universe, and on the other by the hosts of Ahriman, whose ingenious cleverness is far greater than that of human beings, and who wants to utterly deny our moral nature and instead make us into intelligent automata.

Rising from below into the human being, as it were, you have the produce humankind must eat, originating in earth and water. We do not draw sustenance from air, nor from mere warmth. The beings who have their corporeality in air and warmth are as undeveloped as those in enmity with Yahweh. Developed, mature beings by contrast live on Mars, Jupiter and Saturn. These beings of air and fire therefore do not simply battle against the ahrimanic powers but also against everything affecting human beings from Mars, Jupiter and Saturn.

Mars, Jupiter and Saturn, these distant planets, affect us—or rather their spiritual beings do—primarily through the external sensory organs of eyes, ears and so forth. Whereas the moon, Venus and Mercury act within us, in our inner organs, Saturn, Jupiter and Mars work in our sense organs. For instance, the actions of Saturn are primarily located in the human eye. These beings—of Saturn, Jupiter and Mars—seek to make us into very earthly human beings, giving us senses properly set into the surface of a physical human organism. They want to give us nerves that pass from these senses and extend inside us. Saturn gives us the senses, Jupiter is responsible for the neural connections with them, and Mars is a potency that gives us speech for example. In other words, these beings seek to endow us with everything close to our surface, our skin—these senses and nerves are infoldings of the human skin.

The beings of air and fire I spoke of again fight tooth and nail against Jupiter, Saturn and Mars. They sit there in their castles in the air and, in particular in lightning and everything fiery in nature, unfold their powers in the atmosphere. They would like to make the human being into nothing really but an entire eye, ear or nose, pouring our whole surface through us to make us beings who do nothing but see and hear.

They would like us not to eat or drink but just see and hear, and thus become a kind of angel being.

Well, the beings of Mars, Jupiter and Saturn behave very decently—if I can say this of such lofty beings—within external nature. They penetrate what appears to us a purely natural world with morality; they bring morality towards us and it actually enters through our senses.

But the beings of air and fire seek to pervade us entirely with our sensory nature so that we simply see with our senses nothing except what is moral—they want to make us therefore into moral automata.

If you observe nature around you, you find that everything expressed in forces and energies comes from the Mars beings, while Jupiter beings are responsible for natural laws and Saturn beings for colour and tone. But the beings of air and fire would like to prevent us from becoming entirely physically endowed, want to allow us only to be force, law—that means thought—and colour and tone. They want to dilute us or dissipate us and, as I said, make us into an angel being of sorts.

In external nature, the moon, Mercury, Venus, Jupiter, Mars and Saturn are in harmony, kept in equilibrium by the sun, but as far as human nature is concerned they are waging a twofold battle. Firstly the ahrimanic and luciferic beings are battling with each other; secondly the luciferic beings are battling with all the planetary powers beyond the sun, of Mars, Jupiter and Saturn. And then the ahrimanic beings, in turn, are battling with everything working through the moon, Venus and Jupiter.

A hard battle is therefore being waged behind the surface of nature and in the human being, and on this battlefield we have to achieve our progress and our freedom. In ancient times this was accomplished through the teachings of the mysteries, but nowadays we must seek to do it by what we learn from spiritual research about the invisible realms underlying nature and below the level of our human life. You see, to be unaware of these things would in future lead humanity into the gravest decline.

From what I have said you will see that the beings I have described as luciferic and ahrimanic are very highly developed in certain different respects: the luciferic beings in relation to morality, and the ahrimanic beings as far as cleverness and intelligence are concerned. Yet despite this, both types of being repeatedly believe that they will achieve their aims, and keep launching fresh efforts to further and attain these aims. But on the earth they continually meet with disappointment, finding their aims are thwarted. Encountering these luciferic or ahrimanic beings behind nature or below the human being, you keep seeing them celebrating euphoric victories on the one hand, holding to their aims and refusing to relinquish them, continually believing that victory is at hand; and on the other they are repeatedly disappointed and thwarted upon the earth. You can say that this mood, of victorious euphoria followed by repeated disappointment constitutes the life of this type of being.

Specifically, they are disappointed on earth by the physical nature of the human being. One gains the very strong impression that Ahriman and Lucifer are profoundly disappointed if you spend any time in hospitals or by the beds of patients, or in mental hospitals. These beings wage a hard battle, as I said, to possess human nature, but every time one side is victorious against the other they find their aims have not been served.

It is somewhat different with Ahriman's victory against the gods of the moon, Venus and Mars, and likewise that of the spirits of air and fire against Jupiter, Mars and Saturn. These are never complete victories however. Their successes against each other seem to strengthen them, but are really only pyrrhic victories, and thus give rise to their disappointment. Picture for a moment that the ahrimanic powers succeed in winning a victory over the luciferic powers in the human physical body—over those powers that would like to pervade us entirely with our outer senses. When the ahrimanic beings are victorious, we succumb to diseases such as tumours, carcinomas or metabolic disorders such as diabetes.

Whenever a disease such as this physically affects us, Ahriman has won a victory against Lucifer, and this will be associated with a potential ruination of our physical nature. And then this physical nature can no longer serve Ahriman—he can no longer draw from it the instincts and drives with which to create his own race of entities. This will give you a paradoxical yet accurate insight into illness. In many cases it is the only means whereby the good powers can save the human being from the clutches of Ahriman.

And when Lucifer wins a victory in our human nature, over ahrimanic powers that seek to harden us and draw us down into their race of mere water and earth beings, we succumb to allergic or catarrhal disorders, or can develop mental disorders. And this in turn renders Lucifer's victory redundant.

These ahrimanic and luciferic powers continually work with all their strength to secure their victories, only to be downcast and disappointed beside sickbeds, in hospitals and in lunatic asylums—for then they find that however much they battle, they cannot possibly ever be victorious in the last resort.

If you gain insight into the human being's etheric nature rather than just our physical nature, then you can discover the conditions which lead to such disappointments for the ahrimanic and luciferic beings. You see, when the luciferic beings are victorious over ahrimanic beings in the etheric body, a person becomes a habitual liar. But thereby he lapses from morality and from the world Lucifer wishes to raise him into. Lucifer seems to pull human beings from the earthly world. But instead of making them moral automata he makes them into liars. And by becoming a habitual liar, in this making of a person into a liar, a weapon is given to the good powers, however paradoxical this sounds—a weapon to draw us away from the clutches of Lucifer. You see we can overcome the lying habit, improve it at least as karma unfolds, whereas if Lucifer were truly victorious the human race would be lost, would be lifted entirely away from the earth.

When Ahriman is victorious in the etheric body, or is close to being so, we become possessed, inwardly possessed by cleverness. But because we are inwardly possessed by intelligence, this cleverness remains within us as possession, pervading the etheric body. And then, once again, Ahriman is unable to drag our instincts and drives down as he wishes since they are now rooted in the etheric body due to this possession.

Thus the success of the adversary spirits, leading either to mendacity or to possession, continually pulls them up short and faces them with their greatest disappointments.

We can consider the astral body here too. Let's assume that ahrimanic powers are victorious in someone's astral body, or close to being so. Then a person can become a crass egotist, completely egotistic. But if he is, he holds his instincts under control, and Ahriman can't get hold of them or draw them forth. And so the crass egotist also deprives Ahriman of his booty.

And if Lucifer is victorious, or close to being so, a person can become an ego-less dreamer in his astral body, someone who isn't really fully present in himself. Such things exist, or at least we can fall prey to such conditions from time to time. This, again, is a great disappointment for luciferic powers. And so you see how many sources of disappointment there are on earth for the ahrimanic and luciferic powers.

But at the same time you can see that we're in the midst of a battlefield. In the times of ancient initiation mysteries this was already so—we stood in a battle that takes place behind the veil of the physical world. In those times the teachers of the mysteries, the first great teachers, were messengers of God the Father. The pupils of these messengers were the gurus, and their pupils in turn were the chelas,[24] of lower rank. But the greatest gurus were directly instructed by the divine messengers from God the Father. Illnesses, as I have described, are sources of the greatest disappointment for Ahriman and Lucifer. Human illnesses in a sense numb and paralyse Lucifer and Ahriman. Despite the fact that ahrimanic beings are so clever and luciferic beings so moral, because their awareness is particularly bright and clear they can become still more befogged and confused by it; and thus the messengers of the gods were undisturbed by Ahriman and Lucifer, finding remedies for various disorders, as I touched on last time[25]—for instance curing a Saturn disorder by means of the moon and suchlike.

This was in the ancient mysteries, where the messengers of God the Father could directly draw a human being out of the confusion he was exposed to in this battle waged behind nature, and below the human level.

In modern times the confusion we can fall prey to is no less than it was in ancient times. It does not matter if we know nothing about it in our normal awareness, the confusion exists nevertheless. People are torn hither and thither in the battle waged around them, behind nature and below it.

And if we cross the threshold and look consciously into the world of spirit, gaze upon this dire battle, if we observe this confusion of activity around the human being, below him and behind nature, we will look in vain today for any messenger of the gods, such as those who, for example, handed ancient mystery physicians the Staff of Mercury and similar symbols for healing. We can no longer hold our own at all in this great battleground between the retrograde upper beings of Mars, Jupiter and Saturn and the lower retrograde beings of the moon, Venus and Mercury. If you cross the threshold you will actually find yourself in the midst of this dire conflict between upper and lower powers, opposing each other like two warring camps: the air and fire beings as lapsed moon, Saturn, Jupiter and Mars beings, and earth and water beings who are lapsed moon, Venus and Mercury beings. And the conflict rages beyond the threshold in dire fashion, so that the sun first flames with fire and then is darkened and obscured, and at last appears as a terrible black disc.

This was not so for the ancient initiates, for they saw through this black disc, and from it came the divine messengers of God the Father to them, for instance bearing a knowledge of healing in ancient times.

In modern times we cross the threshold and find this terrible battle raging. The sun grows red, grows black, but remains a black disc. And we are repulsed and to find our way, to survive in this confusing battle, have to search upon the earth itself.

And here we are guided to the Christ who stands there as a spiritual being who bound himself to the earth through the Mystery of Golgotha, and says to us: 'Do not despair that the sun has grown black. It is black now because I, the Sun God, no longer dwell in it but have descended and bound myself to the earth.' If we then approach Christ with the greatest inner humility and devotion, and with clear insight into what comes to us through knowledge of the Mystery of Golgotha, while the sun does not brighten again—it remains a black disc—it begins to make audible everything Christ speaks to us; and then we learn of Christ's affinity with the sun. Though it remains a black disc, the sun becomes the being who enables us to hearken to Christ if we have first developed in ourselves the right inner relationship to him.

And then it is the Christ who tells humankind of the means to reconcile the upper with the lower powers, how one can reconcile the powers above the black sun disc—who manifest around our earth as beings of air and fire—with the lower beings. And as human beings, specifically, we acquire guidance, precepts, both for healing illnesses and for understanding all the other evils that continually disappoint Lucifer and Ahriman. Through the power of Christ and the power of the Mystery of Golgotha, we come to the point of being able to say this wondrous thing: 'You creatures of Ahriman and Lucifer, you are disappointed by the evils that must arise on earth through you, as you achieve your only partial victories. But these disappointments will keep recurring since you will continually engender sick or possessed people, and the liars, egotists and ego-less. And thus you will continually swing back and forth between euphoria and disappointment.'

But when the earthly human being finds the right relationship to Christ, he will not despair at the moment he witnesses the despair of beings higher than he is, who follow a different path from the divine beings to whom the human being belongs, and with whom he should keep faith as earth goes on evolving. At the core of these divine beings is the Christ being, who once spoke through the sun's disc to the ancient initiates, and who now continues to speak to us from the earth with the sun's aid. And so, in speaking of Christ today, we are speaking of the one who can stand beside us on earth, as the guide who leads us away from the dire conflict that ahrimanic and luciferic beings wage both with one another and against the upper and lower worlds of the gods.

LECTURE 9

LONDON, 19 NOVEMBER 1922

TODAY I would like to round off the themes we have been considering here recently. You already know what destiny awaits us immediately after death. First we lay aside the physical body and therefore find ourselves in a situation different from that allowed by ordinary consciousness during earthly life. We now have our I, our astral body and ether body around us. Between birth and death, the ether body remains united with the physical body, and during sleep our I and astral body emerges from the ether body and physical body to sojourn outside them. After death we still have our ether body or body of formative forces for a short while—only a matter of days—and during this time we can look back on the whole course of the life that has just ended. This life is in fact contained in the etheric body. I have often stated in public lectures that if we liberate our ether body through initiation, we can then survey the whole panorama of our life on earth.

But we cannot retain the ether body for very long after death since it is connected with the whole cosmos and seeks always to spread out into it. If we were ever to lose our physical body for a moment during life, the ether body would immediately acquire the tendency to dissolve into the whole cosmos, as if by elastic energy. It coheres during life only by virtue of the physical body in which this ether body is always contained. When we lose this cohesive power of the physical body, the ether body starts to spread out, and after a few days will have spread so wide that it is no longer present to us. As you know, if we take a small water droplet and heat it, it soon disperses into the atmosphere and is no longer there—you can't see it any more. In the same way the ether body diffuses after death and is no longer present after a few days.

Initiation wisdom shows us that this period lasts only a few days. In a sense we make artificial use of the ether body in earthly life through initiation science: the etheric body stays within the physical body but we use it by taking no account of the physical body, and by doing so can look back on our life so far. But in this review or retrospective vision, the ether body also gives us a shimmering reflection of the whole universe. The whole starry heavens are at the same time contained in the ether body. You cannot actually see the ether body as separate from the physical body without this ether body revealing the celestial world of stars and planets too; and these celestial bodies, the planets and fixed stars, ultimately absorb the ether body again. You see, initiation science, initiation wisdom can only retain for three to four days at most the pictures it gains in this way in the ether body. Then they fade and vanish and, prior to this, if we wish to retain any connection at all with them we have to return to our physical body to ensure the ether body remains coherent. This ether body also fades from us a few days after death, but because of this we incorporate ourselves increasingly into the starry world.

Having laid aside the ether body, we initially feel alien in the celestial world. Moon forces are the only aspect of it that seems familiar to us. The moon appears and gives us an after-image of our physical form, but at the same time we immediately learn to perceive more precisely the spiritual powers connected with the moon. We learn to recognize that the Yahweh power of the universe is connected with the moon, as I described last time.[26] For a human being who has passed through the gate of death, the moon transforms into a colony of spirit beings led by Yahweh. And now, after death, we become familiar with something initiation science can speak of by virtue of gaining pictures of these things during life on earth still. We learn to recognize what dying on earth means—the significance of death is brought home to us by the moon and Yahweh powers.

When we consider death on earth, we see that a person's physical body becomes lifeless. Soul and spirit, and etheric life that previously imbued the physical body, vanish from it. The physical body is absorbed by the forces of the earth, the elements of earth, either by terrestrial and watery forces if the body is buried or by fire and air if it is cremated. And so the human physical body, laid aside by the human entelechy, is taken over by earth forces. What does this mean really: the human entelechy lays aside the physical body, and this body decomposes? It is like this: when we are born and bear childhood growth forces in us, and also before birth in the embryonic state when we already belong corporeally to the earth in our mother's body, then these same forces which we meet as destructive, decomposing forces at death, the same forces which abandon the human physical body when we die—appearing in death because the physical body decomposes—are the very same forces that now help build and form the physical body. We pass through our ether and then astral experiences into a world of spirit, but here on earth something becomes detached from the physical body and appears as spiritual quality, as something that in a sense emerges from the human body. We could put it like this: the true human being goes in one direction, and in this other direction another entity emerges from us. The physical body lies there in death and we depart from it, but at the same time it is true to say that another being departs from us too, consisting of the moon forces that also live on earth. You see, the moon forces are concentrated in the celestial moon, but their action extends far and wide, if I can put it like that, and this becomes apparent on earth in the forces of death—which are at the same time birth forces. They lead us into life and they appear also when we depart from life. Thus we gain a kind of understanding of the connection between birth and death. And if we think of all the human beings who die successively, the apparition of death emerges from each one of them and reunites with the spiritual atmosphere that surrounds the earth like our ordinary atmosphere, and contains what death releases and birth in turn receives. From forces that rise from human corpses human beings are born in turn. Indeed, our forces of growth have an intimate spiritual connection with the death forces surrounding the earth—that is, with forces that emerge and appear through death.

Now consider this. These death forces, which are also birth forces, are moon forces. And mixed into these moon forces are all the moral values that we accumulate during our lifetime. If we have been good in a particular respect, a distinct being who exists in this sphere of moon death forces will contain a strength retained from this goodness of ours. This being will also contain everything remaining from our immoral actions. And while we live on earth we develop this being. Ordinary consciousness knows nothing of this, but we bear this being within us. Each night when we fall asleep we depart from it—it remains behind in our physical body when we detach ourselves from the physical body. I have told you that our moral and religious feelings are left behind in the physical and ether body; and we also leave behind there too a real being, which we develop during life as the bearer of our karma. This being remains connected with us as long as we are in the sphere of moon forces after death. Sustaining us in the moon forces after death, while we are still in proximity to the earth, this being keeps us connected both with the moon forces and with our karma so that we actually have to re-experience, in reverse sequence, all our actions on earth between birth and death; we re-experience them spiritually, three times faster than they occurred, as I said in the public lecture.[27] In reverse sequence we go back through them, spending a period after death connected with the death moon forces, though no longer through the physical body that we have now laid aside. As beings of soul and spirit we have to perform actions that are intimately related to our actions on earth. And thus we pass through the course of our life again in reverse, and by this means first become fully aware of our karma.

Now things that are spiritual in nature must also be treated as such. If you have loved another person on earth, you may feel sorry that he has to re-experience all the bad or imperfect things he may have done in his lifetime. From your earthly and physical perspective you have a sense of regret about the person concerned having to undergo all this. But if you asked him whether he sees things like this, he would say no. He would reply that he would not lose the opportunity of passing through these experiences again after death, with the judgements and perspectives he now has as a being of soul and spirit, so that he can fully enshrine them in his deepest soul being. You see, if I have done something that shows me to be imperfect and do not have the chance to experience this again, I could not feel the urge in myself to redress or balance it. I would seek to liberate myself from this imperfection. The very fact that I can re-experience my actions from a soul-spiritual perspective gives me the motivation to redress them through a more perfect action. The dead would not relinquish this opportunity at any cost, for it gives them the power to attain their full humanity. Just as a landscape looks different when you see it from down in the valley or from the top of a mountain, so life seen here on earth looks different when perceived from beyond the threshold. And so we can often find that we misjudge the way earthly life is connected with super-physical life after death.

Let's take another instance. Let us say you are committed to anthroposophy, are very inspired by it, but that another member of your household, someone you are closely connected to, hates anthroposophy, regards it as his worst enemy. You may deeply regret the fact that you cause the other such pain by being an adherent of anthroposophy yourself, while he hates it. From an earthly perspective that might be the right way of seeing it. But very often things will look different from the other side. The other person might have had karmic reasons why he could not get anywhere with anthroposophy, perhaps because of constraining factors he brought with him from another life that have led him to intellectually reject anthroposophy. His head cannot approach anthroposophy, and he immediately grows restless or irritable if he hears anything about it. This does not mean his heart is necessarily against it. When the person dies, he may develop a very intense desire for anthroposophy after death. And so it will often be right to send thoughts drawn from anthroposophy to someone who has died, although he hated it when he was alive.

However paradoxical this sounds, some family members who have raged about another member of the family becoming an anthroposophist turn into keen adherents after their death. You should take seriously what I said here last time, too[28]—that from an after-death perspective things look very different.

A person becomes quite different after death. Consider that during life your brain sits there in your skull, and lower down you have your lungs and then the other organs and also your outward senses. You perceive the external world by means of all this. And now you emerge from physical life. First of all the stars only shine into your ether body, but when you have laid that aside too you identify yourself with the stars. Previously you had a brain inside you, and now you have incorporated into you the spiritual intelligences of Venus, Mercury, the sun and so forth. And just as you possess lungs, heart, kidneys and so on upon earth, so now you have moon, Mercury and the sun within you. Your interior is identical with the universe. Do you really imagine that the universe sustains the same kind of rationality for you as your brain? The world looks a very different place now. When we look down from the sun to the earth, the earth looks different from when we look up to the sun from earth. Staying connected with the moon, Mercury and Venus, we pass through our life in reverse, re-experiencing everything; and during this time we have only a weak connection with the outer celestial bodies of Jupiter, Mars and Saturn, and a still weaker one with the fixed stars.

Having gone back in reverse through our actions during life in this way, back to birth, we have in fact judged these actions from a celestial standpoint. The reverse reflection and re-experience of our life also offers a forward perspective: we realize that we need to do certain things in future to redress one or another action. This phase of after-death life lasts for around 20 or 30 years, depending on how old we were when we died—around a third of our lifetime on earth. Children pass through this phase very quickly, and for infants it is but the twinkling of an eye, as you can imagine from what I have said. So that is what happens: we experience a soul-spiritual connection with our earthly life, going back through it in reverse. And arriving at our birth we find that we retain a memory of all this. And now it is as if we lay aside yet another body. You can say that we lay the astral body aside, but what actually happens is that the living activity in which we were previously engaged transforms into a thought picture, except that now a quite different consciousness thinks, a celestial consciousness, whereas before an earthly consciousness was thinking.

And now you continue your journey in the world of spirit, dwelling with beings whose physical reflection embodies the sun, moon and stars. You have to continue dwelling now with the spirits of the stars, and into this life you bear the memory of your karma that you laid aside with your astral body. But here 'laying aside' means only that everything we were actively involved in before is now a memory we possess as a cosmic human being. We enter a pure world of spirit, but burdened with the memory remaining to us of our life on earth.

As long as we pass through this reverse experiencing of our past life on earth, we remain in the planetary sphere. While we progress from the spiritual moon forces to those of Venus, Mercury, sun, Mars, Jupiter and Saturn, and in other words dwell somewhere between the moon and Saturn sphere, still feeling ourselves to be within the planetary cosmos, we are still involved in this journey back through our previous earthly life.

In recent days I have said how the moon forces and Saturn forces work against each other. The moon contains the powers that bring us down to the earthly realm, and continually seek to bind us to earth. Saturn seeks to lead us out into the starry universe, not so as to see the stars' physical reflection but, between death and a new birth, so that we live with the beings who belong to the stars.

As we pass beyond the sphere of Saturn after death, therefore, we become ready for an experience of the pure world of spirit. In my book *Theosophy* I characterized this as the transition from the soul world to the spirit world. Because the memory of our past life still clings to us, though, we are not able to make this transition by our own powers, but need a helper in the world of spirit.

I have also previously described the nature of this helper. During the time before the Mystery of Golgotha, the initiates of the mysteries told their pupils that they could, if they sent up their powers of worship into the world of spirit in the right way, find the sublime sun being who accompanied them from the time they left the sun sphere. This spiritual being, they said, would accompany them also to the other side of existence where the sun shines out spiritually into the universe, in the same way that it shines down physically upon earth. This sublime sun being, said the initiates, will accompany you and bring you to the Saturn sphere, and then beyond this into the star sphere. The spiritual sun will shine for you, said the initiates to their pupils, so that you can make the transition from the soul world into the spirit world.

This sun being descended to the earth through the Mystery of Golgotha, and took on corporeal form in the human being Jesus of Nazareth. By turning our sensibility, our feelings towards the Christ and the Mystery of Golgotha we can already receive on earth the power, the strength, to pass beyond the sphere of the sun and Saturn and enter spirit land—that is, to enter the celestial world of stars. Thereafter our condition is one we continue to pass through between death and a new birth. To describe this condition to you which now, after the Mystery of Golgotha, we can undergo through the power of Christ that we have absorbed, I will need to say the following. I first have to make you aware what it really means out there in the world of stars, that is, in spirit land, to recall one's life on earth. This will become clear to you if I say the following.

As we pass beyond the sphere of Saturn we enter what older traditions called the zodiac, representative of the heavens with their fixed stars, or in other words of spirit land in general. But precisely when we encompass all the separate stars that compose the zodiac we delineate the path the human being now has to pursue. The human being takes this path in order to be able to develop the spirit germ of his next physical body from the whole cosmos, in cooperation with the spiritual beings of the hierarchies.

You would be quite mistaken if you thought that such work is far less interesting than what we do here on earth to further human culture, if you thought the work we do after death to create our own future body must be very monotonous. Everything you can do on earth together does not approach the grandeur and diversity of what you accomplish as you form the human body, this temple of the gods, out of the starry worlds. Such work is far more varied and magnificent. And as you will see in a moment, you do not only form your body in isolation but in a way that makes it part of all humanity. Having come together with one or another person through karma, you now create your new body in a way that endows it with the tendency to meet these same people again in the right way, in order to balance and redress karma with them. You are actually working for humanity in a much loftier sense here than you can do on earth. And how do you do this work? I'd like to describe this in detail, but please be aware that, as I said last time, I have to use metaphors in speaking of these sublime worlds, since human concepts today do not allow one to express these things in other than pictorial ways.

You do actually have to develop the spirit germ of your whole physical body, which is composed of different, specific aspects of the universe. For instance, as you dwell for a while with and in those spiritual beings whose physical reflection we find as Aries, you work with the Aries hierarchies to form your head, your future head, which is actually a cosmos that later contracts in the physical body. In your head you bear the whole cosmos, as seen from Aries. But now, as you work in the realm or arena of Aries with the hierarchy of Aries, the planets shine forth spiritually, just as they shine down upon earth but now in a different, spiritual aspect. Let us assume that you continue to work, and in doing so work your way from Aries to the constellation of Taurus. As you work in the constellation of Taurus with the hierarchies, you develop the connection between your larynx and your lungs. And as Mars shines up out of the planetary sphere towards Taurus, the movement of Mars expresses everything you failed to do or did rightly on earth through your organs of speech. As you work your way through the constellation of Taurus, Mars spiritually shines into the sphere of Taurus every untruth you spoke. So you can picture the kind of memory that is here embodied in our own actions. After death we find this memory inscribed into the universe, and indeed it speaks forth from the other side of the universe as Logos. In relation to our speech organs, we are compelled to work in either a disrupted or supported way depending on whether we spoke the truth or lied.

And then in passing, for instance through the constellation of Leo, all our imperfections are illumined by the sun—all those imperfections due to our superficial or deeper heart, our sympathies and antipathies which on earth are connected with our temperament and blood circulation. And so we build up our future body in accordance with the way our whole former life resounds into cosmic space as planetary utterance.

This is so, yes, however strange it may seem from our earthly perspective. Gazing upon planetary movements from these far realms— seeing, let us say, how Mars performs its movements in relation to Taurus—we find these movements writing a script, one that simultaneously resounds; and this is the star script which our own deeds have inscribed into universal space. No wonder, therefore, that when we return again we prepare what will belong to us in accord with our karma. You see, we can only prepare our future physical body through the influence of this continual language of the stars.

We work our way through the realm of spirit; and the length of time we take to pass through it is greater the longer we have spent in a consciousness different from that of the child, as I also said in the public lecture.[29] As a child we still lived dreamily. We are now in a state of consciousness that surpasses the one we possessed on earth. On earth, as adults, we are in a state of consciousness that surpasses the dreamy awareness of the child. There are three states of consciousness. If we lived to the age of 30, and lived in dream consciousness until we were five, then we lived six times longer in a higher consciousness. And now we therefore live, in turn, six times longer than our whole life on earth in that higher state of consciousness we have out there in the starry worlds. It is easy to see therefore that if a child dies he needs only a very brief period between death and a new birth. The older he becomes, the more time he must spend there; and this is because his super-earthly consciousness, which he passed through after his previous death, has been darkened and obscured all the more during his life, and he must therefore work all the longer to illumine it again. We have to find our way into full illumination after death.

In entering into full illumination we arrive at the time between death and a new birth which I have referred to in a Mystery Play[30] as the midnight hour of human spiritual existence—the midnight point between death and a new birth. At this time, roughly midway between death and a new birth, we have the brightest awareness, one allowing us to live in the world of spirit amongst beings of the spiritual hierarchies. But at the same time we also have the strongest experience that everything we did as a human being remains below in the planetary sphere and we must not ignore it. This—one says to oneself—cannot be amended here; it can only be amended if you descend to earth once again.

At this point begins the urge, the drive to descend to earth once more, in a sense to decide between Saturn and moon. Once more we follow the dawning moon forces to embark on the path back to earth— after centuries in the case of someone who grew to adulthood in a previous life.

And as we approach the planetary sphere, entering the sphere of Mercury, Venus and the moon, the awareness we had in community with spirit beings of the higher hierarchies fades. In other words, we acquire a state of awareness which encompasses only the manifestations of these spirit beings. Previously we felt ourselves amidst and immersed in them. Preparing our future head we feel we are collaborating with spirit beings; now, though, they appear to us as though in pictures. But instead the action of the moon forces surfaces in us, and we feel ourselves once more to be a being who should be self-contained. We are not yet in a physical body but we gain a presentiment of individual life and of being at one remove from the cosmos again. We no longer have spiritual beings immediately before us as they are, but only in images.

And as we pass through these images, we lose sight increasingly of the spirit germ of our physical organism that we have developed. We have to realize that this spirit germ of the physical organism has faded from us and has now descended to physical parents, is becoming incorporated in the powers of the reproductive stream on the physical earth. The germ of the physical body we prepared does in fact contract, and falls away into the reproductive stream of our physical parents. We are left behind as a being of spirit and soul who feels a sense of belonging with what has lapsed from him, yet cannot directly unite with it. We can only do so when we draw the ether forces in the whole cosmos together to form our ether body. After the spirit germ of our physical body has fallen away from us to prepare our physical body in the mother's womb, we gather the powers to form our ether body, with which we then unite when the embryo has been developing for a while in the womb.

This is the process whereby we return to earthly existence. Having reached the stage of seeing only images, reflections of spirit beings, we now incorporate into us all the memory of our karma, only being able to do so by virtue of the moon forces. We reincorporate this into us as real forces. We take these into the ether body, incorporate them into it. And this is why we appear on earth in a guise that enables us to live out our destiny, our karma. As we pass through the moon forces we develop a longing to live out our karma on the earth.

This is the cycle we undergo between death and rebirth, rising to an experience of independent consciousness in the spirit sphere and then descending to a dimmer consciousness where the spirit sphere is present to us only as picture. While in this latter condition, we introduce will into our karma and return to the earth in order to work further in our physical body. Eventually, through a series of earthly lives, we become able to embark on a further metamorphosis of our existence.

At present in our stage of earthly evolution, as we descend from the sphere of the stars we have a memory of our former life on earth, and reconnect with this memory. We ourselves prepare our physical body in the sphere of the stars, and unite with this physical body as we descend. But this current period of earth's development is a very important one, as we can only understand if we know that we prepare and develop our physical body in the celestial sphere and then mantle ourselves in it as we descend to earth. You see, in this present age of ours, something vital is being prepared.

I have often spoken of how in the last third of the nineteenth century, changes were initiated in the world of spirit in relation to the whole course of human life on earth. I pointed out that in a sense our portal of knowledge opened to the world of spirit, and that now, if we ourselves do what is needed, we can actually gain knowledge of the world of spirit and enter this world. This was not possible for many centuries while knowledge of material things was developing. The changes that came about in the world of spirit arose when a being we can call Michael— because his qualities closely resemble those of the Michael being of tradition—succeeded former overarching beings. We can say that this Michael being took over spiritual leadership of humanity. Michael's intervention in humanity's life of soul and spirit finds its correspondence in the increasing numbers of people who really are pervaded by the sense that they are not only connected to the earthly realm through their physical body but continually also to the world of spirit through their soul and spirit.

Our growing into spirit knowledge is connected with Michael's dominion. The other side of this, though, is that a true, honest and deep engagement with this science of the spirit has an effect on our human sensibility, our human soul. As the light of this science of the spirit spreads and broadens, it will not remain mere theory but will stream into human feeling and exist as an increasing compass of human love.

The knowledge we have stored up over recent centuries is really only head knowledge and does not stream through our whole being. It is like a soul tumour actually, something that gradually hardens because it does not gain the right forces from the rest of the organism. If we continually grow cleverer in our heads alone and do not imbue this cleverness with the necessary feeling drawn from the rest of our organism we will become beings who suffer, really, from a soul-spiritual cancer, a soul-spiritual carcinoma. Even the head cannot thrive, in spiritual terms, if the rest of a person does not stand lovingly in the world, also with active will towards what he loves.

What Michael's dominion intends within us is something we only understand if we approach this Michael dominion ourselves with our own qualities. And we can only do so as we grow spiritually enlightened and filled with a general human love originating from this same spiritual enlightenment. Then we will increasingly understand the meaning of this Michael dominion.

The Old Testament people also spoke of Michael's dominion, believing Michael to be the servant of Yahweh in those times. In other words, back then Michael worked through the Yahweh powers. He served Yahweh, combating all the ahrimanic powers of which I have been speaking in recent days. In our age Michael is destined to become, increasingly, the being who serves Christ. Thus to say that Michael's dominion will come to regulate human destiny means at the same time that Christ's dominion is truly to spread across the earth. In a sense Michael precedes Christ, bearing before him the light of spiritual insight, and Christ follows bearing a call for universal human love. But this means not only that something changes for the earth but also that much changes in respect of the life we lead between death and a new birth.

From ancient times of earth's evolution human beings have prepared the spirit germ of their future physical body as I described, and have then taken up this body as they entered upon earthly existence. But since the beginning of the dominion of Christ-Michael, humankind increasingly finds itself in a position—so far this is true of only a few, but their numbers will continually increase—of making a decision before descending to earth. You see, the light of spiritual knowledge shines in a way that illumines the earth and the super-physical realm at the same time; and so, through Michael's dominion, a human being can learn to make a decision after taking up his karma in the etheric body and then embarking on the journey towards his physical body. As spiritual knowledge spreads increasingly on the earth, so that human beings experience universal human love to an ever greater degree, the following will become possible for humanity in future as souls descend into their earthly life. The human being will find that, having prepared this body and sent it down to the earth, having taken up his karma in the ether body he has gathered from the cosmos, this karma involves grave injury he has done to another human being in former lives on earth.

We always run the risk of harming others by whatever we do. Judgement about the injury we have inflicted on another will become especially vivid while we are in the ether body without having yet entered the physical body. In future, the light of Michael and the love of Christ will also illumine this moment, and we will become able to change our decision and give to someone we have especially injured the body we prepared for ourselves, and take on the body that the other has prepared. This is a mighty transition that will increasingly occur in the life of the human spirit as we move forwards into the future.

We will become able to take upon us a body which a person whom we have particularly injured has had to prepare; and the other will be able to enter the body we have prepared. By this means there will be a whole new scope for karmic redress on earth. We will become able to exchange our physical bodies with each other.

The earth could never achieve its aim if this were not to happen—for never otherwise could humanity become a unified whole. And this must happen! In preparation of future stages of planetary evolution of the earth, a time must come when it will be impossible for any individual to enjoy anything on earth at the expense of another. Just as the single leaf of a plant or the single petal of a flower feels itself to be part of the whole plant, and shares in the whole plant's suffering or joy—metaphorically speaking—so a future must arrive on earth when no individual desires his own good fortune or happiness at the expense of the whole of humanity of which he feels a part. The spiritual equivalent of this, however, is that we also learn to prepare a physical body for another.

As humankind, therefore, we are gradually relinquishing a time when each person experienced a certain continuity in relation to his physical body. We are entering a time instead, brought about by the dominion of Michael, when each will also work for the other in preparing the spirit germs of human physical bodies. During the course of our earthly incarnations, this reciprocal service in the spirit will—though this sounds like a complete paradox it is true nevertheless—prepare a more distant era when the souls of people on earth will be able to take upon themselves the very bodies they have most injured, taking the other soul into their own body. This will come about once the earth itself has evolved into different conditions. But what I have described today is the preparation for this, arising through the dominion of Michael in the world of spirit.

This example demonstrates very clearly the nature of ideal magic. If, here on earth, you allow illumination that comes from spiritual science to act upon you, you are supporting and furthering the dominion of Michael. You are furthering the powers of human reciprocity so that people can live for one another, to the extent even of allowing their decision about the physical body they will take on, their choice of physical body, to be governed by what is best for humanity as a whole. In preparing this on earth by embracing human wisdom and love of humanity, you are fulfilling something that is a reality in the world of spirit. This really is ideal magic—which people in olden times called true white magic. It is the condition humanity must embrace.

I wanted to highlight this important moment which has now begun to inform humanity's evolutionary trajectory. Let us be courageous and not draw back in fear when realities of the world of spirit that play into human life are unveiled. You see, the future of humanity depends on us learning to live with the world of spirit in the same way that we live with the physical world here on earth. We can only further humanity's future if we come to be at home again in the world of spirit, as ancient mankind once was, by properly understanding the words of Christ 'My kingdom is not of this world'.[31] He said, 'My kingdom is not of this world,' and yet he descended to the earth and united with humanity. Ought he not to have said, 'My kingdom *is* of this world'? No, he did not say this because he wishes slowly to make the earth into a kingdom that is not subsumed in earthly things, but which gradually flows into a spiritual condition. His kingdom is no longer as it was until the Mystery of Golgotha, and as it has also persisted since then to some degree. His kingdom is such that the spirit will prevail here on earth. And this will come about when the dominion of Michael is properly understood—which it only will be when spiritual illumination and Christian love of others is sought as I have described.[32]

LECTURE 10

LONDON, 17 NOVEMBER 1922[*]

THERE is no doubt that many people today keenly desire to know something of spiritual, of supersensible worlds, and in recent times even scientists or people in the academic world have been seeking ways of gaining insight into these worlds. Yet they are always hindered in such efforts by the nature of authoritative evaluation and judgement implicit in modern science. In seeking to draw knowledge of the supersensible world from one source or another, they come to the conclusion that exact knowledge, as they are used to developing in science, cannot exist in relation to supersensible worlds, for there is nothing to base it on, no solid ground.

By contrast, anthroposophic spiritual science, which I will speak about today and over the next few days,[33] seeks a really precise knowledge of the supersensible world. It is not an 'exact science' in the same sense as recognized by scientific enquiry into the physical world, based on experimentation. Instead it requires the development of inner capacities of the psyche which slumber in us ordinarily both in daily life and in mainstream science. These capacities are developed so that the acuity of human awareness is maintained in a way that only otherwise occurs in the exact sciences. There the ordinary consciousness one has is retained while applying exact methods to enquiry into the surrounding world. In anthroposophic spiritual science we embrace what I would call an intellectual modesty, saying something along the following lines: 'I

---

[*] First semi-public lecture.

was once a child and had capacities that were nowhere near as sharp as those I possess now as an adult and which I acquired through education and life experience. In the same way as I developed certain abilities from childhood on, so there may also now exist capacities still slumbering in me that I can draw on through certain methods.

In the anthroposophic spiritual science I am speaking of here, such capacities must be drawn forth from the soul in the following way. Before gaining deeper knowledge, we apply the methods first to our own development, or in other words we cultivate this inner development in a careful, precise way. We prepare ourselves to see into a higher world by basing this preparation, applied to ourselves, on an exact method. By such means—as I described in my previous lectures here in this hall[34]—we can arrive at exact clairvoyance, acquired in a precise, methodical way, in the same way that scientists enquire into the natural world by using precise methodologies.

I will not go into much detail today about how one acquires this exact clairvoyance, since I have spoken of these methods in the lectures I referred to; and you can find out more about them in the book translated into English as *The Way of Initiation*.[35]

Instead I first want to draw your attention today to factors that ordinarily hinder people from penetrating higher worlds. This is primarily due to our capacity to perceive the world only at each present moment. Our eyes see only the present moment, the world and its phenomena as they appear to us now. Our ears can only hear tones in the present moment, and the same is true of our other senses. The past that we have experienced is something available to us only as memory, thus in thoughts whose immediacy has faded. We can sense this fully if we think how vivid and real were the experiences we had ten years ago whereas the thoughts we have of those experiences now are pale and shadowy by comparison.

Anything reaching back before the present moment lives in us only as shadowy memory in our ordinary awareness. And yet this shadowy memory can be kindled into higher life and flare up brightly. And this is achieved through methods which, as I said, I will not give a full account of today—methods of thought meditation, concentration, self-development and so forth.

Someone who applies such methods to himself learns to live in thoughts as intensely as one otherwise only lives in outward sense impressions, and by doing so he acquires a certain capacity: he is no longer confined to observing the world in the present moment only. But such exercises, which allow us to observe the world above and beyond the present moment, must—depending on each person's disposition and innate possibilities—be practised for a long time in a careful, systematic way, thus in exact meditation and concentration. Some people, especially in our present times, are already born with the capacities of perception developed in this way. Such abilities are not immediately apparent but they emerge from within at a certain point in the person's life, and it is clear that they could not have arisen in this way if they had not been an innate endowment. I am speaking of the capacity to live in thoughts in the same way that one otherwise lives in the world of senses through one's body.

Such a statement should not be taken too lightly. It is worth reflecting that we owe to our experience of the sensory world everything that gives us the sense that we exist. But we can come to experience a second existence when we eventually reach the point of no longer relying on the impressions of our eyes, ears and other senses, instead developing an inner life that is as inwardly intense as the life of the senses—an inner life that lives not only in shadowy thoughts but in inwardly vivid thoughts. We then experience our thoughts as we otherwise only experience our sense impressions, and this gives rise in us to a second existence, a different awareness of self. We then experience what I would call an awakening: not outside our body but within us, where we awaken to a life despite our physical body being as tranquil and unreceptive to sense impressions as it otherwise only is during sleep.

If we examine ourselves we discover that in ordinary life we really only know what we have absorbed through the senses. Direct perceptions do not tell us anything about our own inner life. Ordinary consciousness does not enable us to perceive our inner organism. When we acquire a self-awareness in pure thinking, however, we learn to look inwards with as much clarity as we can otherwise only look outwards.

And then we feel something like the following. In looking outwards at the world, the sun or some kind of light must be there to cast its rays on external objects, and this light outside us enables us to see these objects. But when we come to awareness in this second kind of existence, in a process of pure thinking, a process of vision, in fact, that is as colourful and intense as our sensory impressions only are otherwise, then we feel a kind of inner light—no, not a kind of light but a real one, though the experience is spiritual—which we can shine into our own interior in the same way that objects are illumined outside us by external light.

It is for this reason that we can call this state of human experience clairvoyance. In awakened self-awareness in the spirit, this clairvoyance initially endows us with the capacity to be fully present again within any moment that we have previously experienced on earth.

It is perfectly possible, then, to experience oneself again at the age of 18—not just to remember one's experience, but to re-experience it, more or less strongly. We are again the person we were at that age—at 18, 15 or 10. Thus we can transport ourselves back to any point in our life, gaining inwardly illumined vision of what, by contrast to the spatial body containing our senses and endowing us with outward perception, we can call a temporal body.

But this temporal body is present all at once. We do not experience it in successive moments, but in its inner mobility. We survey our whole previous life, otherwise recalled only in shadowy memories. And yet we illumine this whole life of ours in a way that allows us to stand within any and every moment of it.

In experiencing this inner illumination we realize that we bear not only a physical body—this spatial body—but also a second, finer body, one really woven from images of our life hitherto. Yet at the same time these images or pictures themselves creatively shape and configure this life of ours on earth—that is, they shape our organism and our activity, the organism in which we exist and the actions we have performed. In other words, we become aware of a second human being within us.

And just as the physical, spatial body is experienced within a physical world, so we perceive this second human being, in fact, in a finer, etheric world—a world which I would call light-imbued. The whole world is there a second time, in finer configurations. Finer etheric configurations underlie all physical existence, and now one can perceive these.

Now the remarkable thing here is that everything one experiences in this finer body can only be retained for a short while. It is usually the case that someone acquiring this exact clairvoyance, and thus illumining his etheric body or body of formative forces, as I also call it, perceives that the etheric world, his etheric self, are impressions that fade very quickly indeed. One cannot hold them. And this gives one a kind of anxiety, a desire to return as quickly as possible to physical perceptions in order to live once more in one's sense of inner stability as a human being, as an individual. In perceiving the etheric body we experience ourselves there and also the things of the higher world—all that is etheric in nature in the higher world. But at the same time we perceive how fleeting all these impressions are, how hard it is to keep a hold of them. In fact we can only hold fast to them by seeking a particular kind of help.

Let me give you an example of the kind of help I myself use to prevent the impressions of this etheric vision from fading too quickly. Each time such impressions are present I try not only to see them but to record them in writing. In this way, the activity practised here is not only performed by the abstract powers of the soul but is also retained by writing. There is no need to read what one has written afterwards. The important thing is to allow a stronger activity to flow into one that is initially otherwise only a purely etheric activity.

In this way one 'pours' what is extremely fleeting and fluid, and rapidly dissipates, into one's ordinary human capacities. All this does not occur unconsciously, as it does for a medium, but with full awareness. One pours this all into one's ordinary human, corporeal capacities, and by this means can retain it. And by this means, too, we become able to see how to hold fast a supersensible world altogether— an etheric one initially, though later we will speak of other supersensible worlds—to hold fast a supersensible etheric world which encompasses the life we have lived so far, and also the etheric realm of nature around us, right up to the world of the stars. We become acquainted with this etheric world. We experience ourselves within this etheric world; and we know that it is impossible to hold fast to this world for more than three days without coming into touch with the physical body again. Having developed these capacities to a very great degree, it is possible to hold fast to this world for two to three days. As a modern initiate one can survey all this by the means I will describe in a moment, and can also evaluate the nature of what is present there—of what, without relying on corporeal capacities, one holds fast in one's etheric body or body of formative forces. This is what we initially perceive from our higher self-awareness when we pass through the portal of death and depart from the physical body, which falls away and is laid aside, and what for this reason cannot be retained in our awareness for more than two to three days after the death of the physical body.

Thus, through the forming of exact clairvoyance, we can experience the initial conditions occurring after death. We experience this as a prefiguring knowledge.

The prefiguring knowledge experienced by the initiate occurs for all when they lay aside their physical body. I will explain later what allows continuing awareness after death, without which a person would have no awareness for the whole time, the two to three days, during which we can retain our ether body or body of formative forces through higher knowledge.

For two to three days after death, the human being has an awareness of the etheric world that lives in his etheric body. Then he lays aside this awareness. He experiences how the etheric body falls away from him in a sense, just as the physical body first fell away; and now he finds it necessary to pass over into a different form of awareness so that he can continue to live after death as a conscious human soul.

It is possible to describe these first moments after death—they *are* just moments in terms of universal existence—if one has acquired the capacity I have described to you of vision of the higher world, since then one can prefigure what otherwise normally occurs to everyone at death. By acquiring this strong sense of self-awareness not dependent on the body, one already experiences these moments directly after death.

One succeeds in illumining one's own higher life, and perceiving in oneself the light that reveals in the first two to three days after death a world around one that is different from the world we have around us when we look at our surroundings by means of our senses during our life on earth.

Once this part of the lecture has been translated, I will describe what happens after these two or three days.

To survey the supersensible aspect of our earthly life, whose character, as I have said, lives on a few days after death, one requires the inner illumination I have described. One has to kindle spiritual light in oneself, a light that shines inwards. Then we can get beyond merely perceiving things in the present moment, as the senses allow us to.

To arrive at further knowledge in the supersensible world we not only have to change our capacities of perception but also the conditions in which we live. In ordinary life our condition is one enclosed within our physical, spatial body. The boundaries of our skin are at the same time the boundaries of our life. Our life extends only as far as these bodily limits. Within this condition of experience we cannot get beyond the forms of higher knowledge I have so far described. We can only come to knowledge of higher worlds reaching beyond ordinary experience by acquiring a form of experience that is not enclosed within confines of the spatial body but which encompasses the whole world that otherwise surrounds us.

This experience can be acquired too, as part of our knowledge of higher worlds. As I have said, I wish only to refer to a few aspects of methods the modern initiate uses to obtain exact insights into higher worlds. The rest can be found in the book I have mentioned.

As well as acquiring the ability to have a second existence in our life of thinking, still enclosed in the spatial body, we can also develop the capacity to live outside our body. We do the former, at a first stage, by allowing thoughts to live intensively and vividly in our awareness. Then, using systematic exercises, we proceed to rid our mind of these thoughts again at will, and thereby to acquire this condition of experience outside the body. Let me give you a simple example of such an exercise.

Imagine you're observing a crystal; it stands before you and your eyes perceive it. Someone who wishes only to work in a mediumistic way or seeks a trancelike condition will stare at this crystal so that the impression it makes on him transports him into an unreflecting or unconscious state. Anthroposophic spiritual science has nothing to do with this approach, and instead calls on very different procedures and practices. These involve first observing the crystal but then eventually looking away from it, abstracting as we otherwise only abstract in thought. Thus we have a crystal before us and we learn not only to physically perceive it but to grasp it inwardly also. Here we no longer use our eyes, although they are fully open, to observe the crystal. We shape our soul perception in such a way that we no longer have the crystal before us—that we erase it from our sight. These exercises can also be applied to erasing a colour from our outward vision so that we no longer see it although it is before us.

Thus in particular we can practise ridding ourselves of thoughts that surface in each given moment in response to outward life or rise up as memories from former moments of our lives. We can empty our consciousness of them, instead simply remaining awake and alert and retaining nothing, really, of the outer world in our awareness.

If we do such exercises we discover in ourselves an ability to emerge from the confines of our spatial body and to go beyond it. Then we can experience the *life* of our whole surroundings, rather than just observing their sensory phenomena.

In this very conscious awareness, something in particular arises which I would compare with a memory of the life we have while asleep. In ordinary sensory perception we are confined to the present moment, and our ordinary life is restricted, likewise, to the condition of our waking life.

If you recall your life so far, the times you were asleep are always void for ordinary awareness. What your soul repeatedly experienced between falling asleep and waking up again does not figure in your memory. In other words, our memories are an interrupted stream, although we often overlook this.

But a mind awoken in such a way that a person can live with it outside his body has before it an intense memory of what the soul experiences during sleep. This is the second stage of knowledge of supersensible worlds; and initially we can perceive here what we undergo as soul when our body, our physical body, rests without sensory perception or expression of will in sleep, as if soulless. By this means, during our ordinary waking life, we can in a certain way remember what we experienced outside the body each time we fell asleep. But we also have to realize that we must properly judge what arises in this experience. What the soul experiences during sleep is, after all, an experience outside the body. And we can only perceive it if we can develop an awareness, a condition of life, outside the body. Here we do not, now, come to know something that is illumined by an inner light, like our own time body, as I described this, but, in our waking remembrance, which has elevated itself to this exact, higher clairvoyance, we learn to perceive what we really experience each time we are asleep. Initially, though, this experience is of a different order from what we are used to. In the ordinary awareness of waking life we live in our physical body, and have within us lungs, heart and so on. While we are asleep, instead, we do not possess a personal human consciousness but a cosmic one. However paradoxical this sounds, clairvoyant vision perceives that we possess a consciousness in which live something like replicas of the worlds of planets and stars. We feel ourselves to be immersed in the universal life of the cosmos. Our perspective on the world is from the cosmos and its universal life.

Each time we fall asleep we experience within us—in reverse—what we underwent in physical life during the last period of our waking life, back to the moment we last woke up. Thus after spending a day awake in the regular way and then falling asleep at night, the last experiences we had before falling asleep, in the late evening, come first in our sleeping life, and then we go back through the day's events to those in the afternoon and so on. We go back over all the day's events in reverse through the night.

As I said, in exact clairvoyance as I have described it here, we can recall these nightly experiences in our ordinary waking life. Just as, in our ordinary memory, we recall things we experienced in waking life years ago, exact clairvoyance enables us to witness this reverse experience of daily life. It therefore offers us something like an expanded memory. We look back upon our sleeping experience knowing that in sleep our experience is outside the physical, spatial body, and that here we experience our daily life in reverse within a real world essence which, in a sense, possesses awareness of the whole world as image, as replica. And then we also find that this reverse experience of daily existence does not take as much time as it needs here in the physical world. Developing real research into this realm, increasingly bringing exact, systematic experience to bear on it, one learns to perceive that this reverse experience happens three times faster than physical experience in ordinary consciousness. In other words, someone who is awake for around two thirds of his life and asleep for one third re-experiences in this one third what he underwent in physical life in the remaining two thirds. Thus we can come to perceive a life that happens outside the body, which runs backwards and three times faster.

As we recall this night-time sleeping experience through exact clairvoyance in ordinary daily life, we find at the same time that this reverse experience has no *intrinsic* importance. What exact clairvoyance gives us in our waking life is of course a memory, whose significance is not intrinsic but only preliminary. How do you evaluate the memory of an experience you had 20 years ago? You find it to be an experience in shadowy thoughts. And yet the very nature of this memory offers a guarantee that I do not live in fantasy but that this is an image of what I actually experienced in my life in the past. Just as a memory embodies an assurance that it relates to something quite different, a reality that once occurred, so the recall of our nightly experiences, of no intrinsic importance in itself, bears an assurance of the future. It points towards the future.

We have no need to prove to ourselves that memory points back to the past; nor, having acquired exact clairvoyance, do we need to prove that our survey thus gained of nightly experiences is not just a present fantasy. We can tell by its very nature that it relates to our future, one in fact when we have in reality laid aside our physical body at death whereas now, in exact clairvoyance, we have simply laid it aside metaphorically.

Thereby we learn to perceive what we experience following death after completing the period of three days as I described it. Indeed, through this memory-like process we also come to understand the significance of the two to three days after death, during which we feel ourselves to be within world consciousness, cosmic consciousness, surveying one last time our own etheric nature from the perspective of the cosmos. Here we look back upon what we experienced during our life on earth. We learn to perceive what we experience subsequently: a life following the event of death which unfolds three times faster than life on earth. This is something we learn to perceive through our clairvoyant vision of night-time experience.

And so we find that the etheric vision lasting only a short time after death is followed by a life that lasts 20, 30 years, or shorter, depending on how old we were when we died. These spans are approximate, but this life takes roughly three times less than our life on earth did. If someone died at the age of 30, therefore, this part of life after death will take around ten years. Or if he died at 60, this reverse experience will take roughly 20 years.

Through exact clairvoyance we can perceive all this, just as memory recalls a past experience or action. We learn to see that supersensible experience follows our death: an experience in the supersensible world, which revisits our whole life on earth in reverse. Every night we re-experience the day that has ended. After death we re-experience in reverse our whole life on earth. We pass through it all once more. And in passing in spiritual form through everything we experienced on earth, we acquire an accurate evaluation of our own moral worth.

During this period we pass through after death we incorporate into ourselves, you can say, an awareness of our moral personality, our moral value, in the same way that here on earth we acquire an awareness of life in flesh and blood. After death we dwell within what we were as a moral human being on earth. Passing through all the events of our life again in reverse, and therefore no longer held back from moral judgement of ourselves by our instincts, drives and passions, but instead surveying them from a purely spiritual perspective, we come to an accurate, true judgement of our own moral quality.

The period I have described is needed to form this judgement. Having completed this after-death period, this inner moral life fades along with our reverse recall of our moral qualities on earth; and then we must journey onwards through worlds of spirit with a different kind of awareness, which can likewise become known to us through exact clairvoyance.

For this we need to learn not only to live outside our spatial body but also in a quite different consciousness from the one we possess here within the physical world. We discover that the experience of our moral quality, taking a third of the time of our past earthly life, is followed by supersensible, spiritual experience. A life in pure spirit follows. To discern its nature, exact clairvoyance has to rise from ordinary consciousness to a pure and higher consciousness, and develop the ability to fully evaluate this higher consciousness.

Thus I have attempted to describe to you two of the states that follow death. Once this part of the lecture has been translated, I will continue by describing the nature of the third condition.

If you consider what I have described as our reverse experience during sleep, you will see that while this is a life outside the physical, spatial body, or alongside it if you like, its nature is nevertheless such that we cannot move within it freely. Basically, we have to carry out what we accomplished during the day in our ordinary awareness, albeit in the reverse direction. And likewise, someone who draws on exact clairvoyance to obtain supersensible insight into these experiences I have described feels that the world he recalls in his waking consciousness through clairvoyance is one that holds him fast, one in which he cannot freely move, that harnesses and chains him. In contrast to this, the third condition of higher knowledge and higher life, which we must seek, is to move freely in the world of spirit. Without this, we cannot develop purely spiritual, purely supersensible consciousness.

In addition to exact clairvoyance one also has to acquire what I will call 'ideal magic', which must be distinguished from the charlatanism of much unreal, externally performed magic.

By ideal magic, I mean the following. Ordinarily when someone surveys his life he discovers how, in a certain respect, he has grown different with every passing year and decade. His habits have gradually altered. He has acquired certain skills while others have declined. Anyone who scrutinizes himself honestly to evaluate the skills he possesses will always see that he has changed during his life. But this is something life itself has made of us. We have given ourselves fully to life, and life schools and educates us, shapes and configures our soul.

By contrast, someone who wishes to enter the supersensible world and perceive its nature, or whoever, in other words, wishes to develop ideal magic, must not only inwardly intensify his thoughts to recognize in himself a second existence, as I have described, but must also emancipate his will from its servitude in the physical body. In ordinary life we can only bring our will into action and movement by making use of our physical body, say our legs, arms or organs of speech. The physical body is the basis for our will life. However, we can do the following—and this is something that a person must very systematically undertake as spiritual researcher if he wishes to develop this ideal magic, thus augmenting his capacity of exact clairvoyance. For example, he must develop a will so strong that he can say, at a certain point in life, that he will rid himself of a particular habit and instead inwardly appropriate a different one.

It may sometimes take years to apply sufficient energy of will to transform oneself so entirely as to acquire certain forms of experience— but it can be done. Instead of just letting life teach us through the physical body, we can take this education, this self-discipline in hand ourselves.

The kinds of energetic will exercise, which I have likewise described in the volumes I mentioned, will enable someone who desires to become a modern initiate to do more than re-experience in sleep what happened to him during the day. He will succeed in bringing about states that are not sleep, which are experienced in full awareness but nevertheless allow him to be mobile as he sleeps, to do something, so that he is not just passive when outside his body, as is the case with ordinary awareness, is not merely passive in the world of spirit but able to act there, be active. Ordinarily human beings do not make further progress while they're asleep. But someone who becomes a modern initiate in this sense has the ability to be active, to act, to engage in the life experienced between falling asleep and waking up again. And when, in this way, we carry the will into our human nature in the condition where our being is outside the body, then we become able to develop a quite different kind of awareness in us, one that can now really perceive what we experience during the time after death that follows the one I described. By means of this different kind of awareness, we really do become able to see into our life after death as well as our life before birth.* We become able to see

---

*Translator's note: Steiner writes here literally: 'our post-earthly earth life' and 'our pre-earthly earth life'.

how we pass through a life that unfolds in a world of spirit in the same way that physical life on earth unfolds in a physical world. We learn to recognize ourselves as pure spirit in a world of spirit just as here, in physical earth conditions, we recognize ourselves as a physical body within the physical world. And now we find that we have the opportunity to form a view of how long this life lasts, after the period of moral self-evaluation that I described before.

By carrying the will into one's life of soul through ideal magic in this way, we become acquainted with the form of awareness that we have as adults, and can properly compare it with the dull consciousness we possessed in infancy.

As you know, ordinary awareness cannot recall the very early years of childhood when we live in a dull consciousness, finding our way into the world in a kind of somnolence. Compared to this dark, dull consciousness of early childhood, our ordinary awareness as adults is bright and vivid. Someone who develops the capacity for ideal magic as I have described it, will come to recognize the difference between his ordinary waking consciousness as an adult and this dull consciousness of infancy. In a sense he learns to see that he develops to a different level, from the infant's duller form of awareness to a brighter form of adult consciousness. And arising from the distinction he knows exists between child consciousness, which is like dream consciousness, and his adult consciousness, he becomes able also to judge the other relationship between his adult consciousness and the illumined consciousness into which he has carried not only exact clairvoyance but also ideal magic so that he can now move freely within the world of spirit.

In early infancy we did not have control of our movements. In the world of spirit we learn to move freely just as, from early childhood onwards, we learned to move our body freely during physical life on earth. In other words, we come to perceive the relationship firstly between child and adult consciousness, but then also, similarly, that other relationship between adult consciousness and the highest, purely spiritual consciousness.

By this means, too, we come to know not only our life after death as a spirit among spirits with whom we work and collaborate, but we also acquire a judgement of how long this spiritual life amongst spiritual beings lasts. Here again I would cite the example of remembering an ordinary event. Just as a memory of this kind bears a past reality within it, so what one now experiences bears within it a correct judgement, a perception that in the higher consciousness of the initiate lives something that has more than personal significance, pointing rather to the reality of a life as spirit among spirits after death. And we learn to see how this purely spiritual life relates to life on earth, as we pass through it between birth and death.

If, as an initiate, we look back to our earliest infancy, we find that it becomes ever easier to look into the world of spirit as we grow older. It is true that there are relatively young people who can do so. But with every passing year this spiritual perception becomes clearer and more exact. We increasingly acquire the ability to pass over into this other form of consciousness, learning at the same time how the one relates to the other. We come to perceive the following. At the age of 40, let us say, one only possesses the ability to look back in memory to the age of 3 or 4. We consider how many more years our 40 are compared to the three or four of the infant with his unconscious, dreamlike awareness. We come to see, likewise, that our life in the spirit after death will last longer than this earthly life in the same ratio that exists between this whole life on earth and our dreamy infancy. In other words, it will last for many centuries. Therefore, once we have passed through the period of moral self-evaluation, we enter a purely spiritual life as spirit amongst spirits, and this lasts centuries. In this experience we engage with tasks in the world of spirit in the same way that we engage with tasks in the physical world during our earthly life.

But these tasks, as perceived by the exact clairvoyance I described, supported by our free movement through the world of spirit as achieved in ideal magic, are distinguished by the fact that we elaborate from the intrinsic nature of the world of spirit in which we live after death all the powers that subsequently lead us back again to another life on earth. This new life on earth stands before us as a goal, from the beginning of our life after death. And this life on earth within us is indeed a real microcosm. This microcosm is elaborated out of a mighty experience in the world of spirit after death.

In the physical world a seed or embryo is first small and gradually unfolds to become a large plant or animal. I would also speak of a spirit germ or seed which we develop after our physical life on earth has ended. We work together with spiritual beings to form a spirit germ for our subsequent life on earth, developing this out of the spiritual powers of the world. This work of elaboration is not a mere repetition of earthly life but encompasses modes of activity, intrinsic essences, that are greater and mightier, of course, than anything that can be experienced on earth. After our earthly existence, therefore, we prepare our future life on earth as we dwell in experiences of the world of spirit.

And in addition to this a cosmic consciousness arises, as I have described. The fact that cosmic consciousness arises in one person, and likewise in another, and that indeed this cosmic consciousness is already present every night albeit in a dull state—so that it is no real consciousness but, if I may use a paradoxical expression, an unconscious consciousness—means that people live as spiritual beings not just with other spiritual beings who never descend to earth, dwelling in a pure world of spirit, but also with all the souls who are either embodied in physical human bodies or who have already passed through the gate of death and dwell in the same condition as they do: a cosmic consciousness that all have in common.

It really is true to say that the threads woven here from one soul to another, in families, among people who find each other by encountering one another in physical bodies, but also therefore finding one another as souls, are laid aside—everything we found here on earth is cast off: what we experience through love, as friends, in connections with those close to us, what we experience through physical encounters in a physical body, is all laid aside, cast off in the same way that we lay these physical bodies aside. But having developed family relationships, friendships, love, this is spiritually transplanted through the gate of death into those experiences in the spirit that work to develop a subsequent life. And here we do not just work for ourselves alone but—already also in the period of moral evaluation of our past life—together with human souls whom we have come to prize and love in the world.

Through exact clairvoyance and ideal magic all this goes beyond mere faith to become real knowledge, informing a person's direct capacities of vision. We can even say that there is a gulf here between souls in the physical world, however much they love one another, since they encounter each other within their corporeality, and can only enter into reciprocal relationships mediated by the physical body. But when we live in the world of spirit it is no longer even the case that the physical body of a beloved person still on earth is a hindrance to our community of soul with him. To look into the spiritual world we have to acquire the ability to look *through* earthly objects, as I have described; and in the same way someone who has passed through the gate of death has community with the souls on earth he is close to by virtue of perception that looks through the body. As long as they are still on earth, until they themselves die, he still experiences them as souls.

Today, at the outset of these three lectures, I wanted to raise these things by way of offering insights into the reality of our supersensible life. I wanted to show that efforts to develop exact clairvoyance and ideal magic enable one to speak about higher worlds in the same precise and scientific way as natural science speaks about the world of the senses. Increasingly there will be people who develop their capacities to orient themselves in these worlds; and it will become apparent that no science, however perfect, can object to knowledge obtained through exact clairvoyance and ideal magic, and offered in an authentic spirit of scientific enquiry, about what we undergo not just here between birth and death but also between death and a new birth.

Tomorrow I will speak further about these repeated lives on earth and about what ultimate end they may reach. I will also describe the Christ event, the event of Golgotha, and what effect it had upon human life on earth. In doing so I will need to show that the kinds of knowledge I have described, inasmuch as they concern each individual, can illumine the whole evolution of the human race during life on earth, and thus also illumine what the entry of Christ into earthly life signifies for humanity.

These lectures, therefore, aim to show firstly that there is no need to fly in the face of the exact sciences of modern times when one speaks of supersensible insights. This will be the subject of tomorrow's lecture: that the event of the very greatest importance for humanity, the Christ event, appears before us in a new form, a more luminous form, when the human soul is willing to accept the insights presented here into the supersensible world. At the same time I will also show how anthroposophic spiritual science relates to Christianity.

Lecture 11

London, 18 November 1922[*]

Opposition to what I call anthroposophic science of the spirit arises from two main quarters. I touched on one of these yesterday:[36] the scientific objection. Scientists consider that supersensible knowledge of the kind I presented yesterday is beyond the reach of human cognition. And from this quarter, therefore, anthroposophy is seen as an impossible venture.

Today we will be more concerned with the other form of opposition, issuing from those who feel that anthroposophy deprives them, and many of those who profess the same faith, of their relationship to the Christ. Such people are mostly extremely pious Christians, in their own way, and their opposition is rooted in this very devoutness of soul. Above all they believe that our human relationship to Christ should be found through a simple, naive piety of heart and soul. It seems to them that all efforts to speak of Christ based on real enquiry will only be confusing for a simple, naive piety, and they would prefer that the search for Christ through the simple, human heart should not be disturbed—in anyone—by efforts to understand Christ through powers of human enquiry.

The feelings that arise in these people should no doubt be respected, and yet they are in serious error as far as anthroposophy is concerned. If they were to acknowledge the truth, they would discover that the path they seek to a sure knowledge of Christ is in fact smoothed by

______

[*] Second semi-public lecture.

anthroposophy. They would discover that the simple piety of their heart, their yearnings for Christ, are greatly strengthened by everything that anthroposophy has to say about the Christ.

I would like to clarify this from various perspectives, the first of which concerns what people have felt to be their religious life, their religious consciousness, at various stages of humanity's evolution on earth.

Let us trace this back a little into olden times; and you will see as I continue that this historical view is not irrelevant to our theme but can in fact clear up various modern misunderstandings. However, we cannot discover anything about these very ancient periods of humanity's evolution through external historical documents but only by means of the spiritual science I described to you yesterday. We can only study them inwardly by using the kind of perception which I yesterday showed to be necessary for understanding the human being's supersensible nature and our supersensible experiences of destiny. Looking back in this way into ancient eras, we find that people in those days attended to what was told them by pupils in the so-called mysteries. There are scarcely any extant historical records of these ancient mysteries, since what does exist is of so late a date that it really gives no insight into them. These mysteries were humanity's cultural and spiritual centres, where art, religion and science were still united. And the great teachers of these mysteries, the gurus, enjoyed almost divine veneration. The rest of humanity, to satisfy the dictates of their piety, attended to what the pupils of such mysteries told them, absorbing insights into the world, the world order, that the pupils of mystery teachers had learned in their devotional, reverent life. To illumine the nature of piety in the modern age, in particular devotion to Christ, I'd like to briefly outline the nature of the relationship between a pupil and his guru, a teacher in the mysteries, in those ancient times.

The first thing to realize is that these teachers were revered as people whose inner life was filled with divine power. When such teachers spoke to their pupils in the inspired words of the mysteries and rituals, the pupils believed that divine cosmic powers were speaking from their mouths, that they were not mere human beings any more.

This was not just metaphorical but a real sense possessed by ancient mystery pupils. You can imagine therefore how deep were the feelings of reverence such pupils had for their teachers—knowing that the divine was speaking to them from their teacher rather than just another human being, that what they considered divine was speaking through the teacher. It seems paradoxical to us today, but is especially characteristic of the outlook which pupils in the ancient mysteries had, that they thought divine, spiritual beings themselves had descended to the earth in still older eras when the earth had first begun, had descended, naturally, in a spiritual form. And these divine, spiritual beings, who did not assume a human physical body but who nevertheless were able to communicate spiritual knowledge to the original gurus, the first mystery teachers, gave the first instructions as to what humankind should be taught to bring it into a right connection with the world of spirit. It was thought, therefore, that what the gods had once conveyed to humankind had been passed on from generation to generation, coming down to the pupils of each era.

You will say that this leads to an explanation of the origin of human wisdom in supersensible worlds. But here we touch on an area where, even today still—if for example we think only of explanations of language—people are very unclear about origins. There are people who think of course that human speech evolved from animal calls, as Darwin proposes. But there are also those, and especially until quite recently this was so, who assign a divine origin to language.

Now I do not wish to dwell on this theme at present, or on what really underlies the development of language, for this is beyond our scope today. It is enough for us to know that, in their pious feelings, the pupils of the gurus believed that what their teachers taught them had once upon a time been given to humanity by the gods themselves.

And what was the goal of such pupilship? The pupil-teacher relationship involved, initially, an infinitely strong feeling of reverence for and devotion to the guru. The purpose of this complete adherence to a teacher was to unite the pupil with worlds of spirit. He was meant, we can say, to regard his teacher as the sole stream through which the divine could reach him. A pupil felt that he owed to his teacher everything within him, all that developed in his soul. And his teacher gave him instructions first and foremost about how to cultivate his thoughts. He was to guide his thoughts in a way that enabled him to learn to think—not by focusing on the sensory world but by turning all his thoughts, his whole sensibility, to the supersensible world, through the power which the guru or teacher planted in his soul in a form of allowable suggestion. When we think, our thoughts usually come up against outward things perceived through the senses. We think 'table': that is, our thinking confronts the table, comes up against it. Or we think 'tree', and this means likewise that our thinking comes up against and is stopped short by the tree. By contrast, the influence of the guru aimed to make thoughts transparent so that the pupil saw nothing that is in the world but instead, through thinking vision, could look into worlds, supersensible worlds, which I described to you yesterday by drawing on modern initiation science. The pupil was also to experience these supersensible worlds, and to do so instructions were given him that related to language, to speech. When we speak in ordinary life, we share thoughts with another person—either thoughts we ourselves have or ones we have received from elsewhere. In a nutshell, what flows into our language lives on the physical earth. Now the guru gave his pupil mantric verses which, uttered in a half-declamatory, half-spoken way, were intended not only to enable the pupil to hear the meaning of the living words in his speech but also to experience in each flowing phrase the stream of cosmic divinity as well. Each phrase or sentence was to be spoken in a way that rendered its human content meaningless yet allowed the divine reality living in the world and in the human being to flow or stream within it. Looking through the thoughts that thus became transparent to him, the pupil was to perceive the divine. Rather than the meaning of these mantric verses, the pupil, as he recited them, was to be led into the rites of worship through the divine power streaming through them. Through what lay in these rites he was to direct his will and his whole human personality towards the divine. Many of the rites and rituals were connected with this. You can still see this today in the cross-legged Buddha posture, where the human limbs are placed in a position that does not accord or engage with earthly actions. Through the very posture or physical stance that is adopted, the position of one's limbs, one is lifted right away from earthly conditions and thereby guided to the divine, as accompaniment also to actions accomplished in one's awareness, in the mind or spirit.

What was all this meant to achieve? Well, through this threefold mindfulness of the self, the pupil's sensibility, his soul, sought to raise to the divine the evil or sinful lapses from godliness which people on the earth become embroiled in, and to pour this upwards into the super-sensible worlds that I described to you yesterday. Yesterday I showed that through modern initiation science also, it is possible to rise into the worlds in which we live as soul-spiritual beings before we begin our earthly lives, and from which we descend in order to connect with the body given us by our mother and father. We return to these worlds when we have passed back again through the portal of death, there preparing another earthly life as I said. The aim of these divine teachers in the ancient mysteries was not only to direct the gaze and thoughts of the pupil up into supersensible worlds but to engender in him also a power of prayerful thinking, a power of mantric recitation in which the divine could flow, a power of devotion to acts of worship—a great power that could guide what was sinful in nature up into supersensible worlds. And these pupils would then in turn teach others to embrace the outlook in which they had been inculcated in these mysteries. This was the cultural content of the civilization of those ancient times.

But what was the precondition for engaging in such a practice? It was based on the fact that human beings live here on earth in a world which, unlike the divine, does not fully encompass their being. This is how the ancient pupil of the guru regarded it, and this was also what the guru taught. This world, he said, in which you live between birth and death, encompasses other realms of nature which in a certain way are one with it, but it does not encompass our deeper human nature. What a person could accomplish between birth and death, his deeds and experiences—leaving aside the fact that this life in many respects was seen as very sinful in those times—was not thought to include the full scope of his human nature. And in those ancient times all pupils of a guru knew clearly, at certain moments of their lives, that they had lived in a supersensible world before they were born and would live in this world again after death. They knew this through an ancient, primitive clair-voyance that they did not need to develop but possessed as a natural endowment, a dreamlike clairvoyance common in those ancient times. And so they believed themselves not to be fully human if they were only connected with what exists here on the physical earth, and only accomplished what is possible here. They felt that they needed to direct their powers up into worlds of spirit. Their full being was not here on earth but above. That was the idea at the root of those ancient mysteries, that what cannot be properly accomplished here on earth could be raised, in the rites and rituals accomplished in accord with clairvoyant thoughts, into the stream of mantras with their divine intonations and led from earthly to super-earthly conditions. Only there, in supersensible worlds, they believed, could human deeds be corrected since these supersensible worlds encompass the whole human being.

This is what the ancient gurus taught their pupils, in a very factual, tangible way: When a person passes through the portal of death, he knows that what he has been able to accomplish on earth is not sufficient for his whole being, and that as he passes through the world of spirit he must balance and redress what can be done badly on earth, can only be done imperfectly and unwisely.

And now, amongst all the knowledge of supersensible worlds one gains by the means described yesterday, one can also perceive how actions that remain imperfect on the earth can be completed and made perfect in the supersensible world.

But in those ancient times things were different and, as we will see in a moment, must become different again today. In those ancient times pupils learned from their teachers that when someone passes through the portal of death and enters the supersensible world, at a certain period he meets a lofty spiritual being whose outward manifestation is the sun and its light. The ancient mysteries called this being the high, divine being of the sun. If we look at someone on earth we say that his soul manifests in his facial expressions, his physiognomy. Similarly, people in ancient times regarded the sun's movements, and solar phenomena as the physiognomy, the outward expressions of the high sun being. In the sun's outward radiance and its predominance in the heavens they saw the gestures of this solar being whom they could not see directly while on earth but whom they encountered when they passed through the gate of death. This same being helped to perfect what remained imperfect in earthly conditions. The ancient gurus or teachers spoke to their pupils as follows. Turn the piety of your hearts, your devotion, towards the lofty being of the sun so that you may find this being, and so that after death this being whom you will encounter in worlds of spirit, whom you cannot meet here on earth, will help you to balance and redress your imperfections, will help you to pass through the world of spirit in the right way.

But as the Mystery of Golgotha approached, ancient mystery wisdom was in decline. There was little left of it except fading traditions. There were still initiates who adhered to the divine Father with the same devotion and piety—the Father God who had once sent his divine messengers to earth to teach the original gurus. And these initiates knew still that the teachings given to mystery pupils in ancient times had granted them great consolation and comfort: the knowledge that after death they would meet the lofty sun being who helps transform all earthly imperfection into perfection, relieving them of the burdensome sense of lapsing from the divine, spiritual world order. But this lofty sun being had to descend to earth and take on the garb of humanity in Jesus of Nazareth and, since the death of Jesus Christ at Golgotha, is no longer to be sought in supersensible worlds but instead amongst humankind.

This was the message of initiates around the time of the Mystery of Golgotha and through to the third century AD. To those who were willing to listen to them, these initiates said that the healing being they had longed for had been present for ancient humanity, but, through a divine deed, had descended to the earth, appearing in human form, and since then had been living supersensibly within humanity's further evolution. Whereas ancient pupils had to enter the mysteries and, in their acts of worship, their rites, learn to look up to supersensible worlds, people of the new era must now gain a direct relationship with the Christ being *on the earth itself*, for he had descended and become a human being like other human beings.

That was the mood disseminated by contemporaries at the time of the Mystery of Golgotha and by many initiates in the first three centuries of the Christian era. Historical records say little about this. Basically all the texts that promulgated this have been destroyed. But by the means I described yesterday one can develop insights that show this mood prevailing in Christianity in the first three centuries amongst those who were still willing to hearken to the remaining initiates—until this Christ mood was lost and must today be renewed. When this part of the lecture has been translated, I will begin the second part.

And so, in the relationship which pupils developed with their teacher, this reverent, devotional relationship, they gradually learned to look up to the divine. And in the teacher himself, the guru, they saw a mediator of the divine, someone who enabled the divine to stream down to the earth, and in turn guided up into the world of spirit the piety which pupils wished to direct there. A wealth of such feelings existed and, by inheritance through generations, took root in the human sensibility, the human soul. Those who became the first Christian teachers—whose powers of inwardness and reverence few have any inkling of today— guided the devotion of those who hearkened to them not to gurus any longer, in the old sense, but to the Christ who descended from worlds of spirit and had assumed humanity in the body of Jesus of Nazareth.

This sum of feelings was perpetuated through centuries, and was directed towards the figure whom external Christian history tells passed through the Mystery of Golgotha, passed through death for the sake of humankind, so that henceforward humanity could find him on the earth.

Modern initiation science, which I spoke to you about yesterday, now approaches this Christ Mystery once again, seeking to grasp the secret of Golgotha. Why is this necessary?

Although a quality of piety and religiosity survived into the Middle Ages, as if perpetuating that current of reverential devotion which pupils had once felt for the ancient gurus, the old, dreamlike clairvoyance increasingly faded as a human endowment. Anthroposophic spiritual science enables us to ascertain, without recourse to historical documents, that in ancient times people were able to immerse themselves in a kind of dreamlike clairvoyance; and by this means they perceived the world from which they themselves had descended to earthly existence. But humanity slowly lost this knowledge of the eternal in the human soul. Under its sway, people could never have attained a sense of human freedom, which is part and parcel of our full humanity, and had to enter humankind. This sense of freedom entered human beings during the Middle Ages, at the same time as that old form of consciousness faded away—since it could never have been intrinsically free. You see, when a person gazed upon the nature of the human being as soul among spiritual beings in pre-earthly existence, he felt himself to be dependent, he felt unfree. One can say that a time arrived when the old clairvoyance grew dim, and in this twilight state in respect of the world of spirit humanity developed its sense of freedom, which reached a certain culmination in our modern civilization. But this also meant that humankind could no longer see into those supersensible worlds from which Christ descended into Jesus of Nazareth. And therefore the reverence practised in Christianity became a more traditional one, with people relying on historical tradition and drawing on what remained in them of ancient guru veneration passed down through heredity. It was still possible for a while to direct towards the divine all human reverence which people had formerly acquired in their relationship with it. But in this twilight consciousness a knowledge of the natural world, such as had been unknown in ancient times, increasingly developed and people increasingly lost any inkling that human enquiry can discover a world of spirit.

But the kind of knowledge I described to you yesterday is a real continuation of our knowledge of nature. All that can approach us as we practise meditation and concentration and thus gain insight into the world of spirit can develop most strongly when we do not accept what science tells us about the surrounding world as the whole truth but instead wrestle inwardly with it, when we absorb scientific thoughts, in their precision and accuracy, but then seek to unite them with our inmost human nature. What arises in consequence is initially undefined—a certain mood or condition of soul. If, in this mood, we practise meditation, concentration in the realm both of thought and will, the soul is guided upwards, as I described yesterday, into supersensible worlds. And by this means we acquire the capacity to understand the nature of the supersensible. We learn to look away from the earth as science describes it into a supersensible world which, however, belongs to the earth, and which must be seen as intrinsic to the earth in particular if we wish to understand the human being.

And then, in the inmost depths of someone struggling for anthroposophic insight, arise questions of the most far-reaching importance.

And in seeking answers to these questions, he will find that they lead him in turn to an understanding of the Mystery of Golgotha.

Having raised our consciousness away from the earth, thus learning to see the realm of spirit, having succeeded in perceiving outside the human body and even, as I described yesterday, in acting through ideal magic, we have learned to introduce our cognition and will into a world of spirit in this body-free condition.

Equipped with this inner understanding of the world of spirit, if we look once more towards Christ, to the earthly event we then see as the Mystery of Golgotha, we do not, as much theology does, stop with the human being Jesus of Nazareth. We no longer have a merely materialistic understanding of what happened at the Mystery of Golgotha. Instead, since we have acquired the capacity for spiritual perception, we perceive how the human being Jesus of Nazareth was permeated with the Christ. With our capacity to see the spirit, we also succeed in seeing this divine, spiritual nature in the Christ once more. Our modern theosophy, which can regain a direct knowledge of the divine, spiritual realm, draws on this knowledge to look upon Jesus of Nazareth and perceive in him, in turn, the Christ who can only be perceived as a spiritual being. Thus the knowledge we develop of the super-earthly realm allows us to approach the Christ, perceiving in the Christ himself a super-earthly reality: the divine within the God who became man.

Modern anthroposophy leads us back to the Christ through a full grasp of the world of spirit, doing so especially if we have properly prepared ourselves through anthroposophy. To render this fully comprehensible, I'd like to show how, as modern human beings, we can approach the world of spirit in either a mistaken or a correct way. Today, you see, there are modern successors to those over whom the influence of the ancient mysteries once held sway, in a dull, twilight consciousness that could look into certain states of pre-birth existence. In this dull awareness they sought through their rites and rituals to let the spirit flow towards the divine. These ancient, pious people have successors today in those who seek a connection with the world of spirit in a very dubious way. In ancient times, the outward soul life of these pious people remained in the soul realm, and they directed their soul towards supersensible worlds. This pious mood was perpetuated among

Christians, as Christian reverence, as I described at the beginning of my lecture. Such people today wish to retain this naive piety. It is naive nowadays because we no longer perceive supersensible existence through our natural consciousness, and this naive piety no longer leads us upwards, as it did the ancient pupils of the guru, to supersensible worlds but instead remains here on earth in the physical body. That is the characteristic quality of this naive piety, that it remains with feelings and sentiments, feelings the soul has when immersed in itself, in its own human nature. When someone dwells in and upon their own human nature, they can in fact gain knowledge that the physical body is not just flesh and blood but also contains spirit. This spirit, which pious people once sought to guide towards the divine, is what the misguided modern successors of ancient mystery pupils today seek to enact in a mediumistic kind of way.

What is a medium? Someone who allows the spirit to speak or write, or announce itself in some other way, through the physical body. It is true that the human body is not merely physical, that spirit can speak from it, but this is a mechanical spirit, of a lower order, and we can see this in the fact that mediums speak when their consciousness—which is what usually produces writing and speech—is dimmed as it once was in the mystery pupils of ancient times. Such mediums not only wish to experience the spirit directly in and through their body, but also try to manifest it there. And this does happen—something spiritual that lives in the body does speak when the medium speaks or writes. The characteristic thing about such mediums is—as you may perhaps know— that they become loquacious, write great quantities, but a great deal that must seem dubious for ordinary logic is mingled with what the spirit announces through their body; and as such they demonstrate that we ought not to reach back to this old form of connection with the divine, spiritual realm, but must instead seek it by other means.

It is this other means that is sought by anthroposophic spiritual science. And perhaps it is legitimate for me to speak about this, for a particular reason. This other way of approaching the world of spirit—at the same time giving due credence to scientific findings and discoveries, and accepting them as the great achievements of modern civilization— is one that finds it extraordinarily difficult, as it seeks to approach spiritual worlds, to move the organs of speech, even to entertain the resulting thoughts, let alone to resort to recording them in mediumistic writing. When the spirit within us of which I spoke yesterday takes hold of us in meditation and concentration, we would like best to fall silent altogether! Whereas a medium grows loquacious and allows a spirit to speak from him through the speech organs, a conscientious, scientifically educated person in whom the spirit develops supersensible knowledge as I described yesterday, would like best to say nothing, not to speak of that delicate experience announcing itself in the soul. One even feels like forbidding oneself from thinking since one's thinking has been learned in relation to earthly, physical things. One would prefer not to let thoughts run on, not to flow into one's soul, because one feels a certain inner anxiety that one might half-unconsciously apply to the spiritual realm thoughts trained through observation of outward, physical, sensory things. If one applies such thoughts to the inner state of soul I described yesterday, one gets the sense not only that the spirit will take flight but also that one is acting profanely, that spiritual reality will be distorted. Least of all does one wish to resort to writing, for one knows that in those ancient times when divine worship was enacted in rituals and actions, writing was never involved. Writing is something that has only developed in humanity along with the sensory, physical orientation of the intellect and reason. One senses writing to be something one wishes to push as far away from oneself as possible when knowledge of the divine spirit takes hold of one. As this capacity to perceive the divine spirit, the supersensible world, grows in one and takes root, one first becomes inwardly dumb and silent in one's thoughts, and even more so in relation to speech or writing about the divine.

As I said, I feel it is legitimate for me to speak of these experiences, since they are in fact my own. They are ones I had when I myself pursued a path of development that took me from science to a grasp of worlds of spirit, to perception of spiritual worlds, through to a vision of the Mystery of Golgotha gained by perception of these worlds of spirit. But you will also understand some of the difficulties faced by a person who approaches the Mystery of Golgotha through this modern, anthroposophic science of the spirit. The Mystery of Golgotha must be grasped in its whole majesty and grandeur, as this is revealed in humanity's history. We have to learn to look upon the historical fact that God passed through death at Golgotha within the human being Jesus of Nazareth. We have to look upon this greatest of all historical events in an entirely sense-free picture. And yet, in the way I have done this, it is extraordinarily difficult to wrestle one's way through to a sense-free grasp of this reality in thoughts, then to present it in words, perhaps also in writing.

But by doing this one acquires inner reverence, inner awe before the great Mystery that took place at Golgotha. Something pours through the soul of someone who has fallen silent in thoughts and words as I described, who wishes to stay very still when the divine spirit draws him to the Mystery of Golgotha. The deepest, most reverent feeling pours through the soul of such a person, so that he refrains from drawing any closer to this experience. And thus we gain not only knowledge on the anthroposophic path. Knowledge comes first, through looking up to supersensible worlds; but this pours into feeling, into awe and reverence—something that takes root in the human soul far more deeply even than the feelings an ancient pupil had for his guru. This feeling first develops as the profoundest need to encompass the experience of Christ Jesus at Golgotha. Through an inner metamorphosis, what is initially supersensible vision is entirely transformed into feeling. And this feeling seeks the God become man at Golgotha, and can find him because it has learned to perceive the spirit. It does not speak of the *human being* Jesus of Nazareth but learns to recognize that Christ can truly be perceived in him within earthly reality as a divine, spiritual being. And so there flows from anthroposophic spiritual science a knowledge of the spiritual Christ, and at the same time a true reverence flows towards the divine by virtue of what can live in knowledge of the supersensible.

How this can lead to a fruitful deepening of Christianity is something I will speak of in the short, third part of the lecture after the second part has been translated.

Someone who, in the way described, would best like to fall silent in thoughts and words when the power of supersensible perception takes hold of him, who would prefer to refrain from using his organism to express what lives in him, experiences a transition point when he decides that he will after all give outward expression to these things; and then he finds something that justifies him in speaking of the spiritual nature of Christ Jesus. At this transition, with the decision to think about the spirit in thoughts, to speak and write of it, you find that in all speaking and thinking about this spiritual reality you feel yourself raised out of the physical body. In fact you cannot then think or speak, since thinking belongs to the physical body, and the physical body is required for speech, and now you feel in a certain way alienated from your physical body. Whereas a medium feels himself fully present in his physical body, even suppressing consciousness and living entirely in the physical body to let the spirit speak from it, the person who perceives supersensibly raises himself out of his physical body through a refined, a heightened awareness. Through everything he has experienced as a world of spirit, the physical world becomes something that is extremely difficult for him to grasp hold of. He finds no language, no naive activity of thinking; he cannot find his arms or his whole physical body. You gradually have to rediscover this physical world, your thoughts and power of speech to convey what you experience in the supersensible world. And this makes you feel as if you had to master life a second time, all over again—like passing through a self-created birth. But this also teaches you about the depths of the human entelechy. For in taking hold of this being of yours for a second time in order to make it into an instrument for thinking about the spiritual, supersensible realm, and to express this, you come to know it. In coming to know it supersensibly, in penetrating your organism with supersensible knowledge of the kind I described to you yesterday and today, you will also find the Christ there, who passed through the Mystery of Golgotha. You experience the Christ—not only the Christ who once descended to earth and passed through death, but the Christ who passed through death in order to pour himself out again henceforth into humanity, the whole of humanity. This is what you experience as you encompass your body once again more fully and consistently through supersensible knowledge. Someone acquiring knowledge of Christ in this way is then able to clothe this knowledge in words that convey a true message of Christ. He has this knowledge: that Christ died on Golgotha, and passing through death poured himself into human powers of birth, living since then within human nature. And human beings can find him when they enter deeply enough into their being. The modern initiate therefore knows that the Pauline phrase 'Not I, but Christ in me'[37] is profoundly true. I will find the Christ within me if I descend deep enough into my humanity.

But the initiate does not have to try to initiate everyone else too, to make them Christians. Instead, equipped with this knowledge of Christ, he discovers how simple piety can also find new ways forward. This simple, primitive piety *can* find the Christ. Nowadays, however, such piety has to find somewhat different ways from the old ones. It is no longer enough to sit at the feet of a guru. The path must be an inward one, since human beings ought no longer to send up their feelings for the divine into a supersensible world but should instead delve into themselves to find within them the Christ who has been living on the earth since the Mystery of Golgotha. Anthroposophic spiritual science can communicate a real truth to those of simple piety—that it is no illusion to find the Christ if you delve deeply enough into yourself for he is there in your depths, he is there because he descended into these depths through death at Golgotha. The anthroposophic spiritual scientist knows he is conveying a truth in speaking in this way to those of simple piety, that he is not merely drawing on a person's feelings, but that he can show him a goal which a person of simple piety can attain. Someone who possesses a simple, pious outlook can also pursue a modern path. In former times, through reverence for the guru, pupils developed transparent thoughts, the divine resonance of the mantra, the gesture of worship, whereas someone who wishes to find his way to Christ in the modern era needs to find, first and foremost, an inwardness of soul. He needs to learn to look inwards, to have an inner content in his feelings, his inner experience, when he turns his gaze away from the external world. And there he must find the power that leads him through the gateway of death, becoming acquainted with it here on earth in a devotion to Christ and the Mystery of Golgotha.

The ancient guru told his pupils, and through them all of humanity, that when they passed through the gate of death they would find the sublime sun being who perfects the imperfections of earth. The modern initiate or teacher says, by contrast: 'If you gain a relationship here on earth to the Christ who descended to us, and to the Mystery of Golgotha, finding your relationship to him with all powers of inner reverence, inner adoration, then within you will stream a power that does not die when you do. You will bear this with you through the gate of death, and it will accomplish for you what you cannot accomplish here on earth as long as you possess a physical body. What the sublime sun being accomplished for human beings in ancient times, the power of Christ will accomplish by remaining in your being when you are free of the body after death.' The Christ power will act in what remains imperfect in us, making it possible for people on earth to find one another in social existence in this acknowledgement of Christ. You see, what penetrates us with an inner power that streams from Christ, as anthroposophic spiritual science can reveal, is a power that can work into human actions, human will, an impulse for such actions which stream, therefore, into our social coexistence. The powers of Christ can indeed stream into the life of our social community.

Today people speak a great deal about social reforms, social progress. But who will be the great reformer of social life, the great innovator who will one day enable human actions in society to be undertaken in the name of Christ Jesus, so that the world can become Christ-permeated? Who will be the great reformer, the social reformer too, who will sow peace wherever there has been social conflict? Only the Christ can do so, when people become able to develop social community together which, at certain moments in life, becomes an act of worship. Then they can look up to the Christ and, instead of saying 'I . . .', say that if only two or three, or many, are united in Christ[38] then Christ is among them. Thus social initiative will become an act of worship, and a continuation of ancient rites of worship. Christ must himself become the great social reformer of our times by working within us in a living way.

This is the Christianization of social existence. But now I'd like to ask this: Is what people long for possible? Is it possible for those of simple piety to find the power of Christ in their souls so that, in acting amongst others in social community they act in the name of Christ, and their actions become worthy of this? Can a person of simple piety acquire the certainty that his actions are done in Christ's name? The modern initiate can tell such people that their experience is based on truth, that what they find in reflecting on themselves and on what lives in them as Christ did arise from the death at Golgotha and does truly flow from Christ. And what you accomplish in social community in the awareness of doing it as Christ impulse is indeed done in Christ's name, for Christ lives amongst us when we find him. And we find him through ourselves, through inwardness in social coexistence; we find true, devotional love which crosses the gulf between one human heart and another, bringing a supersensible element into our feelings, like the light which shines inwardly, a supersensible element into our perceptions and insights.

It is therefore possible for people of simple piety to learn that their path of simple devoutness is not hindered or disrupted by anthroposophic spiritual science. Not at all! The perpetuation of a purely outward science would gradually dim and darken this natural piety. But anthroposophic spiritual science, in conveying knowledge of the supersensible realm and thus a true knowledge of the Christ being as a supersensible being, can give to those of true piety the very thing they long for: a certainty about what lives in their souls; a certainty about what lives in their hands and loving actions done in the name of Christ, in harmony with the Christ impulse. The very thing a devout person longs for will be able to enter the world as certain knowledge through what anthroposophic spiritual science seeks to be. It does not obstruct the paths of the truly devout, does not lead people away from the Christ. It does not enter the world of spirit in denial of modern science but carries this science forward with it, and with respect for it. Anthroposophic spiritual science knows that humanity cannot go forward into its future without the Christ; it does so with the Christ, with the truly perceived and felt Christ, with actions in the world that summon his being to work here in the world.

LECTURE 12

LONDON, 19 NOVEMBER 1922[*]

As I have outlined in the past two days,[39] anthroposophy does not seek to be a merely theoretical outlook, one that might enable people to ignore unpleasant, painful aspects of life and take flight into a mystical world. Its aim, instead, is to engage fully with life as it is lived. It has to become practical, to inform real life; and this is because the mode of spiritual perception I described yesterday and the day before must lead us to fully encompassing and perceiving the world of spirit—which does not have some detached and separate existence but is implicit in all material realities. Whenever we meet another person we are by no means only concerned with what our eyes can perceive of him, what our linguistic understanding can grasp of what he says, or anything else our ordinary awareness can receive as external expressions of his being. We are also involved with his being of spirit, with the spiritual entelechy living in him—with a spiritual, supersensible being that continually engages in his material organism.

The kind of knowledge we acquire through our ordinary sensory perception, and the intellect connected with this, is unable to give us much understanding of the world. People subscribe to the illusion that they will eventually come to understand the world better as science improves, by means of human intelligence, sensory observation and experimentation. But in fact, as the two lectures I have given sought to show, sensory observation and intellect alone can only encompass the

---

[*] Third semi-public lecture.

mineral realm. Even the plant world already asks more of us: an understanding that much subtler laws and powers are at work there, originating from the cosmos, than human logic and sense alone can grasp. This is even truer when we encounter the world of the animals, and most of all so when we consider the human being. In plants (though least so in these), animals and human beings, the powers working in their physical organism, in the material realm, act like a kind of ideal magic. It is very mistaken to think that a material process observed in the laboratory can be observed in the same way in an animal or human organism. In the animal and human organism, a purely physical process is embedded in an ideal magic. We start to understand the nature of this ideal magic and what is at work in the human being by looking through and past his material processes to see how the spiritual realm is continually working in him.

We can only grasp such spiritual magic through insights I spoke of here both yesterday and the day before. As I said, the first level of such insight shows us that the human being not only has a present and momentary relationship to the world but can also transpose himself back to any age since he was born. I gave the example of going back to when we were 18 or 15, and experiencing what we experienced then—not only as shadowy recall, but with the same intensity and vigour as one actually experienced it at the time. You *become* 15 or 12 again. You undergo this inner spiritual metamorphosis; and by this means you become able to perceive a second organism within the human being, a subtle organism which we can call 'etheric' because it has no weight like a spatial body—it is a subtler organism. But this finer organism is also a time organism. All at once you perceive, in a complete overview, everything that constitutes this etheric organism as a temporal process. But at the same time you know that this is an organism, and you learn to see that we dwell within this subtler temporal organism in the same way we otherwise live in our spatial organism.

If for instance you observe someone suffering from, say, a certain kind of headache, you must be able to realize that a cure might well have to proceed from a particular inner organ of the body, and that it cannot be effected simply by treating the head itself, for the cause may be rooted in an organ far removed from it. In the spatial organism we inhabit, everything is connected. But the same is true also of the etheric time organism which is especially active in earliest infancy though it also remains mobile throughout life. It bears within it forces that act in the following way for instance. Let us assume that at the age of 35 we have an opportunity to reshape our life situation. If we find we are equal to this new situation and find that we're able to act in the right way in it, we may become aware that a long time ago, as a 12-year-old or 8-year-old, we learned the most important part of what has now enabled us to find our way rapidly into this new situation. At the age of 35, a certain joy radiates from what came towards us in childhood through a carer or teacher, say, when we were 8 or 10. What happens in a child's ether body in response to the work of a teacher, to his teaching, works in the same way as an organ a good way distant from the head can, when we heal it, have a curative effect on the headache syndrome. What we experienced at the age of 7 or 12 continues to act in us when we are 35 and still later, engendering a joyful mood or depression. A person's whole outlook, even at a very advanced age of adulthood, is dependent on what the teacher developed in the child's ether body in the same way that one organ of the human body is dependent on another. If we ponder this we will realize that this insight arising from perception of how the etheric body develops, how its separate realities are interrelated, is the only proper basis for educational work with children. Think this thought right through and you will see that just as a painter or other artist has to learn his craft and technique, so it is necessary for a teacher to acquire a craft and technique of teaching. Just as the painter must develop an eye—superior to that of the amateur—for the forms he observes, for colours and their interplay or dissonances, and then base his handling of colours on these observations, the way he handles his brush or pencil, acquiring something that works right through him and is based on his skill in observing, so the teacher must be able to draw on his observations of what acts spiritually in the human being and makes his biography a living whole. You see, education cannot be a science. It has to be an art. And in developing artistic capacities we first have to acquire skills in observation, then also skill in engaging with and shaping our material as we go on observing it, go on wrestling with it. In the sense intended here, therefore, spiritual science, anthroposophic science of the spirit, can provide a foundation for a true, authentic art of education.

But it does so also in another way. If education is to be really effective it has to properly cultivate what seeks to emerge from deep within a person in childhood. In this art of education a teacher really has to be able to regard the child as a divine, moral mission entrusted to him. We can only find the strength to work alongside the child so that all his potential unfolds from within him when we raise ourselves inwardly, morally through this educational work, so that it is imbued with something like religiosity or reverence. In other words, all teaching has to be a moral action, must originate in moral impulses; and these impulses must be applied to the kind of human insights and observations that I just described.

If we take full account of this we will find, however, that a human life falls into different periods in a much more defined way than we usually realize. People recognize, outwardly, that second dentition occurs in a child around the age of 6 or 7, and that certain physical changes accompany it; but they do not observe more carefully to discover what transformation occurs in the child during second dentition. But someone who knows how to properly judge what a child was like before the age of 6, and what he is like after this, will see that after this age, 6 or 7, powers develop from the depths of the human being that were previously deeply concealed within it. If we consider this properly we will find the following: second dentition is not just a sudden, unique event in human life. The second dentition that occurs around 6 or 7, and never recurs again, is nevertheless something that has filled all of the child's life so far, from the emergence of the first teeth through to second dentition. Throughout this time, the powers that eventually enable the second teeth to emerge from within the organism are surging and pushing. And at second dentition we have only a conclusion of what is active throughout the child's life so far. There is no third dentition. What does this mean? It means that up to the age of 7 or so the child has developed in his physical organism the powers he needs until the second teeth emerge, but which he no longer needs for his physical organism thereafter because there is no further dentition to accomplish. What happens to these powers or forces?

We can find these powers again, when we study the human being through supersensible perception, in the child's altered soul life between second dentition and puberty. The nature of his inner life changes, and the soul acquires a different type of memory and a different relationship to his surroundings. If we know how to observe a child spiritually as well as physically, it becomes clear to us that what we see in the child's soul between the ages, roughly, of 7 to 14, previously lived in his physical organism—and in other words was as yet an activity connected with second dentition but not wholly encompassed by it. This activity also instigates many other processes in the human organism. Around the age of 7 it ceases to be physically active and begins to be active in the soul, in inner life. And so to understand the distinctive powers at work in the child's soul between the change of teeth and puberty you must consider what occurs physically in the child from birth to second dentition. Soul powers are at work then, manifesting soul-spiritually still in the physical organism. And this means that a proper understanding of the child— especially in infancy but in a certain respect also through until the change of teeth—shows us that he is entirely sense organ, not in a coarse sense but a subtler one. In a subtler kind of way, the child is entirely a sensing eye. Just as the eye forms inner after-images of what is outside us, giving us an inner picture of the objects in our surroundings, so in his infancy a child has an entire form of perception, though not specifically visual. He is entirely sense organ if I can put it like that. Let me try to make this more tangible. Think of an infant. As adults, we have our sense of taste on the tongue and the palate. The young child—and we can learn this through spiritual science in ways I have described to you these last few days—has a flow of taste throughout his organism: he is entirely taste organ. He is also entirely an organ of smell and also, in a certain inner sense, entirely an inner organ of touch. So his whole organism is sensory in nature, and this sensory nature radiates through his whole organism. This means that until the age of 6 or 7 the child's disposition is to inwardly echo everything that occurs in his surround- ings, and to develop his own being in accordance with it. If we observe a child with finer senses, perceiving him also by spiritual-scientific means and see how he relates to himself every gesture someone in his environment makes, inwardly echoes it and seeks to embody it himself, and if we see how the child lives entirely in what people do in his surroundings, then we discover he is an imitative being until the change of teeth. And the most essential gift in the first period of life arises from this imitation: human speech, based entirely on the fact that the child lives into what people around him are and what they do. By inwardly adapting to what happens in his surroundings, and imitating it, a child develops the ability to speak. Carers and educators with responsibility for a child in this early period of life must therefore regard this principle of imitation as the most important thing to consider. We can only nurture and educate a child by engaging in activities and conducting ourselves in ways that the child should imitate if he is to become strong in spirit, soul and body. The constitution that the child will have throughout his life originates here, in what is implanted at this time not only in his spirit and soul but also his body, in the inner strengthening of his organs. The way I behave around a child of 4 is something he will carry with him until he is 60, so that, in later life, he will feel the effect of my conduct as his destiny.

Let me give an example: When you concern yourself with such things someone might well come to you and say something like this: 'I just don't know what has happened. My child was always so good, never did anything wrong; and now he has done the most awful thing!' He may for instance have stolen money from his mother. If you have some experience of child development you would first ask how old the child is; and you hear that he is 5. In other words, at this age the imitative principle is still active. It turns out that the child has seen his mother taking money out of a drawer every day. He simply imitates this. It's nothing to do with good or bad; he just has an impulse to do what is done around him. We will be barking up the wrong tree completely if we think we should manage such behaviour with moral commandments. We will only achieve something by offering the child an example to imitate. This even includes the way we think. Ah yes, between a carer and a child a fine, spiritual connection exists! And in proximity to the child we should try to cultivate thoughts and feelings which the child can inwardly imitate. You see, the child is an entirely sensing being, perceives what is occurring in his surroundings in the subtlest movements and actions, far beyond anything our adult senses are aware of.

Having passed through the change of teeth, powers that previously sat deep inside the child's organism now become soul faculties. Whereas the younger child was given up to his surroundings, now he lives as a soul meeting souls. The feeling of this age, compared with the earlier imitative instinct, is one of complying quite naturally with the authority of those around him. It really is like this: in the early years of childhood until second dentition we seek to unite with our surroundings, wish to give ourselves up entirely to them. This is a kind of physical counterpart to religious sensibility. Religious sensibility is one where our spirit surrenders itself to the spirit; and likewise the child surrenders himself, with his body, to his physical surroundings—the physical correlation or counterpart of religious sensibility.

Once the child is over the age of 6 he no longer gives himself and his body up to his physical surroundings, but instead surrenders his soul to other souls. The teacher comes into his own now, and it is necessary for the child to regard the teacher as a source of all good and ill for him, and to participate as fully in what the teacher says and teaches him as before he participated in every gesture and outward action in his surroundings. A child between the age of 6 or 7 and 14 experiences the urge to surrender himself to a natural authority. The child wishes to become what this authority is for him. His love for this natural authority, his hearkening to it, is now a principle that works just as much as imitation did before.

You may be surprised that someone who wrote a book entitled *The Philosophy of Freedom* in the 1890s[40] is now propounding something you perhaps regard as unjustified: the principle of authority. But what I mean is this: it is a kind of natural law in human life that, roughly between the ages of 7 and 14, a child inevitably regards teachers and educators as sources of natural authority. This is not an intellectual matter—not discernment of what is good, true, bad, wrong or ugly—but the child, rather, finds something good because his teacher considers it good, and beautiful because his teacher finds it beautiful. All mysteries of the world approach the child in this indirect way, through the person of the beloved teacher. This is the principle at work in human development between, roughly, the ages of 6 or 7 and 14. And so we can say that in his early childhood the child is filled with a sense of surrender to his surroundings, as a physical counterpart to religious sensibility, and between the change of teeth and puberty with an aesthetic absorption of his surroundings, one permeated with love. He feels the urge to take pleasure in what the teacher presents to him, and to avoid what the teacher wishes to keep at a distance from him. The educational approach for this age should enter our inner perception, our inward sensibility. The carer, educator or parent must be a worthy example in early childhood, whereas in the second phase of childhood the teacher must be, in the noblest sense, a natural authority in his whole being and character. Then, as teachers, we bear within us something which enables children in our proximity to educate themselves. Moral education relies to an important degree on the self-education of the teacher. I will speak further of this in a moment, when the first part has been translated.

If one can say that the child is entirely sense organ up to the age of 6, then after the change of teeth, from 6 onwards, we must regard the principle of sensory absorption as having risen away from the inner organism to its surface. But it continues to be the case that sensory impressions entering a child at this age cannot yet have an ordering, regulating effect on the sense organs. Between second dentition and puberty, we find that the child wishes to be feelingly surrendered to his whole sensory organization but is as yet unable to participate in this sensory organization from within outwards with his will. Involvement in the sensory organization from within gives us intellectual people, and we only become so after puberty. Only then, really, are we able to judge the world intellectually. You see, judging the world intellectually means at the same time to judge it in personal terms, out of our inner freedom. This is a capacity we only acquire once we have entered puberty. But this in turn means that between the change of teeth and puberty we should not educate children in an intellectual way, nor in an intellectually moral way either. In his first 7 years, the child wants to have outer sensory reality there before him to imitate. After 7, the child wants to hear from his authoritative teacher what he can do and what he can't, what he should regard as true and false, right and wrong and so on.

But now, between the age of 8 and 9 something extraordinarily important starts to stir in the child. A teacher who observes human nature very carefully will know that at some point between the age of 8 and 9 a child will be in very special need of something. He does not yet have intellectual doubts, but an inner restlessness—something like an inner question that, in his childlike way, he is asking of destiny. He cannot express this in words, and does not need to, but he senses it in a dreamy kind of way, semi-consciously. If we have observed children properly, with the real eye of a teacher, we can experience how children approach this age. They want something very particular of the teacher who they look up to with love. This question of theirs cannot usually be answered by some intellectual response. It is instead a matter of developing an especially intense and intimate relationship of trust with the child at this age, giving a child the sense that one is offering him a great deal of loving attention. This question the child asks of life, which is of the very greatest significance, is answered when he receives love in this way and can have trust in his teacher. What is the nature of this question really? As I have said, it isn't a question the child asks rationally, but in his feelings, with the whole of his subconscious being. He does not formulate it in words—but we can do so. Up to this age the child has naively accepted his beloved teacher's authority, without further question. But now a need has awoken in him to feel good and bad in a new way, as if they were present as powers in the world. Until now the child looked up to the teacher, but now he wants to look *through* the teacher and say to himself: 'This teacher is not just someone who says something is good or bad, but he says it because he is a messenger of the spirit, a messenger of God. His knowledge comes from higher worlds.' As I said, the child does not formulate this rationally but this is what he feels. And this special question of his, which also rises in his feelings, tells us what a child now needs. It shows us that what we say is good or bad, or true or false, must now be rooted in something deeper. And then the child finds new trust and confidence in the world.

This is also the moment when moral education can enter a different phase from mere imitation, or our word that something is good or bad. At this age, between 8 and 9, we can start to present morality to children in a pictorial way—not intellectually, for the child is still given up to the senses uninformed by intellect. We should generally educate in a pictorial way between the change of teeth and puberty, teach him in pictures, pictures for all the senses. Although a child at this age is no longer entirely sense organ, he still lives in the senses that are focused, now, at the surface of his body. Tomorrow, in our evening lecture[41] I will elaborate on how we need to educate children aged 6 or 7 through reading or writing in general. But now I want to examine the moral aspect of education.

At this moment between the age of 8 and 9, we should start to present pictures to the child that especially stimulate his imagination: pictures of good people, evoking a feeling of sympathy with the deeds of such people. Please note: I specifically do *not* say that we should inculcate moral commandments or address the intellect with moral judgements and precepts. Instead we should approach the aesthetic realm, the imagination. We should awaken pleasure or displeasure in the child in response to what is good or bad, or right or wrong— pleasure in nobility and moral actions, but equally in redress accomplished, wrong deeds put right. Previously we had to act as moral exemplars, as an embodiment of what is right. Now we add to this pictures that act only on the faculty of imagination expressed within his sensory nature. Until puberty the child should absorb morality in his feelings. He should develop a certainty in his feeling judgement that he has sympathy with what is good, and antipathy for what is bad. Sympathies and antipathies, feeling judgements, must be the foundation of morality in him.

If we understand that the human temporal body is, as I have described, an organism in which everything is interrelated, then we can see that we need to do the right thing at the right time for a child. You cannot ask a plant to grow in a way that produces a flower immediately. Flowering emerges from earlier development. The plant first has to develop roots. It would be nonsense to expect a flower to emerge instead of roots. In the same way, if you teach a child intellectually formulated moral precepts between the change of teeth and puberty, this is like trying to turn a root into a flower. You first have to nurture the seedling, the root, in other words: morality in feelings. Once a child has cultivated morality in his feelings then after puberty he will awaken to intelligence; and then he himself will elaborate and inwardly develop what he possessed as feelings between second dentition and puberty. Then he can awaken moral, intellectual judgement within himself. And this is something so vital for life, upon which all moral education must be founded! Just as you cannot turn the root of a plant into its flower but must wait until the root has developed, then leaves, until finally the plant unfolds its flower, so likewise you must cultivate the root of morality in feeling judgements, in a sympathy for moral actions. And then you can stand back and allow the individual himself to bear these feelings into his intellect through his own autonomous powers. And then, later in life, he will have a profound inner sense of satisfaction that what lives in him are not mere memories of principles that a teacher gave him about what is right or wrong, but instead that inner joy, inner energy filled his whole emotional life so that he himself could awaken to the freedom of moral judgement at the proper time. By doing this we avoid educating a child to slavishly adhere to some moral orientation. Instead we prepare in the child something that can itself flower as moral compass from a person's free-growing being of soul. Instead of equipping the child with fixed moral judgements this endows him with moral strength. And this is something that shows us repeatedly, if we're seeking a spiritual foundation for education, that we must always try to bring things towards the child in the right way at the right time.

Now you will ask me this: if you're going to educate a child in a way that implants a moral sensibility in him between the change of teeth and puberty rather than by giving him moral exhortations that appeal to his intellect, then what are you appealing to in him? Well, you are drawing on his relationship with you as a natural authority, the imponderable aspects of the connection between the teacher and child. Let me illustrate this with an example. I can try to teach a child something, pictorially, about the immortality of the soul—pictorially and not by some theoretical argument. The child really isn't available for scientific or academic argument until puberty. I must weave nature and spirit together for him and convey something that I perhaps form into an artistic image: 'Look at the cocoon or chrysalis of a butterfly,' I might say. 'The butterfly crawls out of the cocoon. And in the same way, the soul emerges from the human body when it succumbs to death.' In this way I stimulate the child's imagination, bringing a living moral picture before his inward eye. I can do this in one of two ways. I can either think I am a skilled teacher, terribly clever, while the child is small and rather thick-witted. And because the child has not yet risen to my lofty height, I will create a picture for him. The image has no intrinsic value for me, but I create it for the child. If I tell myself such things and, with this underlying outlook, try to convey the image to the child, it will not work in his soul—it will just go in one ear and out the other. You see, imponderable factors are at work between the child and the teacher. But if instead I realize that I am not in fact a great deal cleverer than the child, or perhaps that the child is, subconsciously, a great deal cleverer than I am … if I feel reverence for the child and, in relation to this picture I wish to convey, think to myself, 'Actually this is not *my* image; nature itself has given us a picture in the emerging butterfly,' and I myself believe as deeply in this picture as the child should believe in it— if I possess this strength of belief, then the picture will also root in the psyche of the child, and things that are not part of coarser reality but live in a subtler world will work between the teacher and the child. These imponderables at work between the child and teacher will fulsomely replace anything intellectual that might pass from teacher to child! This allows the child, also, to develop freely *alongside* the teacher. The teacher thinks: 'I live in proximity to the child and must create opportunities for the child to educate himself as far as possible. But to do so I have to stand alongside the child with a sense that I am not hugely elevated: I am just someone who is a few years older than the child.' Relatively speaking, we do not always become cleverer as we grow older. We need not think ourselves superior to the child but instead should see ourselves as helpers in his development. If, as a gardener, one seeks to nurture a plant, one does not push the sap in the stem to get it moving from root to flower, but just prepares the surrounding soil so that the sap can flow. As a teacher one should be selfless so that the child's own inner powers can develop. This is good teaching, and then a child will thrive as he should.

If morality is developed in a child in this way, then, in the same way as a plant grows naturally, one aspect after another emerges. Initially, in full harmony with human nature, it manifests in the imitative human organism. It is consolidated there in the way described and gives a person in later life the necessary inner strength, also sustained by his physical organism, to be morally assured. Otherwise, his physical organism might weaken, grow weak so that a person may have a good sense of morality but be unable to adhere to it. If a child has good, clear, strong examples in infancy, his moral stability develops. And if from the change of teeth to puberty a person's powers of sympathy and antipathy for good and bad have properly taken root in him, later he will be able to overcome the kinds of depression that might prevent him from doing what is morally necessary. As an imitative being he has developed within his organism what his soul will need for its moral sensibility, its feelings of sympathy and antipathy as these are cultivated in the second seven-year period. And in the third seven-year period, now oriented to the spirit by life itself, intellectual moral judgement awakens in free human development in the same way that a plant awakens to flower and fruit through sunlight. Morality will only really take proper root in the mind and spirit if body and soul have been prepared for this in a way that allows it to awaken through and in life, just as the flower and fruit awaken through and in sunlight.

But when morality is developed in a person in this way, with respect for him, for his inner freedom, moral impulses will connect with him inwardly and allow him to really feel that they are part of him, belong to him. Then he will feel his moral faculties and moral actions in the same way that he senses the circulation of his blood and growth forces within him. He inevitably feels that the natural life of the body belongs to him and pulses everywhere in his organism, endowing him with strength right through to the surface of his skin; and in the same way he will feel morality as a power intrinsic to him because he himself has developed it.

And what does this mean for him? It means that he realizes that without this moral sensibility he is in a sense crippled. Just as someone is actually crippled without a physical limb, so the kind of moral development I am speaking of will give people the sense that if they did not have a strong moral compass, if they did not imbue their actions with morality, they would be a kind of cripple in life.

If people have a strong inner sense that they would be crippled without morality, then their education has provided them with the strongest possible morally motivating force. As long as we help a person to develop in the right way, he will want to be whole; and specifically when morality approaches him in this way, this means in turn that he will by his own powers and motivation also develop an inner inclination for the spirit. And he will see the good that streams through the world at work and active within him just as he sees natural forces at work in his body. He will understand what one means, metaphorically, by saying for example that an iron horseshoe has inner forces, can be used as a magnet. Someone else will dismiss this other aspect of iron: 'What's that to me?' he will say. 'Iron is iron. I'll use it to shoe my horse.' This is like someone whose various stages of development have not enabled him to see the spiritual at work within us as whole human beings. This is because he has an eye only for outward things, for immediate utility, rather than for the spiritual reality that works and holds sway in human beings. To educate someone without helping him to develop the right way of understanding life, without developing the powers he needs, is an education that, metaphorically, fails to create in people an awareness that magnetic iron shaped as a horseshoe can be used as more than a horseshoe. They will not develop a full view of life or unfold the right powers. If we understand this in the full, spiritual sense, feeling it and transposing it into our will, this will also be the strongest motivating force in social coexistence.

Our time is dominated by social questions, with great justification. I wish I had time to speak about these issues at greater length, but my time has run out. I will end just by saying this: the social question has a great many aspects, and much work will be needed to address all its diverse details in a way that may eventually lead in future to a reform of society such as any open-minded person will wish for. But all the outward institutions we can possibly conceive of and introduce in practice, all the possible schemas people nowadays formulate about society, appear in the following light to someone who has a spiritual view of morality: trying to address the social question without including the question of morality in it is like trying to look for something in a room devoid of light.

The social question can only be seen in the right light if we fully encompass the question of morality as well. If we survey all the interconnected aspects of life we will find that the moral question really is like the light that must illumine social community. The social question must come to be fully and authentically a human question, must acquire a religious dimension. What is needed today above all, also as far as the life of society is concerned, is for people to gain a relationship to the question of morality. I believe I have been able to show that what I have called a spiritual science, an anthroposophic spiritual science, also tackles the great issues of contemporary life in an authentic way, and that it gives serious attention to the question of morality and the way in which education can help human beings to develop moral sensibility.

LECTURE 13

LONDON, 20 NOVEMBER 1922[*]

IT might appear strange to you that I wish to speak about practical matters of education from the perspective of a particular world-view— that of anthroposophic spiritual science. In fact, my reason for speaking about education originates here from educational practice itself.

As you have just heard,[42] the art of education which I will speak about tonight is being realized at the Waldorf School, and this has led me to broaden and elaborate the scope of anthroposophic ideas and aims for education. A few years ago, when educational questions were very much in vogue, the industrialist Emil Molt[43] decided to found a school, initially for the children of the people working in his factory. He turned to me, asking that I give this school a fitting pedagogical curriculum and orientation.

Initially the pupils who attended, therefore, came from a very specific social milieu, the proletarian children of the Waldorf company; and there were also a number whose parents were members of a society with a distinctive world-view, the Anthroposophical Society. But the school's remit very soon broadened. We began with around 150 children in eight school classes but before long we had eleven school classes with over 700 children. Following a lecture series on the art of education which I gave at Christmas at the Goetheanum in Dornach, attended by several members of the Anthroposophical Society, I was invited, in August this year, to give a cycle of lectures here in England, at

---

[*] Public lecture.

Oxford,[44] about the principles on which this Waldorf School is based. These lectures in Oxford led to the founding here of the Educational Union,[45] with the aim of introducing more broadly in England the educational principles which I will speak about this evening.

I wished to mention this context so that you do not have the impression that my discourse here tonight is merely theoretical. What I have to say is drawn from a real, practical art of education. It is all the more important to stress this since tonight, of course, I will only have time to give a few outlines. The ideas I describe will inevitably remain incomplete since the educational principles I will speak of are not a fixed programme but a living practice. And this means that one can only offer examples drawn from this practice. It is of course easier to start from a theoretical programme, and offer general phrases, general maxims. But this is not possible in relation to the distinctive nature of the educational principles on which the Waldorf School is based As I have said, this form of pedagogy and education has arisen from a spiritual-scientific world-view, one which can lead to real insight into human nature and thus also to real insight into the nature of the child.

When a painter or an artist in another medium practises his art he needs to develop two capacities. Firstly—let's take the example of painting—he needs a certain skill in observing colour and form, must be able to create his works out of the nature of form and colour. He cannot start from theoretical knowledge but only from a living immersion in the nature of form and colour. Then comes the second skill, the craft and technique of painting itself. From the perspective of anthroposophic spiritual science, pedagogy is not seen as theoretical knowledge but as a real art, one that works with the noblest material in the world, with the human being himself, with the child. From year to year, even from week to week, we can see the spirit and soul deeply concealed in the child as a divine dowry from worlds of spirit, emerging in his countenance, his gestures, and in every other way the child expresses his being. The pedagogical approach I am speaking of starts from the view that, just as a painter needs to acquire skill in observing colour and form, which turns in his hands, soul and spirit into craft and technique, so the educational artist needs to be able to observe and trace the way human nature develops and manifests in the child. This can't be done, however, unless we move on from a form of human observation implicit in ordinary consciousness to faculties that can really observe the life of soul and spirit. This in fact is precisely what anthroposophic spiritual science seeks to do. What we call 'knowledge' today is really only able to concern itself with corporeal, sense-perceptible reality. As modern human beings, how do we learn to recognize soul qualities today without developing actual spiritual knowledge? We can only do this, really, by finding the soul's expressions and activities within ourselves. By trying to practise self-observation, we become familiar with our own thinking, feeling and will, which are faculties of the psyche or soul. You can say that we only know about the soul by forming a view or judgement about it. Sensory impressions are given us, and we perceive them. But we only know about the soul by forming a view that something like a soul is at work in our own inner nature.

Anthroposophic spiritual science in the sense I mean it does not start from this ordinary form of consciousness but seeks to systematically develop powers slumbering in the human soul so that—and please do not be alarmed by the expression—a kind of exact clairvoyance arises from them. In this way you can look *through* soul expressions to find the intrinsic nature of the soul. And then you can come to know this soul nature through spiritual perception in the same way that you can familiarize yourself with sensory colour impressions through the eyes or sensory tones through the ears. But ordinary consciousness can only discern the spirit that holds sway in the world by deduction. In our ordinary awareness we can only ever say that we see natural phenomena, expressions of soul. From this we conclude that all this has a spiritual foundation. Our thoughts are concerned to discover a soul and spiritual quality underlying corporeal reality. But anthroposophic spiritual science develops powers slumbering in the soul—the spiritual sense organs, if I can use this paradoxical expression—by means of which we not only deduce the existence of spirit but experience it ourselves in living thinking.

Only when one perceives the soul, when one experiences the spirit in living thinking, can one gain real insight into the human being. Spiritual science can develop such a living knowledge of the human being that it can grasp human reality and observe at any moment in the life of the growing child how the spirit and soul are working in him. It not only enables us to see the child from without as it were, through the senses, but also discerns how the soul reveals itself in sensory expressions. Rather than just basing its understanding on the way the soul expresses itself outwardly, it directly perceives soul substance as clearly as the eye can see colour. It starts from insight into how the spirit works within a child, by drawing on a form of knowledge that encompasses the spirit itself in living thinking.

The art of education I am speaking of is therefore based on living knowledge of the human being, on insight into the developing child at every moment of life. Only when we really perceive the nature of this noblest of all materials we can employ in art, the material used in the art of education, when we understand the human being in this way and act in truly pedagogical ways, can we discern things quite different from those available to ordinary awareness. Based on this kind of knowledge, this direct vision of the soul and spirit, one can then give guidance to teachers and educators on ways in which, through actual practical involvement with the child, they can develop this soul and spirit in him.

From living observation we can discover that the spirit is no less present in the child than in the adult; but this spirit is deeply sealed within and still has to master the body. When we ourselves can see the spirit we gain a sense of the wonderful way in which it works in the child's organism as a divine gift—before the child can speak to us in language, before he can display intellectual thinking. We gain a sense that there is no divide between a person's physical and spiritual nature. We perceive the spirit working inwardly and immediately upon the child's physical nature, much more than can ever be true of the adult: the child's physical nature wholly imbued with spirit. As adults we possess spirit in the sense that our minds need it to think about the world. The child by contrast possesses spirit by virtue of needing it, like a spiritual sculptor, to first shape his own organism. Far more than one thinks, our physical organism is created for the whole of our life by what the spirit immanent within this physical organism accomplishes in childhood. But to avoid dwelling too long in abstract ideas, let me offer a few specific examples of what I mean.

If we regard the child only by outwardly scientific means, his anatomy or physiology, rather than with spiritual vision, we fail to see how every gesture in the child's surroundings acts on his physical organism and takes effect there. Let us imagine someone shouts at a child who is engaged in doing something. It is a quite different thing to shout at a child or at another adult. If we shout at the child we should remember that his organism is as yet in a quite different condition from the adult. The adult's sense organs are focused at the surface of his organism, and the impressions he receives through them are mastered by his intellect. He counters his sense impressions from within with his fully developed will. But the child is wholly surrendered to the outer world. If I can put it like this—I'm not speaking metaphorically here, but in real terms—the young child is entirely sense organ. I want to be very clear and precise here. Think of an infant. If we perceive him outwardly it seems to us that he experiences the world, observes the world, in the same way as an adult, with the only difference being that his intellect and will are not as developed as an adult's. This is not so. An adult tastes things, for instance, only on his tongue and palate. What in the adult has come to be focused at the exterior of the organism delves much further inwards in the child. We can say that when he eats the child becomes entirely taste sensation, and entirely light sensation when light and colours enter his eyes. It is not just metaphorical but reality to say this: light not only vibrates through the child's nervous system but through his breathing, blood system, through his whole organism, whereas in adults it is really only active in the eye. The child is entirely sense organ. And in the same way that the eye is given up entirely to the world and light phenomena, the young child lives entirely in his surroundings. He bears within him spirit so that he can absorb all that lives in his physical surroundings with his whole organism. So imagine that you shout at a child; his organism responds in a very particular way. Something vibrates within him in a much stronger way than in adults who can resist this through the powers active within them. Your shouting will cause something like a faltering of the child's soul-spiritual life, and the effect of this will be transferred directly to his bodily organism. If we shout at a child often, and also alarm or frighten him, we are not only affecting the child's soul but his whole physical organism. The health of an adult, right into old age, lies in our hands and is strongly affected by how we behave in his proximity.

The most important aspect of educating a child in infancy is how adults themselves behave around him. If a child is exposed to perpetual hurried activity and busy rush, everything around him quick and fleeting, his whole physical organism will acquire an inclination to rush inwardly too. If we have developed discernment for the activity of soul and spirit in a child, we can tell by the time he is 10 or 11 whether he has lived in a restless, hurried environment, or one more calmly measured, or one where activities were too slow or static. We can tell this from the way the child walks, from his step. A child who has grown up in surroundings where things were too rushed and where impressions kept rapidly changing, will step softly and tentatively, not firmly. How a child absorbs his surroundings works right through his physical organism into his step, his way of walking. We will find that a child in surroundings that have not offered enough stimulus but have left him perpetually bored will by contrast later walk with a far too heavy tread. I mention these examples because they are especially striking and show how we can become more subtly observant of children. In infancy the child is what I would call an imitative being; he imitates his whole surroundings, but he also looks to the adult to imitate what he should feel inwardly or morally. Let me give an example of this.

A father once came to me and told me that his son had always been a good boy, behaving in ways that elicited his parents' approval. But now, suddenly, said the father, he has been stealing money! If we have some real knowledge of a child at this age we will immediately ask something like this: where did the child take the money from? It turns out that he took it from a drawer, where his mother keeps it, taking money out of it every day. The child is an imitative being, given up to his surroundings as soul-imbued sense organism. He brings his own being into movement to do the same as what he sees going on around him. In the first phase of childhood, exhortations, commands and prohibitions have little meaning for him. They do not take root in his soul very strongly. The child is oriented only to what he perceives in his surroundings. But we have to remember that he sees things far, far more accurately than the adult, even though what he perceives does not come to full awareness.

All he perceives around him shapes and informs his organism; and so his whole organism becomes a reflection of what he perceives.

In modern views we greatly overvalue inheritance, genetics. Seeing what someone is like later in life we assume that he is the way he is mostly because of purely physically inherited characteristics. But someone with the capacity to observe the child properly and to understand human nature will see how the child's muscles develop in response to impressions he receives from his surroundings, to the way we treat him with gentleness, love or in other ways, how his breathing and blood circulation develop according to the feelings the child experiences. If a child often experiences someone approaching him lovingly, and instinctively finding a tempo of experience with him that nurtures his inner being, the finer, subtler aspects of his respiratory system will develop in a healthy way. If you wonder where an adult acquires the foundations for a healthy physical organism, you should look on the effect his surroundings had on him as a child, when he was one entire sense organ—the words, gestures, the whole behaviour of people around him, and how this worked upon his muscles, blood circulation and breathing. You will find that a child is not only an imitator as far as his language development is concerned—which relies entirely on imitation once the child has developed and strengthened his speech organs—but that the child's whole physical body, and its subtler patterning, is an imprint of what we do around him.

And therefore the way we live right through into old age, which is bound up with us having a stronger or weaker physical organism, and the extent to which we can depend on this, is something we owe, for good or ill, to the impressions our surroundings made on us when we were infants.

I am speaking here of the first phase of childhood, when we are imitative beings. Real insight into human development shows that this lasts from birth to the change of teeth, until the age, roughly, of 6 or 7. After the age of 6, the child changes in more ways than are commonly realized. I will describe the child's further development, along with sure foundations for educational practice and a real art of education, in the second part of the lecture, after the first part has been translated.

Around the age of 6 or so, at second dentition, this physical sign of change accompanies a deep-seated transformation of the child's being. Essentially an imitative being until the change of teeth, and dependent on the powers of imitation for developing his physical organism, the child around 6, at the change of teeth, starts no longer to be *physically* surrendered to his surroundings but instead to need to give his *soul* life to them. Whereas up to the second dentition the child's being is deeply informed by everything in his surroundings, in this second phase, from the change of teeth to puberty, he is informed and formed by everything founded on the natural authority of those who bring him up or teach him. The child is not intrinsically drawn to learn the skills adults possess that he is taught, such as reading, writing and so on. It is a huge mistake to think the child has the least intrinsic urge to acquire these skills of communication and expression of what you as adults have mastered! Everything that really helps the child to develop arises from his loving openness to your natural authority. If a child learns things it is not because of any rationale intrinsic to what is taught. The child learns because he sees that the adult knows these things and can do them, and because he hears from the adult who is his unquestioned authority as a teacher that this or that is the right thing to do and the right way to do it. This extends also to moral principles.

Up to the change of teeth, as I showed, the child inevitably absorbs his sense of morality through imitation. From around 6 or 7 to 13 or 14, from the change of teeth to puberty, everything must be absorbed through the child's loving devotion to the teacher's natural, self-evident authority. There is no point in trying to impose moral precepts intellectually, stating as a principle that something is good or bad, but rather the child must develop within a feeling context in which the natural authority of adults shows him what he should consider to be good and likewise should consider bad. For the child there should be no other foundation for his pleasure in good or displeasure in bad than what is conveyed as such by the authority figure who stands beside him. He accepts this not because something appears to him intrinsically good or bad as an intellectual concept, but because his teacher finds it so. That is the important thing in a real, authentic form of education. Between the change of teeth and puberty all moral education, and all religious education too, must come through an authentic human presence. The human relationship with a teacher is the all-important thing. When we appeal to a child's power of judgement we are teaching him in a way that actually deadens a great deal within him. He is no longer entirely sense organ, it is true, and his senses are now focused more outwardly, on his body's surface, but his whole soul is within. He gains nothing from the intellectual element by means of which, as adults, we organically regulate and order our senses. A child at this age can however give himself to the natural authority of a teacher if everything is presented to him in an ensouled picture.

This means, though, that between the change of teeth and puberty, we must shape education in a thoroughly artistic way, and always take art as our starting point. In our modern culture the letters we present to children so that they can learn to write and read are something the child has no real relationship with at all. In certain civilizations as we know, the forms of letters originated as visual representations of outer things and processes, as picture script. When we teach letters to children we have to start again from pictures. That is why, in Stuttgart, in our practice of the art of Waldorf education we don't actually start with the letters as such at all, but with lessons in painting and drawing. This is hard with children starting school at 6 or 7, but these difficulties will be overcome if we stand next to the child with a natural authority so that he gets the feeling he wishes to copy what the teacher is creating out of colour or form—that he wishes to become like the teacher. This is how everything should be learned at this age, and can only be through an inner, not just an outer, relationship between child and teacher in which all lessons are imbued with aesthetic feeling. You see, imponderable factors are at work between the teacher and the child: not just the skills we may have acquired as a teacher but above all our inner sense of things. Feeling and sensibility are at work, and the teacher's whole inner stance; and this acquires the right orientation if, as teachers, we can approach the spiritual nature of the world.

Let me give another example to illustrate what I mean—and it is one I especially like to give. Let us assume we want to activate a moral, religious sensibility in a child. The right time to do this, roughly, is around the age of 8 or 9. The kind of education I am proposing makes it possible to perceive from the child's development what we should teach him in each school year. Let us say that when he is 8 or 9 I wish to teach him the idea of the soul's immortality. I can speak about this intellectually. Yet not only will it make scarcely any impression on the child, but his inner life will in fact grow more arid in consequence, for to lecture intellectually to a child about moral or religious matters involves nothing of an inner nature! His inner life, his soul thrives instead on imponderables that must be at work between him and the teacher. Instead I can convey an image to the child, a symbol, an artistic picture, of what I wish him to grasp of the soul's immortality. I can say: 'Look at the butterfly's cocoon or chrysalis. The butterfly breaks through this, flies out of it, then flutters about in the sunshine. The same is true of the human soul: it lives in the human organism as the butterfly does in the cocoon; and when a person dies, it leaves the organism and henceforth moves through a world of spirit.'

But there are two ways in which one might do this. As a teacher it is rather easy to think oneself very clever: to think I am clever while the child is not, and he cannot understand my clever or complex ideas about the soul's immortality; I will therefore make these concepts into a picture for him so that he can grasp them in that lesser form. If I cobble a picture together in this way, and feel myself to have a more sublime understanding, the impression the image makes on the child is only fleeting, and it will also cause something to wither in him. But I can approach the child differently, with feeling sensibility, and actually believe in this picture myself. I have not, I realize, fabricated it, but divine, spiritual powers themselves place this butterfly cocoon, and the emerging butterfly, into the natural world, offering me a picture, an authentic one, something that lives in nature and embodies what I need to understand of the soul's immortality. I encounter the immortality of the soul at a simpler, more primitive level in the emerging butterfly. God himself wished to show me this. You see, only if I myself believe in the images I convey to children will this remarkable, invisible supersensible connection exist between us. And if I present to children something that really is my own deeply held view, this picture will take root in them and remain in them throughout their lives, developing as they do. If between the change of teeth and puberty we can transform everything into pictorial teaching of this kind, then we succeed in avoiding the inculcation of fixed concepts or precepts the child is supposed to adhere to in exactly the same form. Doing so, it is like trying to harness a hand to a machine so that it cannot freely develop according to its own laws. Instead we should convey inwardly mobile concepts to the child that grow as limbs do; and then what is presented in this way can change and grow through the decades, becoming different when someone is 18 or 20, and quite different again when he is 40.

But to fully understand what is needed here so that it really enters the whole art of how we teach, we need to do more than just observe the child in the present moment and ask what he needs and what developmental powers are currently at work in him. We also have to survey the whole of life. Let me give an instance. Let us assume that we succeed, between the change of teeth and puberty, in eliciting the child's inner sense of devotion to the teacher as I described. The inevitable later consequence of this appears in a particular kind of strength and quality. Those who have some insight into such things will know what good fortune it is in much later life if they had the chance, in childhood, to look up to someone in reverence. Imagine, perhaps, that a child hears he will soon see a much revered relative whom he has never met before. He is going to be allowed to visit him. After everything he has heard about him, the whole picture that has been conveyed to him, he makes his way to see this relative. In shy awe he sees the door opening. To look up to someone or something with such reverence is a huge thing, and in the soul of those who have had the good fortune to do so something takes deep root and bears fruit much later, very late sometimes in life. The same is true of everything that has been conveyed to the child in mobile, living concepts rather than being inculcated or imposed on him. If a teacher manages to enable children to really look up to him as a natural authority this engenders in them something I would express as follows. We know that there are people who, at a certain age, are a boon for the people around them. They may not say very much but their words are a blessing to others. There is something in their voice, rather than the content of what they say. It is a blessing for children to come close to such people. If we look back to the childhood of someone with this quality, who may now be 50 or 60, and see what he was given between the change of teeth and puberty, what he learned then, we will find that he learned to revere, learned a moral reverence which taught him to look up in the right way to the higher powers in the world. He was someone who learned to pray in the right way, if I can put it like that. The reverence that develops through learning to pray truly is transformed, when he is older, into powers of blessing, into powers that make him a boon and a blessing for all around him. And I would say this too, to make it as vivid as possible: someone who has never learned to fold his hands in prayer as a child will never develop the strength in later life, either, to pour out blessing upon others.

Instead of forming a few abstract ideas and foisting these upon the child, therefore, we need to know how to work in a way that will develop something in his soul and be fruitful for him throughout his life. Thus instead of inculcating abstract reading and writing directly, we start with writing, but conveyed artistically, allowing all the abstract letters of our alphabet to arise from pictures. And by teaching children to write in this way we meet their need to be fully, actively involved, rather than just to use their head and faculties of observation. When a child learns to write in this way, out of pictures, and with his full involvement, we give him what he needs. Once he has learned to write, he can then learn to read.

Those who are too deeply rooted in mainstream education today will be worried that children would learn to read and write more slowly by this method. But it is worth questioning whether the age and speed of learning these skills is right in modern education! Basically the child should only begin learning to read after the age of 7, and in a way that develops everything out of a pictorial and artistic element.

Someone who has gained real insights into human nature through true perception of the human soul and spirit will be able to observe things very subtly, and from this observation develop an art of education. Let's say we have a child whose gait and step are too heavy. This will be due to the wrong kind of influences on his psyche before the change of teeth. But we can do a good deal to remedy such problems through the pictures we bring artistically to the child, which enliven him inwardly, invigorate what has been configured in someone before the change of teeth. Someone who has gained deep insights into human nature will therefore get a child with a heavy step or tread to spend a lot of time painting and drawing. A child, by contrast, whose step is too light or tentative needs to engage more in music; and in fact his whole character development later on, profound aspects of morality, depend on this. In each specific instance, if we are able to bring real understanding to bear, we can say how we need to approach the child with material that has been formed pictorially.

Until the change of teeth the child's natural surroundings are those provided by the proximity of his parents and family. But we must support this with nursery schools, play schools. We will only do the right thing for young children in helping them play and be active if we know how such things enter a child's physical organism. You should try to imagine that a child's blood circulation becomes sluggish, and his physical organism is disturbed if he is given a ready-made doll, a so-called 'beautiful' one with a beautifully painted face, all finished and 'perfect'. We have no idea what harm we do and how this works upon the child. If instead we ourselves make him a doll from a couple of cloths which we tie together in his view, then paint some eyes on—so that the child sees the doll being created in front of him—he will take this into the mobility of his organism. It will pass into his blood and his breathing and have an enlivening effect.

Let's say we have a melancholic child before us. Someone who thinks in external ways rather than with soul vision will say that the darkness in a melancholic child must be alleviated by having very lively colours in his surroundings: toys coloured yellow and red perhaps, and bright clothes, as vivid as possible to awaken the child from his melancholic state. No, that's wrong! You see, this would just give the child an inner shock, driving all his life forces in the opposite direction. Instead we should surround a child who is melancholic or introvert with blue or purple colours and toys, and we should stimulate a child who is inwardly active by surrounding him with bright colours. This allows each to bring his own organism into harmony with his surroundings. A child who is too nervous or flighty will come into a healthier state through bright colours and movement around him.

True insight into human nature therefore gives us direct help for the smallest details of our educational practice. If we educate in this way we can see that ordinary assumptions about what a child learns at any age, what we should foist upon him and how we should go about it may need to be reconsidered. You see, a child can only draw from his surroundings what is already present as potential in his organism. And this realization leads us to deal more sensitively with children. Think of a child who tends to work in small or fine detail, artistically, rather than to be robustly active in the material world. If we are determined to make him work more robustly, outwardly, his inner disposition and inclination for finer, subtler work will actually wither, while the capacities we wish to draw out of him because we obstinately think everyone should master them will disappear even more completely. A child will do what he is asked to between the change of teeth and puberty, but none of it will stick, nothing that is simply foisted upon him from without. The educational principle I am describing requires the teacher to have a fine sense of what is at work in each child, and then, from what he observes as the child's physical, soul and spiritual constitution, to find the right instinctive educational measure at any moment.

In this way, really, the teacher can observe the educational needs of a child as he grows. In the Waldorf School the curriculum is developed from this careful observation. Everything that does not have to be done on an ongoing yearly, weekly or monthly basis must be drawn from observation of the child so that we can give him what his inner nature requires. The profession of teacher is one that requires the greatest selflessness, and therefore will get nowhere at all with predetermined programmes. It must be focused entirely on working with the child as we stand beside him, through the relationship we develop with him, in a way that basically offers the opportunity for the child to develop in his own way and by his own powers.

This can best be achieved between the ages of 6 or 7 and 14, at elementary school age, if we refrain completely from appealing to the intellect, instead allowing an artistic sensibility to govern everything. At this age, everything directed at educating the child's body, soul and spirit can be clothed in images. Moral issues, especially, should be clothed in pictures when the child is 8 or 9. We ought not to give moral commandments, saying something is good or bad but instead tell children about good people so that they can feel sympathy for them; or also tell them stories about bad people, so that they can develop antipathy towards what is bad or wrong. Through images we can awaken morality in a child's sensibility.

These are only brief hints and indications relating to the second phase of childhood. I will describe in the third, very short part of the lecture, after the second part has been translated, how all this can become the foundation of a thorough, lasting education—not just one tailored to the brief years of childhood but for the whole of a person's life.

You will best be able to understand how the art of education I have described can, from childhood on, have the right effect on a person's whole life from birth to death if I illustrate this through one specific example, the art of eurythmy. Artistic eurythmy, performances of which have been given here in London in recent days,[46] also has a pedagogical aspect.

The art of eurythmy involves individuals or groups invoking movements from the depths of human nature so that all such movements flow from the human organism in as lawful a way as human speech or singing. There is nothing arbitrary at all in a single gesture or movement of eurythmy. What we have instead is language made visible, music and song made visible too: a speech and singing through movement. In our speech, the whole human being's capacity for movement is restrained, held back; and what is metamorphosed in the audible tone is configured in the art of eurythmy into a visible speech.

Now we introduced eurythmy into the Waldorf School, for the lowest primary class through to the oldest class. And it has become apparent that the child lives into this visible speech in which, just as every audible inflection expresses meaning in audible language, so every movement of fingers, hands or the whole body is likewise really a speech sound, but one made visible. We have found that children at the change of teeth and beyond, through to puberty, live into this language as naturally as a very small infant finds his way into speech sounds. It becomes evident that the child's whole organism of body, soul and spirit—for you see, eurythmy is at the same time a kind of gymnastics for the soul and spirit—finds its way into this eurythmy language in as self-evident a way as ordinary language was acquired; and the child feels that what he is given here flows directly from his whole organism. Eurythmy thus complements gymnastics, which originates more in observation of the external physical body, for here a person not only feels himself as body, as ensouled body but also as spiritualized soul in a body shaped by the soul. So to sum up: in the art of eurythmy we experience something that works on our potential in an enormously living way, and likewise has a very fruitful effect on the whole of our life.

However well you practise gymnastics with children, if it adheres only to the laws at work in the body this will not protect them later from, say, all kinds of metabolic disorders, and rheumatism itself—in brief, from disorders that later become metabolic diseases. What is drawn from gymnastics tends in fact to harden and condense the physical body. But if you draw every single movement from the spirit and soul, this will give a person mastery of the mind and body throughout his life. External gymnastic movements in childhood will not prevent a 60-year-old body from becoming frail. But if you educate a child to perform gymnastics drawn from the soul, giving him a pictorial education between the change of teeth and puberty in which an image that otherwise remains an inner one passes soul-spiritually into the body, you will prevent the body from getting brittle as it would have done. You see, this picture language is nothing other than ensouled, spiritualized gymnastics; and this ensouled and spiritualized gymnastics helps the child develop evenly in body, soul and spirit so that what we implant in him in childhood will bear fruit throughout his life. We can only do this if our attitude resembles that of the gardener who cultivates a plant. He does not try to artificially interfere with the movement of sap, to graft something alien onto it, but simply creates conditions, an environment, where the plant itself can grow. He is quite naturally wary of intervening in the inner workings of the plant. Such reverent wariness is something we too must have in the face of what is seeking to unfold into life in the child. We will not therefore keep trying to teach a child something in a one-sided or narrow way. The principle of authority I have described must hold sway in the child's soul in the profoundest way. And the child must be able to absorb things that he cannot yet understand intellectually, but picks up on because he loves his teacher. If we teach in this way we are not robbing the child of the possibility of experiencing certain things in later life. If I understand everything while I'm still a child, the following, for instance, will never come about. Let us assume that when I'm 35 I have an experience of something which recalls what I once absorbed from a beloved teacher, a beloved authority figure, which I simply took then on loving trust. Now I am older and more mature, and suddenly a quite new understanding of what he meant dawns on me. This experience, of returning at a later age, with more mature understanding, to something we once absorbed but did not yet understand, which now acquires new life, gives a person inner assurance, an empowering of the will. And this is an experience we ought not to deprive people of if we have sufficient respect for their freedom and wish to educate them for freedom. The educational principles I have been describing here are based on educating people as free beings. This is also why we should not constrain the child's will by imposing intellectual moral judgements on him. We need to realize that if, between the age of 6 or 7 and 14, we allow the child's sensibility to develop moral pictures through his own feelings of sympathy and antipathy, when the child becomes an adolescent with more intellectual understanding of moral feeling and what he himself wishes, then the aesthetic feeling developed when he was younger, which imbues his will, emerges from the will and comes to life in relation to morality. And because it kindles in a living context, in freedom, it endows a person with strength and inner certainty.

Someone who tries to practise this kind of educational art is not just thinking of childhood but of a person's whole life through to old age. He wants what he implants into the child to be like a flower that grows and thrives in the living context of its surroundings. When we plant a flower we cannot try to force it too quickly. We wait patiently for it to develop in its own good time, from root to stem to leaf, then to flower and fruit, freely unfolding in the sunlight. This is the goal we keep in mind for a true art of education. In the child we want to cultivate the root of his life in such a way that the life of body, soul and spirit we help to thrive in childhood and youth gradually transforms in versatile ways. Then we can be sure that, with full respect for human freedom, our education enables a person to take his place in the world as a free being, and that really the root of education can develop not by our grafting onto it something that enslaves it but so that later in life, right into old age, a person can develop as a free human being in whatever circumstances he finds himself.

These educational principles, of course, make the greatest demands on a teacher. That is certainly true. But surely we cannot imagine that the most highly perfected being here on earth—the human being—can just be treated superficially and simply, without us fully entering into his distinctive nature? Ought we not to approach the task of education with something like reverence, and sometimes even as a kind of religious service? The art of education, as we need to realize, requires the greatest selflessness of us, so that we forget ourselves entirely, immersing ourselves in the child's being and seeking there already for qualities that, in the adult, will help the world to thrive. Selfless care and the will to penetrate human nature with true insight, to keep deepening this insight, are the fundamental conditions for a real art of education.

Education, after all, is the very finest aspect of human life, from which of course it is drawn, so why should we not devote our heartfelt energies to it?

This is what makes for progress. The human progress we cultivate through education means that young generations whom we receive as a gift from divine worlds can develop by virtue of what we older generations have ourselves developed, moving humanity on a step further. We serve humanity, therefore, when, as an older generation, we draw on the best and most beautiful qualities we possess to serve the younger generation, when we practise the finest art of education in a way that most fully accords with human dignity.

Lecture 14

STUTTGART, 4 DECEMBER 1922

I am very pleased to be able to speak to you again today as I pass through on my travels, and I would like to use this opportunity to expand a little on the subject of my last two lectures here.[47] Previously I spoke about the human being's relationship to the world of spirit in so far as this can be perceived by shedding light on processes that occur during sleep, which are unconscious for ordinary awareness, and also by spiritual-scientific investigation of experiences we pass through in the world of spirit between death and a new birth.

Today I want to describe how the life we lead here between birth and death is a kind of transformed image of what we live through in spiritual worlds between death and a new birth. We only understand human life on earth if we can relate the diverse ways in which this life comes to expression to what corresponds to them in worlds of spirit—where, we can say, the major part of our existence is spent.

Firstly I would like to speak primarily of how the psyche expresses itself, how the soul manifests on earth, and how this can be related to experiences in the world of spirit. You will have seen from what I presented in my two last lectures here that the experiences of the human soul in the spiritual world between death and a new birth are essentially different from those we have here during life on earth. Here, all our experiences are mediated by the body, whether the physical or etheric body. Nothing we experience on earth can be experienced without the support of corporeality. We might very easily believe that thinking is a purely spiritual activity, and that the way in which it occurs on earth in the human soul has nothing to do with bodily existence. From one point of view that is true; but however spiritually autonomous human thinking may be, this thinking could not happen here in our earthly existence if we could not rely on our body and its processes. Let me use a metaphor that I have often used in relation to these things. When we walk over the ground, it is true of course that the ground does not itself constitute the human being, who bears his essential attributes enclosed within his skin. But without the support of the ground, we could not exist here physically.

The same is true of thinking as a process living in the soul. By its intrinsic nature it is not, certainly, some kind of brain process; and yet it could not happen if it did not have the brain to sustain and support it here in physical life. Only by seeing things in these terms do we form a correct idea of the spiritual nature but equally of the corporeal dependency of human thinking. There is nothing in us here in earthly existence that does not have to rely on corporeal existence, in which we possess physical organs—lungs, heart, brain and so on. In a condition of ordinary health our awareness is not filled with perception of our inner organs. Only when we suffer from some disorder of an organ do we start to perceive it, doing so also in a very imperfect way. We can never say that direct perception of an organ gives us full knowledge of it, unless we study anatomy; and then we only have the dead and not the living organ before us. We can never say that we have as clear a perception of an inner organ as we do of an external object before us. It is characteristic of earthly existence that our own inner corporeality is not directly available to our awareness. Least of all do we know anything about what is usually regarded as the most valuable part of our body, the interior of the head. When people do start to become familiar with it, this is usually a very unpleasant familiarity caused by headaches and all associated disorders. In spiritual existence between death and a new birth, the very opposite holds true. Here we do really know our interior. Imagine that here on earth we did not see the trees and the clouds outside us but within, as if we were looking inwards always and seeing lungs, heart or stomach. In the world of spirit we look into our interior; but what we see there is the world of spiritual hierarchies, the world we know from our anthroposophic literature as that of the higher hierarchies. That is our interior world. And between death and a new birth we feel ourselves, really, as the whole world. If I say 'the whole world' this is relative, but fully true nevertheless. Each of us feels himself to be the whole world. Within us, particularly at the most important moment of our spiritual existence between death and a new birth, we experience the world of spiritual beings within us, and our consciousness originating in them. We have an awareness of our interior as constituted by the spirits of the higher world whereas here on earth we have no awareness of our interior, of liver, lungs and so forth. This is the characteristic nature of spiritual experience—that basically everything is the reverse of physical experience here. But only through initiation science do we gradually come to realize how we should conceive of this reversal.

Now there is an important process, or really I could say a group of processes, which relate precisely to this inner community of ours with beings of the higher hierarchies. We could never come to ourselves if in the world of spirit we only perceived the world of higher hierarchies within us. We would know that certain beings live in us, but we could not gain any sense of ourselves in the spiritual world. Our experience between death and a new birth, therefore, is subject to a rhythmic alternation—between looking inward and experiencing the world of spiritual beings described in our anthroposophic literature, and then, you can say, the dulling of this awareness. In relation to our spiritual interior this is similar to what happens in sleep, when we close our eyes and our ears no longer hear anything. Yet sleep has a different significance here on earth. When we turn our attention—if I can put it like that—from the world of spiritual beings within us, we start to perceive ourselves instead. This is however as if we were outside ourselves; but we know that we ourselves are there outside us. In other words, in the world of spirit we perceive, in alternation, ourselves or the world of spiritual beings.

You see, this recurring rhythmic process is one we can compare with two things in physical existence here on earth—firstly, with our inbreath and outbreath, and then also with sleep life and waking life. Both of these are rhythmic processes, and both can be compared with what I have just described. But now it is important not just to have some abstract idea of processes like this occurring in the world of spirit between death and a new birth in order, if you like, to satisfy your spiritual curiosity, but instead we should see that earthly life is a reflection of super-earthly life. So then we must ask this: what occurs here in earthly life that is like a capacity to remember this immersion of ourselves in the world of spiritual beings alternating rhythmically with an experience of our own self? We do not ordinarily have this capacity; it is one that beings of the higher hierarchies would have. What occurs here in physical life on earth that resembles such a memory?

If we did not have this kind of experience between death and a new birth, by means of which we can gaze into ourselves to perceive the world of spirit, there would be no morality here on earth. What we retain from this experience of beings in the world of spirit when we pass through the embryo stage and enter earthly life at birth is an inclination for moral life. Our inclination for it will be all the stronger the more our experience of this community with spirits of the higher world has been one of bright clarity between death and a new birth. Someone who has the right spiritual insight into such things knows that people who are immoral here on earth are so because their experience was too dull when they looked into this spiritual existence. But it is also true that if, between death and a new birth, we could only experience what makes us one with beings of the higher world and never came to ourselves in the world of spirit it would be quite impossible for us ever to become free, develop an awareness of our freedom, a sense of who we are, of our individuality—which basically is identical with our sense of freedom. The morality and freedom we develop here on earth are memories of this rhythm we experience in worlds of spirit between death and a new birth.

By studying the soul we can see even more accurately what remains within us as echo of these experiences—of becoming one with spiritual beings alternating with spiritual self-awareness. The echo in our soul of being one with spiritual beings is the capacity to love. This ability to love is more closely connected with moral life than people think. You see, without it there would be no moral life on earth. All moral action arises from the insight with which we meet another's soul, arises from efforts we make to ensure our actions accord with our insights into another soul. Our capacity to behave selflessly towards others means that we can become moral in love; and this is largely an echo of our community with spiritual beings in the world between death and a new birth. And what remains from what I would appropriately call our experience of loneliness, the lonely experience of our self in the world of spirit? Actually in a sense we feel lonely when we breathe out. Breathing in is like an experience of spiritual beings, while breathing out is like an experience of the self. Our sense of loneliness, the echo of this sense of loneliness is, on earth, our capacity to remember. We would have no power of memory if this were not an echo of the sense of loneliness I have described. We are human, really, in the world of spirit by virtue of the fact that we—to say 'withdraw' is not strictly right—can liberate ourselves from what exists in us in the form of higher spirits. This makes us human beings, autonomous human beings in the spiritual world. And here on earth we become independent human beings because we can remember our experiences. Imagine what kind of autonomy you would have if you could live only in the present moment in thought. The thoughts you remember compose your very capacity to have an inner life, make you an individual on earth; and this ability to remember is indeed the echo of that experience of loneliness in the world of spirit that I have described.

Why do we actually descend into the physical world here from worlds of spirit? From what I described to you here last time you can see that the powers that keep us in community with the higher spiritual beings gradually grow weaker. Here in physical life we grow old because the powers that keep us one with the physical earth grow weaker. In the spiritual world, the powers that keep us one with spiritual beings likewise grow weaker. In particular, the powers weaken that enable us to grasp ourselves within beings of spirit, and to be autonomous human beings. In the spiritual world—a fairly long time before we descend to earth—we first lose our capacity to live as one with beings of spirit. I described this last time I was here: together with spiritual beings we form the spirit germ of our physical body, sending this down first, then we take the ether body and follow after. First we lose the capacity—it fades—to live in community with spirit beings in the world of spirit. And we sense ourselves approaching ever closer to the earth by virtue of moon powers. We feel ourselves to be a self, but we feel our ability to grasp ourselves, sustain ourselves within the realm of spirit to be diminishing, waning. Increasingly we feel as if we are growing faint and weak in the world of spirit. And this induces us to feel we must support this feeling of self, which we can no longer sustain within us, by investing it in something external, in our body—to underpin it with a body. One can put it like this: we slowly forget how to fly and have to learn to walk. That's putting it metaphorically, but the metaphor is in turn a truth, a reality. And so we live our way into our body. The sense of loneliness is sustained by the body and becomes the faculty of memory, while our feeling of community is something we first have to regain here on earth. The whole significance of what is regained here becomes apparent if we study the state of sleep by spiritual-scientific means.

I described the state of sleep from a certain angle when I was here last. But now I wish to add to this picture some other processes. I realize that these things can easily be misunderstood. It repeatedly happens that people wonder why one description I give of, say, our experience during sleep is different from another that I present. My dear friends, if I were to tell you on one occasion what a privy councillor does in his chambers, and on another what he experiences at home with his family, these things would not be contradictory. They interrelate. And in the same way things are interrelated in my accounts of sleep life.

Between falling asleep and waking up again we experience a kind of reverse repetition of what we did during the day. Sleep may be brief too, then these things are compressed or telescoped. It is not just that we look back on the day's experiences between falling asleep and waking up—unconsciously of course—but that when the soul really becomes clairvoyant during sleep, or if it recalls clairvoyantly what it experienced then, it becomes apparent that we really do experience in reverse order everything we did during the day. The last event we experienced before falling asleep figures first. In this way our whole sleep has a remarkably balancing effect. I can only tell you things as I find them to be in my spiritual-scientific research. If you sleep for quarter of an hour, the beginning of your sleep already knows roughly when it will end. And in this quarter hour you remember in reverse what you have done since you last woke up. However extraordinary this seems, everything is properly distributed through the available period of sleep. And this reverse experience lies somewhere between full reality and appearance. It's like this: if you have a memory picture of something you experienced in life 20 years ago, your healthy powers of reason tell you that you are not experiencing this now; it is a memory picture of a past experience. And someone with clairvoyant perception of what the soul experiences in reverse during sleep will not relate it to the present moment but to the future, after death. The memory of an event experienced 20 years ago recalls the past; and in the same way someone who studies sleep clairvoyantly sees that it is a prefiguring of what will be experienced after death—and that in other words we will have to recapitulate in reverse all the deeds we did on earth, re-enacting and recapitulating them. This picture during sleep is therefore half reality and half appearance, for it relates to the future. For ordinary awareness, therefore, it is an unconscious passage through what we must undergo in the soul world—as I called it in my book *Theosophy*. And the states of Intuition and Inspiration as I described them in *Knowledge of the Higher Worlds* can observe sleep and thereby perceive what we must undergo in the first after-death phase. These are not things I've randomly invented but ones that can be observed once the capacity to do so has been acquired. Between falling asleep and waking up again, therefore, we recapitulate without our body what we did with our body while awake.

Now, though, we arrive at an extremely subtle idea. Imagine that we must re-experience our deeds from without through our I and astral body. The capacity to do this is one we acquire increasingly as we become better able to love. That is the secret of life as far as love is concerned. If a person is really able to go out of himself in love, in a sense loving his neighbour as himself, he learns what he needs in sleep in order to fully re-experience in reverse what he must experience, but without torment. For in this condition he must be completely outside himself. If a person is unloving this gives rise to a tension when he must re-experience his unloving deeds outside himself. It constricts and confines him. Unloving people, if I can express this in an image, sleep in a tight-chested way. While we sleep, what we implant in ourselves through love in our life becomes very fruitful for us. And, as will be apparent from what I have said today, what develops during sleep endows us with what passes beyond the gate of death and continues to live there in the world of spirit. In our life between death and a new birth our community with beings of spirit in higher worlds gradually wanes; but then we regain it germinally during our life on earth, through love. You see, love reveals its meaning when a person is outside his physical and ether body with his I and astral body in sleep. Between falling asleep and waking up, a person's human nature widens and broadens if he is loving, preparing itself well for what is to happen with him after death. His being grows narrow and constricted on the other hand if he is unloving, and is ill-prepared for what is to happen with him after death. The germ of what occurs after we die lies primarily in loving thoughts and actions.

During life on earth, between birth and death, memory is something extremely fleeting—just pictures in our mind. Consider for a moment how little of our experience remains in our memory pictures. If you think of the deep pain you may perhaps have experienced at the death of a loved one and recall vividly how you actually felt at the time, then picture what remains of this as inner experience when you think back to it ten years later, you will find that it has grown pale, almost abstract. That is the nature of memory—things grow pale and abstract compared to the fresh immediacy of actual experience. Why *is* our memory weak and shadowy? It is because it is, in fact, the shadow of our experience of ourself between death and a new birth. This experience contains our capacity for memory, and so really gives us our existence. What gives us flesh and blood here on earth endows us with the capacity for memory between death and a new birth. There, memory is strong, fresh and vivid—if I can use such expressions for spiritual reality. Then it employs the flesh and grows weak. And when we die, for a few days, as I have often described in my books, the last remains of memory are still present in the etheric body. When we pass through the gate of death we look back upon the whole of our past life, and then this memory fades. But from this memory emerges what our strength of love on earth has given us as strength for life after death. And thus the strength of our memory is the inheritance we bring with us from our pre-earthly life; and the strength of love is the germinal power for what we have after death. In other words, earthly life and experience relate to the world of spirit.

But you remember that I compared what we experience in community with higher beings in the world of spirit, and its alternation with an experience of the self there, with breathing, with inbreath and outbreath. In turn we can see our breathing process, and all that is connected with it, processes of singing and speech, as a picture or reflection of this breathing in the world of spirit. You see, our life in the world of spirit between death and a new birth occurs in the following way: insight into our own interior and oneness with beings of the higher hierarchies; then a view from our own interior, and oneness with the self. This occurs like inbreathing and outbreathing, except that there we breathe ourselves in and breathe ourselves out, and this breathing is a spiritual process. Here on earth this breathing process becomes memory and love as I have described. And in fact memory and love also work together here as a kind of breathing in physical life. If you can study this physical life properly with soul vision you can actually discern the interplay of memory and love, even physiologically, in an important manifestation of breathing, in speech and singing.

One of the most interesting aspects of the young child up to the change of teeth is the way the power of memory gradually develops. Initially this is very elementary. The child has a certain ability to remember but this only acquires autonomy towards the time of second dentition. It is enormously interesting to observe how the power of memory develops and emerges in the first period of childhood, and is really only fully developed when the child is ready for school. Only then can we draw on the child's remembering capacity. If we draw too much on his memory at an earlier stage we will make a person too rigid and inwardly sclerotic later in life. Up to the change of teeth it is important that the child receive the right immediate impressions from his sur-roundings. We can only start building on his memory between the change of teeth and puberty.

Nowadays physiologists are not yet able to describe these processes accurately. Spiritual science can do so, and physiology will no doubt catch up at some point, since these things can be observed through accurate study of human nature. When we speak a sound or sing a tone, we can say that the head is involved initially. But what participates in this in the head is the same capacity that gives us memory as an inner faculty. Here, in a sense, it shoots into the speech sound or tone; this comes from above. It is easy to realize that no one can speak without some memory ability. If we always forgot what lies in the speech sound or tone we would never be able to speak or sing. Tones and speech sounds are, on the one hand, embodied memory. On the other hand, love plays a part too, also physiologically, in what becomes speech and singing in the breathing process; and a clear sign of this is that in the second phase of life—when love comes to physiological expression—the full inner wealth of tone arises in the male sex. It arises from below. And here you have the two elements together: from above what underlies memory physiologically, and from below what underlies love physiologically. These form speech sounds and sung tones in reciprocal interplay. In a sense this too is a breathing process that lasts throughout life. In the same way that we breathe in oxygen and breathe out carbon dioxide, so the power of memory combines in us with the power of love, and these encounter each other in speech and song. So we can say that speaking and singing involve a mutual interpenetration in us of the power of memory with the power of love. This is extremely significant for fathoming the real secret of tone and speech sound.

There really is some truth therefore in the view of ancient cultures that language expresses the sum of universal powers and thoughts, as the Logos, and that this is the supersensible aspect of what comes to physical expression in speech. We not only breathe higher beings in and out between death and a new birth but in a sense we speak—although this speech is at the same time singing—in this mutual interplay between oneness with spiritual beings of the higher world and coming back to ourselves: we speak with the beings of the higher hierarchies. This is a spiritual speaking. In the condition of becoming one with beings in the world of spirit, we look upon them, albeit within ourselves. When we release ourselves from them again and return to ourselves, we have an after-echo of this, and there we are ourselves. There they impress their own being into us, telling us what they are; and there the Logos lives in us. The reverse is true when we come to ourselves on earth: here we express our own being when we speak and sing, express our intrinsic human nature in song and speech. We express our whole being in breathing processes, whereas between death and a new birth we receive the whole nature of the world in the Logos as we withdraw from community with spirit beings.

Now as we make the transition from the world of spirit to the physical world, at the same time in a sense we pass through a great oblivion, through forgetfulness. Who still perceives in the shadowy power of memory in ordinary consciousness an echo of what we really were as a self in the world of spirit? And who still recognizes in speech, in the aspect of it originating in memory, the after-resonance of the self? Who, with ordinary consciousness, recognizes in our shaping of language, in singing and speech, in the development of language's formative power, the echo of beings of the higher hierarchies? And yet it is true, isn't it, that if we know how to listen to speech without focusing on its utilitarian aspect, if we can hearken to what tones intrinsically express in their very nature, especially if we have an artistic sensibility, we can have an inkling that speech and singing reveal more to us than is encompassed in ordinary awareness. And why, in fact, do we transform ordinary language, with its utility as means of earthly communication, by ridding it of this utility in song and using it instead to express our own being in the heightened speech of poetry or in singing? Why do we transform it in this way? What are we actually doing here?

We gain the right notion of this if we acknowledge that we were in the world of spirit before we descended to this earth, and lived there as I have described. Then the great forgetting occurred. In what your mouth speaks, in what your soul remembers and how your soul loves, you do not perceive the echo of what you were in the world of spirit. But in art in a sense we take a step back from life and a few steps nearer to what we were in pre-birth life and what we will be in life after death. And if we can recognize that memory, on the one hand, is the echo of what we had in pre-earthly life, and loving thoughts and deeds are the germ of what we will have after death, if we can bring to mind in us the past and future of human existence through spirit knowledge, then in art we can call into the present moment—as far as this is possible for us in our physical state—what connects us with the spirit.

You see, art acquires its distinctive luminosity by transposing us, albeit naively, into the immediate presence of the world of spirit. Someone who can look into the heart of human life will see that human beings usually only remember things they have done in their earthly life so far. But the strength with which we recall these earthly experiences is only the diluted strength of our actual self-experience in pre-earthly life, our existence there. And the universal human love we can develop here is the diluted germinal power of what will come to full flowering after death. Here we have past and future. And just as in singing, for example, and in the heightened speech of poetry, a connection must really exist between what a human being is, that is, memory, with the way in which he can give himself to the world, as love, so in all art we experience in the present moment a harmony between our self and the outer world. And unless we are capable of bringing to the surface what we are, what life has made of us, and what basically is the content of our memory, in one respect we cannot be artists. But nor can we be artists either if we seek to be extreme egotists. Only someone who in a sense seeks to flow out into the world, to become one with others, who demonstrates love, can unite this loving openness with his own inner being. Here altruism and egotism flow into one; they do so most inwardly of course in the musical arts, but also in the pictorial arts. And if we deepen our powers of perception sufficiently to discover how our past and future are connected with a supersensible world, at the same time we can see that we have a present inkling of this connection in both the creation and enjoyment of art. Art never really comes into its own if it does not involve some kind of resonance with religiosity. This does not mean it has to be over-pious, since humorous art can also touch on a religious quality.

But we can see this clearly from the way art has developed. It was originally intrinsic to religious life, integrated into rites and religious worship in the ancient days of humanity. The images of the gods that people made gave rise to sculpture. Goethe refers to the Samothrace Mysteries in Part II of *Faust*,[48] where he speaks of the Cabeiri. At my studio in Dornach I tried to depict these Cabeiri. What emerged was very interesting. I simply set myself the task of discovering through direct vision what the Cabeiri in the Samothrace Mysteries must have looked like; and what I got were three jugs, though they were artistically sculpted ones. I was astonished myself to begin with, although Goethe also speaks of jugs. The whole thing only became comprehensible to me when I discovered that these jugs stood upon an altar and were used to hold something like incense. The rites were sung, and from the power of these words, which in ancient times still possessed a quite different resonance-awakening power from today, the incense smoke formed into an image of the god who was invoked. Thus in the midst of religious worship you have this resonating song which comes to immediate expression in the forms of the smoke.

Humanity really did draw art from religious life. And Schiller is right when he says, 'Only through the dawn-red light of beauty do you enter the land of knowledge,'[49] which is usually printed in books as, 'Only through the morning door of beauty do you enter the land of knowledge.'[*] If an artist makes a mistake when writing, posterity naturally perpetuates the error. Of course he meant, 'Only through the dawn-red light of beauty do you enter the land of knowledge.' In other words, all knowledge arises from art. Fundamentally there is no knowledge that does not have an intimate affinity with art. Only knowledge that relates to externalities, to utility, seems to have no connection with art; but such knowledge can only encompass, say, what a paint manufacturer knows of painting. As soon as one goes beyond mere paint-making in chemistry or physics—I'm speaking metaphorically but you understand what I mean—science becomes artistic too. And when the spirituality of artistic endeavour is properly understood, then it gradually becomes religious. Art, religion and science were once one, and we should still sense their common origins. We can only do so however if humanity's civilization, humanity's evolution, returns to the spirit again, and when we give serious attention to the relationships that exist between human life here in physical earth existence and in the world of spirit. We need to make this our certain knowledge from a range of different perspectives.

I have addressed one of these perspectives today to show how we are connected with the spiritual world. I hope that we can continue these observations in the not too distant future.

---

[1] Translator's note: the difference involves only the reversal of three letters in German.

Lecture 15

I am very pleased to be able to speak to you here again at this branch group of our Anthroposophical Society where, for many years, I was fortunate enough to develop a good deal of my work.[50] Today I want to speak to you about things that I think are particularly important at present: about how we human beings are connected with the supersensible world.

This of course is a theme always current in the anthroposophic movement. But you will by now have accustomed yourselves to the fact that we can only come into full possession of truths about supersensible worlds when we consider them from the most varied points of view. As I have often pointed out, we can then gain an overall sense of things from pictures taken, as it were, from different angles.

Human life is of course divided into two divergent states, occurring at different times: that of full wakefulness, and that of sleep. As you know, spiritual-scientific research has shown that during sleep the aspects of our nature that we call the physical body, the etheric body (or body of formative forces), the astral body and the I are separated. We leave our physical and etheric body behind, as it were, in the physical world, and lead an initially unconscious existence in our astral body and I being outside of the physical body and etheric body. When we rise to higher knowledge it is not true to say that by this means alone, through knowledge, we gain anything for our human nature itself, just as little as theoretical knowledge of digestion will directly improve the latter's functions in the normal state of our organism. Higher knowledge does not of itself introduce anything new into us. What higher knowledge reveals is already present in us. And yet it is also true to say that what introduces nothing new into us nevertheless points us to what remains hidden from our ordinary awareness and which, when we not only perceive it but also experience it with the full content of our soul, does then infuse a higher reality into the human being—not knowledge as such, but an experience of this knowledge.

Here, though, I am referring to something I would like to present in terms of a threefold anthroposophic endeavour. First of all there must be individuals who develop spiritual-scientific methods to a degree that enables them to offer knowledge of supersensible worlds gained through higher vision. It is not so important what name we give to the acquisition of this knowledge. We can gladly speak of clairvoyant knowledge as long as we do not associate this expression with some kind of nebulous, mystical idea, as is very often the case. Clairvoyant insight does give rise to a living content that must increasingly inform human sensibilities in our present era.

The second aspect is this: that ordinary, healthy common sense, if people's minds are sufficiently open, can see the validity of what clairvoyant knowledge reveals. I have said this on many occasions: a person does not need to be clairvoyant himself in order to see the value of what clairvoyant research brings to light. But it is also important that someone who himself develops clairvoyant vision can translate what he sees into ordinary human concepts. For people today, at our current stage of development, the important thing is precisely that clairvoyant knowledge be translated into human concepts prevalent in modern civilization. Whether or not one is clairvoyant, one has to be able to understand what clairvoyant research reveals.

The third thing is that clairvoyant research translated into human concepts, and thus pictured or understood, must then become a living content in people so that they realize they are beings whose existence is not bound solely to earthly reality between birth and death. They must know that they are beings for whom earthly life is only a phase, a transitory stage of metamorphosis. Everything that can inform human sensibility as living content of this kind, through anthroposophy, must take root in the soul. Then people know that they belong to worlds of spirit, and also that the tasks of earthly existence are given them from these worlds. But secondly, too, this gives them a sense of responsibility towards worlds of spirit. It raises them beyond mere earth existence—though not in a way that induces them to flee it or denigrate it in a kind of airy-fairy mysticism. No, our tasks in life, and consequently the whole character and cadence of our life on earth, must be drawn from the supersensible world.

In our times it is particularly important that we first learn to attend to what can be stated through clairvoyant research, and that we then endeavour to understand the content of this research by our healthy common sense, making this content into something we work upon in life, illumining life with the tasks that arise from it, and enhancing our sense of responsibility towards worlds of spirit. These introductory words aim to set the mood and tone of my observations today, which offer various new aspects of our relationship with worlds of spirit.

Living here on earth, we open our senses to the physical world. And looking inwards we perceive, in a sense, our thinking, feeling and will. What we perceive through our senses and make into the content of our soul is also what we call our earthly surroundings. As earthly human beings in our physical surroundings we are really very familiar with what we call the 'outer world', the natural world around us, but by comparison our ordinary state of awareness tells us very little about what lies within our own being, even physically. External science does provide knowledge of our inner organs but really only by making these organs outward entities, for knowledge about them is gained largely through dissection and so forth. By looking inwards with his ordinary faculties, a person cannot gain knowledge about, say, his lungs or heart. At the most we might be able to feel or perceive these organs when they are malfunctioning. In a healthy state, we do not really perceive what is happening within us. It lives in us, functions within us, but precisely because it is in us and constitutes us we do not perceive it as we perceive the surroundings from which we distinguish ourselves.

This can show us that our perception of what is outside and around us gives us a world, a content, whereas our gaze inwards gives us only the general, vague feeling of an I. If we are honest we will admit that this is a very dim and unclear perception. We alternate between this inward gaze, a fairly unclear and opaque experience in the soul, and our experience of tangible, detailed surroundings full of specific content. Basically, this alternating experience fills our awareness between birth and death.

Between death and a new birth our experience is very different, and especially different at the midpoint of this existence, corresponding if you like to the middle period of earthly life when, as 30- or 40-year-olds, we are at the peak of our physical powers. This midpoint of life after death is diametrically opposite to earthly life: we gaze inwards with the different consciousness we then possess, and in doing so we see things in as specific and tangible a way as we observe our outer surroundings here on earth. But when we observe our surroundings on earth, we see the three or four kingdoms of nature—minerals, plants, animals and the physical aspect of human beings. They surround us as the content of our sensory perception. But when we gaze inwards during the time I am referring to between death and a new birth, instead of the things of nature we find within us a world of beings, those we describe as beings of higher, spiritual realms, of the hierarchies. Here on earth we have outer perception of the world, perception of things, while in the world of spirit we have inner perception, perception of beings. We look into ourselves but we do not find there organs such as those we possess on earth; instead, as long as we can have the right awareness of this, we find the whole world of beings. Someone who describes these beings of the higher hierarchies is really describing nothing other than the human being's outward experience between death and a new birth. And when, in the same way as we can here direct our gaze away from the outer world and look inwards upon ourselves, we direct our gaze outwards, away from the beings of the higher hierarchies within us, then we discover our self, come to ourselves. After death the outer world really becomes inner world, and inner world becomes outer, in the way I have now explained.

The world within us we perceive as full of spiritual beings becomes a kind of image or reflection in earthly existence. Here we see the sensory reflections of those beings whom we perceive within us between death and a new birth. We do not see the beings themselves as such but instead their dwelling places, and these are—since there are always a host of these beings together—the starry heavens around us. What therefore are we describing when we speak of the stars or the sun, for instance, when we speak with full knowledge rather than the mole vision of ordinary awareness we possess between birth and death? The sun offers a certain image to our sensory gaze, but what we see as the image of the sun here is something we perceive between death and a new birth as a realm of spiritual beings. We see a realm of spiritual beings, not the image we see here. Here in earthly existence we have a kind of memory which tells us that this realm of spiritual beings corresponds to the sun we see from an earthly perspective. And this is true too of the other stars. So our spiritual awareness between death and a new birth is a cosmic one. There we are not enclosed within our skin as we are here, but have truly become the whole world. But we should not think of this in spatial terms. We become the whole universe, and carry the starry heavens within us. Just as we have our lungs, heart and stomach inside us here, so between death and a new birth we carry the sun, the moon, Saturn and the other planets and stars inside us as our inner organs; but they are spiritual beings. We carry in us their spiritual correlate, their spiritual archetype.

If we were always in this condition in the spiritual world we would never come back to ourselves, would always feel ourselves to be one with the world of the higher hierarchies. But that cannot be. That would be like always only breathing in and never out. This is why our life between death and a new birth consists of a rhythmic alternation: a life within these higher hierarchies and—in a cosmic form of consciousness—in looking outwards, which there means coming back to ourselves. Just as we alternate here between inbreath and outbreath—or I could also say between being awake and being asleep—so there we alternate between an experience of the hierarchies, the world of spirit, and an experience of ourselves, where we come to ourselves and feel the loneliness of our contracted soul. Thus we have a recurring rhythmic alternation of experience between being spread out through the whole universe and coming back to ourselves.

This life between death and a new birth in the spiritual world, whose physical reflection is the world of stars, is certainly not less rich than life on earth. In earthly life, though, we can only really see the *result* of what we experience between death and rebirth, and only in a very indistinct way. Think of it like this: here in life on earth, one person may make shoes, another makes dresses, a third is a hairdresser, a fourth is an engineer and so on. As we do these things here on earth, what is called human culture develops, civilization. If you now imagine that from time to time the emergence of this whole civilization, its artefacts and effects, were to be summarized in a kind of overall outcome in a quite different realm, say on the sun, it would not be immediately possible to perceive it, with sun consciousness, as the result of earthly civilization. On the sun there would just be many specimens of a single outcome. This is in fact the reality of what we do in collaboration with the beings of the higher hierarchies between death and a new birth: we work there with these beings to create the spirit form of our physical body on earth. And this work, done in collaboration between human beings and the beings of the higher hierarchies to create the spirit form of our future physical body, is truly a richer and more diverse kind of activity than goes into the cultural artefacts we create in physical existence. This is true even though the physical human body standing before us may not immediately betray the fact that it is the result of the work of divine beings in collaboration with the human being during his existence between death and a new birth. But older civilizations were aware of this when they called the body a 'temple of the gods'. As little as we normally realize this with our ordinary consciousness here on earth, this human body is the most complex thing existing anywhere in the universe. A single human body is the confluence and totality of the work of countless beings, of whom we too are one. We help to work on the body with which we clothe ourselves in an earthly incarnation. We would not be able to elaborate it individually for ourselves but have to create it in community with countless spiritual beings of the most diverse ranks.

From an earthly perspective we are used to regarding a seed as something that is small to start with and then unfolds to occupy greater physical space. If we call what we elaborate between death and a new birth the 'spirit seed' or 'spirit germ' of the physical body, this spirit seed is in fact as vast as the universe, and grows ever smaller physically as it passes through the embryo stage. The small fertilized human ovum contains a reflection of this great spirit seed that has been elaborated by the human being together with higher beings. If we use spiritual vision to study the world human beings live in between death and a new birth, we find how the tasks of the macrocosm give rise to the microcosm, the human body, which is continually configured anew. And this task is more sublime than all cultural endeavour accomplished by human beings during life on earth. The life we spend there, working from the universe upon the human seed, is more varied and richer than what we accomplish here on earth when, say, we make shoes or clothes, teach children, rule nations and so on. I could of course go on and on with the list. Anyone who really wishes to understand the world must grasp the fact that it is an extraordinarily sublime thing to share in this task of the universe in configuring the human body as it exists here on earth in physical reflection, and that the nature of this task is incomparably more sublime than what we accomplish here on earth—even when we are involved in creating the most valuable cultural products of physical life.

Between death and a new birth we dwell in the world of spirit. Our outer world is our self. Our gaze looks towards our future life on earth, and with this in view we contract and come to ourselves. When our consciousness is filled with this view of our future life on earth, and with looking back to our past life, we are aware of self. When we work together with beings of the higher hierarchies at the task of creating the spirit seed of our complex human body, we are in a sense outside ourselves and have become one with spirit being, live with spirit being out in the universe. Specifically at the culmination of our experience between death and a new birth, which I called 'the midnight hour of human existence' in one of my Mystery Plays,[51] the human being experiences his inner life as the starry heavens he sees here on earth in reflected form, the heaven of fixed stars. The world of fixed stars or their representative—as older cultures called it—the zodiac is, from our earthly perspective, the physical image or reflection of the spiritual world in which we live between death and a new birth, and which we then experience as our inner world.

This continues for a certain period, and then we depart in a sense from this living, active work, which must appear sublime from an earthly perspective, and is accomplished in direct collaboration with spirits of the higher hierarchies. The next experience we have is that of witnessing the revelations of higher beings. We are no longer directly involved in their work but they still show reflections of themselves to us. In earthly terms we can say that we find a transition from the world of fixed stars to the world of planets. As we pass through the planetary sphere in our progress towards an earthly existence, we no longer feel the life of higher worlds as our inner life. Previously we felt it to be our inner life. Here in the physical world we feel the circulation of our blood, our breathing and so on as the inner workings of our organism. There, in life between death and a new birth, we feel the life and being of the higher hierarchies to be our inner life. We stand within a spiritual reality and participate in it. But now, from a certain moment onwards, we realize we are no longer participating. Instead it is as if an image appears to us of something we have previously worked on. Before we were actually in the spiritual world, now we are in its manifestations. But this means in reality that we have left the sphere of the fixed stars and have entered the planetary sphere.

Here, initially, we have to overcome a certain difficulty, which involves entry into the Saturn sphere. Specific spiritual forces emanate from Saturn. You see, once we have passed through death, we first enter the planetary sphere and then that of the fixed stars, tracing the path I have just described in the opposite direction. As we depart from earthly life, Saturn is the dwelling place of beings who do not want us to remain on earth, but lift us away from it and seek to liberate us from earthly forces. They try to convey us onwards, out into the world of pure spirituality. In my book *Theosophy* I described this endeavour from another perspective as the transition from life in soul land to that in spirit land. These two accounts relate to each other in the same way that one can photograph a tree from different angles. The tree is the same, but looks different from different sides. As we return to a new life on earth, therefore, we again fall under the sway of Saturn beings. And those whose karma, due to their previous life on earth, allows Saturn forces to exert a strong influence on them as they return easily become people without a strong earth connection—who either rhapsodize about earthly things having no worth, and take flight into some cloud cuckoo land of ideas or who, regarding human relationships and circumstances in a superficial way, are inclined to get involved in spiritualist séances and suchlike, inviting the rampant activity of very diverse spiritual beings. All this is due to the fact that in his last life a person acquired a karma that led him into a stronger connection with Saturn forces as he returned to the earth.

But as we enter the planetary sphere on our passage towards the earth, we also fall under the influence of beings opposite to those of Saturn: those who dwell on the moon. The primary task of these beings is to lead the human being into earthly existence again. Someone who absorbs this influence will stand fast in earthly existence although, on the other hand, moon forces can also mean that we are too strongly involved in purely physical life, and develop a preference for this physicality.

In our life on earth we walk around amongst trees, flowers, grasses, animals and so on, while between death and a new birth we wander about amongst the stars. You can form quite a full and real picture of this if you think of it like this: in earthly life you are here on earth, while after death you pass through the spheres of the planets, leaving the moon sphere and with it an inclination for earth life, passing through Saturn, then spending a relatively long time compared with your life on earth in the sphere of fixed stars; then returning, entering the planetary sphere again and especially, as you come under the moon's influence, finding there, though still in supersensible existence, the impetus to return again to earth. You are drawn strongly back to earth life. In the same way that we have a certain relationship with what we call our sensory surroundings, the same is true as we pass through the world of stars. And all this has great significance for our collaboration with the beings of the higher hierarchies to create the spirit seed or spirit germ of our physical human body. As we reach the planetary sphere in our downward trajectory towards our future life on earth, we decide whether we will become a man or woman. For quite a while this remains undecided while we dwell as soul-spiritual beings in the planetary sphere. In the sphere of the fixed stars something resembling our earthly gender distinction would be nonsensical. But in the picture I am trying to convey you can see things like this: here is the moon, seen from in front; but in the world of spirit you see it from behind. Venus, Mercury and the sun you likewise see from behind, then you see the zodiac sphere and so on. But in your passage through these spheres, what is a physical image or reflection for us here is transformed into a wealth of spiritual beings whom you perceive. As you regard the moon from behind you see spirit beings, for instance those who were of prime interest to the initiates in Old Testament times: the Yahweh being, and beings belonging to him. But when you now return to the earth and approach the moon sphere, as a result of your former karma you can seek out the point in time at which, from the earth's perspective, the full moon is in the sky. On earth you would see the illumined face of the full moon; but from behind, approaching the earth, you see a black disc. If you choose this moment to approach the earth, when the black moon sphere, uninfluenced by the sun, acts upon you and when therefore it is full moon on earth, you will be born on earth in female form. If instead you choose the period when we do not see the moon here on earth—new moon—when sun influences shine unhindered through the cosmos in all directions, then you will be arranging life for yourself in a male body. Right down to the physical gender we assume, you see, we have to trace the effects of what we experience as we pass through the spiritual sphere between death and a new birth, and see these effects from an opposite perspective to that on earth. These things can be traced in every detail of our life here. In the same way that we can discover the different effects of eating cabbage or eggs or meat—for our physical existence on earth is dependent on such things—so likewise there are all kinds of connections in spiritual worlds which come to expression in our form and inner vitality on earth. Here on earth we eat eggs or meat. In the world of spirit between death and a new birth, in accordance with our karma we choose either to pass through the moon sphere at the time of new moon or full moon, and thereby become a man or a woman. The full scope of our human existence in relation to the cosmos is something we can only understand if we lift our gaze from what happens between birth and death alone to see that what occurs during this life on earth is connected with what happens between our death and rebirth.

Today people do not yet grasp the full, real significance of this. Yet our knowledge of the human being is about as extensive as a mole's knowledge of museums. A mole may burrow below the floor of a museum and might even be able to tell us of his experiences underground; but his account will have very little to say about what is above his head. Sciences that confine their gaze to the earth are roughly like this. The difference is that a mole can do perfectly well without the things over his head; he doesn't have much use for museums, whereas we are intimately connected with the supersensible world, are really connected with it, and we ought to gain an awareness of this world once more. A dull awareness of such things did once exist, illumined by the ancient mysteries, albeit using ancient methods. These mysteries were not narrow enclaves of worship, a state of affairs that has really come about only in modern times. Today people have to celebrate their rites in ways that are distinct and separate from the rest of culture, and this is because humanity has become egotistical, and seeks some assurance of its immortality. That is all well and good; such an assurance can be given. But people today have a great capacity to keep things separate, sundered. At the time of Paracelsus this was not yet so; medicine was still a form of religious worship. We do need distinctions and yet we ought to come to see all earthly activity as the fruit of spiritual influences and activity again. Today people pass through their experiences on earth in a way that is sundered from the spiritual world, and this is necessary for otherwise we could not achieve a sense of freedom. And yet the time has now passed when human beings should keep separate from spiritual existence, shut themselves off from it. Our consciousness must once again imbue itself with the inner illumination of spiritual existence, and we can no longer use ancient methods for doing this. We have to learn how this can be achieved today by modern means.

Just picture this for a moment: an ancient mystery site took care of the concerns of its surrounding area through the knowledge enshrined in it. This duty of care extended to all the affairs and activities of those living in the vicinity, all the matters that could only be organized through insight into a connection between life on earth and the world of spirit. Let us assume that a person fell ill. In olden times no one asked what substances had been tested for their effect on the human organism. Still less did anyone enquire into the effect of substances that had been tried out on animals. Such empiricism inevitably entered modern life, and I am not criticizing medicine today, just surveying how things developed through evolution. In ancient times someone who fell ill sought assistance from the mystery centres, since priests were simultaneously artists and physicians. Art, religion and science were still one, and were cultivated in mystery centres. In those days a complete, holistic view of the human being still prevailed. When someone of a certain age contracted a particular disease, people knew this was not just to do with the chemical mix or disorder of substances in him, but from a higher perspective they saw it was connected with experiences he had undergone as he passed through the starry worlds, and started to seek his new earthly existence there.

Think of someone who fell ill, say, between the age of 14 and 21, and turned for help to a mystery centre, which was at the same time a centre of healing and medicine. Though the knowledge at work there would be instinctive and dreamy, the examination given to such a patient would often reveal more than modern consultations with a doctor do. I have known doctors who, in discussions, showed they knew nothing about certain vital aspects of their patient, not even his age. One can't of course help improve a person's health without knowing what age he is! You see, a person needs a different remedy at different ages since the character of human life is constantly changing. No one would think of planting a petal in the ground and waiting for a new plant to grow from it, but we take a seed from the fruit and plant that, since we know how plants develop. Human life should be regarded in a similar way. So if a patient aged between roughly 14 and 21 came to seek help from a mystery physician in those times, the latter knew that there were a number of disorders connected with the human being's passage through the sun sphere as the soul descends from the planetary world into the physical world. If the patient was aged between 35 and 42, the mystery priest knew which illnesses were connected with the soul's descending passage through the Saturn sphere. In other words, he would enquire chiefly into the way our experiences in the life between death and a new birth are connected with earthly life. He also knew how the external nature of the stars, as seen from earth, their physical reflections, related to the beings of the higher hierarchies. Certain plants have a more intimate connection with the sun, while others are more closely related to Saturn and so forth. By bringing a healthy instinct to bear upon the profuse flowering of some plants you can see that they have a different relationship to the sun than a fungus or the lichen on a tree. Someone aged between 14 and 21 suffering from a disorder of the stomach or heart will certainly not be cured with tea made from Iceland moss,[52] and the ancient mystery centres would have been aware of this too, and would have looked to the juice from a sun-related plant, knowing this through their insight into the connection between human life and the cosmos.

Knowledge of this kind has been lost. Humanity has passed through a period of darkness, and must regain these insights but at a higher level now, illumined by our modern intelligence. They must and can be rediscovered; and the anthroposophic world-view is the start of this rediscovery of humanity's spiritual illumination in all areas of life.

The human being descends into the planetary sphere, and a time arrives shortly after the moon has begun to exert its influence when he loses the spirit germ of his physical body, which has already contracted and shrunk a great deal—these expressions are naturally coarse ones, but you will understand what I mean. This spirit germ of the physical body descends in advance of the human being himself, is passed to the parents, implants itself in a fertilized human embryo and there becomes the growth element before the human being descends himself. In other words, the germ of the body is already given over to earthly life at a time when we ourselves are still in a sense looking down upon the earth and seeing what will become of what we will be part of. As yet we still live free in the cosmos. Now the human being draws from the etheric world of the cosmos the powers needed for his etheric body, so that his being now consists of I, astral body and etheric body. And having acquired his etheric body in this way, he now unites with what his physical germ has become, which he himself first sent down in advance.

There is a huge wisdom in this sending down of the physical human germ in advance, and the subsequent coalescence, if I can call it that, of the etheric body. Imagine what would happen if in the pre-birth world we retained the configuration of our physical body while gathering our etheric body together, and the physical body was not yet infused by physical substance but only consisted of the forces that could later be infused with it in the womb. Imagine we did not send it down in advance but already imbued it with the etheric body before we had arrived in the substance of the physical embryo, and with what is offered us there. What would happen? By grasping what would happen we can feel great wonder at the wisdom at work in the universe. If things were not as they are, then with every thought we formulate, every tendency towards evil we possess would stand before us. It would be as if we had a living memory continually of the slightest evil of any kind we had done on earth, even one committed in thoughts or feelings. The content of our conscience would run rampant in us, especially any kind of transgression, and then we would be unable to form any neutral thought about anything—for instance we would be unable to develop a knowledge of nature. If we wished to observe plants objectively and discern the natural laws at work in them, our observations would easily be tinged with thoughts such as these: 'What an awful person you were when you were 16, and what terrible things you did!' This would colour our observations, and make it impossible to form a neutral or objective view. The fact that we can keep these things apart, our simple, neutral observations from our moral or immoral instincts, is something we owe to the fact that we first send down our physical spirit germ and only then unite with this physical body once we have drawn our etheric body together. By virtue of this we hold these two aspects so far apart that in the physical body our memory can be held back, and not always impinge, leaving us free so that our whole moral life, especially, is not always present before us, and we can form thoughts in the etheric body of a neutral, reflective kind.

I have therefore now described how the human being descends from the world of spirit up to the moment when he unites with physical earth substance so as to be able to live on the earth. What emerges from this? As I said, it becomes apparent that there is great cause for wonder at the wise guidance at work in the universe when we realize that we first send down the configuring powers of our physical human body and then follow ourselves. If I really grasp this vividly I need not stand there empty-headed like someone who manufactures a machine and feels no need to admire it. I would have to be very arid indeed if I gazed on the revelation of such huge wisdom without an outpouring of wonder. The same is true of all anthroposophic insights.

The ordinary earthly knowledge we grasp in our waking minds

largely addresses our rational nature, and less so our feelings. This is not true of the insights we acquire from the world of spirit in inward experience. These address our whole being; in fact, they reorganize us entirely as we acquire and assimilate them. Spiritual-scientific insights will not, unlike physical knowledge, leave us cold, but this does not make them any less objective. If someone were to say that insights that engage our sensibility are not objective, are subjective, we can consider the following. If you stand in front of the *Sistine Madonna* by Raphael you'd have to be pretty thick-skinned to have no sense of wonder at it. But no one would dream of saying that the picture is simply subjective, and Raphael's *Madonna* has no objective existence. You see, we do not have to suppress all feelings of sympathy or antipathy in our souls when we look at an objective phenomenon. It is a matter only of ensuring that our subjective response does not disturb its objective reality. Of course, if we think something is an objective perception because it pleases us to assume it, this is due to our own predilection and therefore not objective! But if we find ourselves before something as objective as the insights I have described and then feel a sense of great wonder, such wonder will certainly not cloud the objectivity of the insight. The essential quality of anthroposophic or spiritual-scientific insights is that they do not address our rational mind alone, our head, but our whole being. Someone who becomes familiar with truths of this kind in increasing number, truths that relate to the life of the human being between death and a new birth, will find a life of feeling springing up in him, and subsequently a will life too. This means that we imbue our impulses for action with the insights we gain from higher worlds. And then we feel our task here on earth to be that of fulfilling what we were in the life of spirit between death and a new birth.

A truly experienced anthroposophy therefore certainly has the intrinsic power to fill the whole human being, just as did instinctive clairvoyance, an instinctive connection with the world of spirit, for ancient humanity. But what has made us such intellectuals nowadays, and why were ancient people not like this? It is because in those times what people knew, the laws they lived by, originated in their whole being. Today for instance we learn geometry, are taught, say, what a vertical is. But for us, mostly, this floats—well, not in the air, one cannot even say that—in an ideal realm, and people fail to see any connection with themselves. We would never actually be able to gain any sense of a vertical if we ourselves had not become vertical, learning to stand upright. We therefore feel the nature of verticality in our movements. And what the whole person experiences his head experiences too and conceptualizes it as the vertical. Similarly, what we experience when we spread out our arms leads to an experience of the horizontal. Originally human faculties lived in our whole being, but this gradually confined itself to the head, which can only represent things pictorially. And what does our head do? When I walk I live in a different way from when I drive in a car—the car drives along and I rest inside it. The head does the same thing really; it is lazy and piggy-backs on the rest of my organism. It allows itself to be transported and everything in it is at rest, like sitting in a train carriage. This is why everything becomes abstract image, an abstract state we have arrived at through the long course of earthly evolution. But we must return to a state that allows us to grasp the spiritual within existence, and this is something that takes hold of our whole being. This is the reverse process from the one that happened with ancient peoples; but by means of it we can again come to enquire into the whole human being, can thus return to a culture and civilization that fills our whole nature and being.

Today there are some who listen to what spiritual science presents and then say: 'How odd these anthroposophists are. They propound spiritual-scientific truths and say these are needed by humanity. No doubt worlds such as the spiritual scientists describe may indeed exist, but what does this matter to us? We can happily wait until we die and then we'll see if there's truth in it. What is the point in exerting ourselves here to understand the nature of a world of spirit?' But they are mistaken. You see, if you wish to understand the significance of spiritual perception—I'm speaking of course of the kind that healthy common sense can entertain once a spiritual researcher has made his findings known—the best way to do so is by engaging with an explanation, arising from spiritual research, of the first stage of supersensible knowledge, that of Imagination. Let me describe a few characteristics of this.

Ordinarily we are only aware of the present moment, conveyed to us by our physical body, which lives in space. Space with its three dimensions represents the present moment, and we are only aware of this. A memory, you see, exists from the present perspective: we do not re-experience what we experienced ten years ago when we remember it, but only have an image of what we experienced, one that is therefore fairly shadowy and abstract. By seriously undertaking the exercises I describe in *Knowledge of the Higher Worlds* to acquire the capacity of Imagination, it gradually becomes possible not just to live in the present but to overcome the shadowy nature of memory and to *live*, also, in one's past memories. Thus in 1922 it is possible to re-experience things that happened in 1911 in the same vivid way as one originally experienced them. If you make special efforts to live in thoughts—and I do not mean living in abstractions, but in something fully tangible which allows you to grasp how living in thoughts brings with it moments of destiny and all kinds of experience, profound sympathy and antipathy, as otherwise only actual, material life on earth—besides your ordinary experience of your spatial body you will also come to an experience of your temporal body. If I cut my big toe for instance, this hurts; and I have an immediate experience of pain and not just a memory of this pain even though the head is a good distance away from the foot. There is of course a spatial connection between head and toe, and the experience of time is different. If at the age of 30 you think back to what you experienced when you were 16, which is now removed from you in time, the memory is pale. Or picture what you felt when you lost a dearly loved person, say 13 years ago, and how pale this pain now is compared to the reality you felt at the time. But if you acquire the capacity for imaginative perception through the exercises described in *Knowledge of the Higher Worlds*, so that you know how to live in thoughts—that is, in pure, sense-free thoughts as I described in *The Philosophy of Freedom*—then you will live simultaneously, with equal vigour, in every part of your temporal body in the same way that you ordinarily live in every part of your spatial body. Then, at 50 or 60, or even 80 you do not just look back five years, but—since present existence extends across the whole of one's life—you are immediately present in every moment of your life. This immediacy and presence, however, is bought at the cost of its fugitive, fleeting character. If you are able to experience with this vividness something that occurred when you were 18, it won't fade quite as rapidly as a dream, but you cannot hold fast to it, you have to forget it again. And as a spiritual researcher, if one found no other aid or remedy, this would place you in a very difficult situation. You would be able to create the connections by means of which you can discern things in the etheric world, but you would immediately forget them again. For this reason you have to resort to all kinds of aids—I described the details of this in *Knowledge of the Higher Worlds*—so that what you acquire through this spiritual-etheric vision does not immediately disappear again. It will certainly fade after a couple of days, with the same rapidity as a person's ether body fades and dissipates after death.

This experience I have described gives one insight into the whole nature of the etheric. Accounts of the life after death are not fabricated but won from living perception. However, if you wish to use aids as I described, mere head activity will never be sufficient. I am describing what I myself experienced when I noticed the fleeting nature of such perceptions in the etheric cosmos. However much you perceive initially, after a week you have to have recourse to something else if you are to tell others of your experiences, but this help is not available from the head's capacities. One excellent remedy for the problem is to write down what has been experienced while it is still vivid, an activity that does not pass through the head therefore but through the writing hand. I do not mean mediumistic writing, nor writing with the aim of recording and preserving the experience. Recording things in this way—even writing down the content of a lecture afterwards—is actually something extremely unattractive from a spiritual perspective. But it is an aid to fixing something otherwise very fleeting by getting the whole organism to participate in it in a way we otherwise only do in drawing or painting. Then it remains in your organism and there is no further need to appropriate it again afterwards. It is just a question of fixing things. You have to fix them through something that involves your whole being, and writing down what you experience is one such means. But be clear that you are not involved here in any kind of intellectual activity. The only thing that counts is the flow of writing itself; or you can also make a symbolic drawing, painting or suchlike.

You can see from this the intimate connection between the whole human being and the capacity to convey in ordinary ideas what one perceives in the world of spirit. Having 'translated' such perceptions one can convey them to others who do not have spiritual perceptions, but who grasp them through these same ideas with their healthy human reason. They then possess the same ideas as the clairvoyant presents to them. To discern and discover spiritual-scientific truths, a clairvoyant art is needed; but to live with these truths one does not need it. One need only bring healthy powers of insight and understanding to bear on what is communicated.

But from what I have said you can gather something else. What we are spiritually in our ether body does not live in space but in time. Consider the physical organism, for instance the eye; you perceive visible things by means of it. If you pluck out your eyes you can no longer see visible things. If you consider our spiritual nature, this is in a sense the whole stream passing from one life to another, existing between death and a new birth, then in physical life on earth, and then again in a life between death and rebirth. All this is a unity. In ancient times people were naturally endowed with clairvoyant faculties on earth. In other words they had a connection with worlds of spirit simply by virtue of natural powers, and this was reconfigured in them so that they could take it with them again through death—as long as their knowledge of the spirit did not cease. In our modern era, this knowledge must not cease either; we must acquire it while here on earth in the ongoing stream of our existence. Once your life on earth has ended, if you knew nothing at all of the spirit while you were alive this is precisely the same for spiritual life as plucking out your eyes would be for your power of physical vision. What you learn on the earth as knowledge about the life of spirit belongs to you—it is the eye with which you later 'see' between death and a new birth. But if you remain 'in the dark' on earth in relation to knowledge of the life of spirit, you will be blind to it after death; and then, between death and rebirth it will be like passing through a valley of darkness. You have to develop your eyes for the world of spirit through what you acquire here on earth, and by negating or excluding any knowledge of it you are actually plucking them out.

Humanity has to become fully aware of this. Now that an ancient, instinctive clairvoyance has faded altogether, humankind must realize that organs to perceive the spirit must again be developed by efforts such as those undertaken in the anthroposophic movement. You can't wait until death. It is not true to say that no efforts are needed to understand spiritual worlds because you will find out what the world of spirit is like after death. Certainly, you'll see something, but for the soul it will be like dwelling in a dark dungeon if, in this life between birth and death, we have not developed an eye for life in the spiritual worlds. The dogma that there is no need to concern oneself with supersensible existence during life on earth is wholly misguided. In fact, we live in an era when we must try to meet our true supersensible obligations to the cosmos, and this is something we only do if we acknowledge that between birth and death we must acquire an eye for the spirit. Then, after death, things will not be shrouded in darkness for us, and we can experience the light that will then be around us.

Some time ago when I was here[53] I spoke of our relationship with the spiritual world and ended by saying this: in our era we have reached the point where it is necessary for a core of people to form who recognize the need for spiritual-scientific insight and knowledge. What I have said today doubly confirms this. We live in an age when the world of spirit wishes to show itself to us during our life on earth. We must not close the doors and windows through which it can enter. We must draw back the curtains and let in the light of the world of spirit, for the sake of life on earth itself; we must let it shine in for the sake of the life we live between death and a new birth. We must hearken to the voices that speak spiritually to us from the world of spirit, and must say: 'It is time for us to perceive the light of the spirit and hearken to the voice of the spirit.' Once we have come to know what spiritual-scientific insights can tell us of the needs of contemporary life, the right outlook will prevail in any domain of work. We will recognize our obligation to lead humanity to the point where it sees that the time has come to perceive the light of the spirit, to hear the voice of the spirit and to understand it.

In times when geographical distance separates us, let us remain united, let us stay connected in these thoughts, and especially in this feeling and outlook. I'd like to leave you with this greeting: 'May the words spoken when destiny brings us together hold sway amongst us as thought, as a spiritually present sense of belonging when we can no longer be gathered in one place.' But nevertheless, I hope I will soon be able to speak further of these things in your midst![54]

Lecture 16

Last time[55] I spoke to you about certain spiritual realities of our relationship with supersensible worlds—I could equally say, of the relationship between our human existence on earth and that between death and a new birth. This is because our life between birth and death is so bound up with the physical, sensory world that it seems to us as if our life consists of this physical, sensory reality. Between death and rebirth, on the other hand, our life is entirely interwoven with the supersensible world of spirit, and seems to be encompassed by that different reality.

Today I would like to continue this theme by discussing several other related facts and also the important conclusions we can draw from them. First and foremost, anthroposophic spiritual science can give us a vivid awareness that in considering ourselves here in the physical world we find before us a real reflection, a picture of the supersensible world. A rock or a mineral is not a direct reflection of supersensible reality in the same way. Its nature is something I have described in my book *Theosophy*. By contrast the human being cannot in many respects be understood at all simply in terms of what we see around us in the physical world of the senses. What surrounds us in physical reality allows us to grasp why salt crystals are cuboid in shape. While scientists have not yet fully explained what causes such things, we can say that a salt crystal can be understood in terms of what can be discovered directly in the realm perceptible to the senses. A human eye or ear, on the other hand, do not originate in, and cannot be explained by, factors in the physical, sensory world perceived by the physical senses. We are born with the inner form and external shape of an eye or an ear, bringing it with us as innate capacity. We do not acquire these either at fertilization or through powers at work in the womb; and the word 'genetic inheritance' will not do, either, as vehicle for all that we do not really understand. This merely perpetuates illusion. The truth is that the inner forming of eye or ear is innate in us as disposition, and is in a sense developed in advance in the spiritual realm of pre-earthly human existence. This happens in collaboration with higher spiritual beings, the beings of the higher hierarchies. Between death and a new birth in many respects we ourselves develop the spiritual form, spiritual germ or seed, of our future physical body, then implant this spirit germ, after shrinking or contracting it to the necessary extent, into our physical DNA. By this means, spirit is filled with physical, sense-perceptible substance, becoming a physical, sense-perceptible embryo. But the whole form, the inner form of an eye, the inner form of an ear, are elaborated from the work we undertake between death and rebirth with supersensible beings of spirit. When we consider a human eye, therefore, or an ear we must not assert that, like the salt crystal, they are comprehensible in terms of what can be perceived around us in the sense-perceptible world. If we wish to understand a human eye or ear we have to resort to secrets we can discover in the supersensible world. We must realize that the form of an ear for instance—let's stay with this now— emerges from the supersensible world, and only after it has been so formed does it embark on its sensory task in the medium of air, hearing physical tones or speech sounds in the earthly realm in a physical way. Thus the human being is a reflection of processes and beings in the supersensible world.

Let us consider the specific details of this for a moment. In tracing the inner form of the human ear we look through the external auditory passage and see what is called the eardrum. Behind it sit the three tiny ossicles which science calls the hammer, anvil and stirrup. Passing beyond these we enter the inner ear, which I will not now describe in full. The very names science gives to these tiny bones shows that it does not have the faintest idea of what is involved there. Illumined by anthroposophic spiritual science, we can find—and I am moving from within outwards in my reflections here—that the 'stirrup' or stapes connected to the inner ear appears as a transformed, metamorphosed thigh bone or femur interlocking with the hip. What science calls 'anvil', this tiny ossicle, appears as a transformed kneecap or patella; and the ossicle pointing from this anvil towards the eardrum, the 'hammer', appears as a transformed lower leg or shank, with the foot attached. Here the 'foot' in the ear is not resting on the ground of course, but on the eardrum. Inside your ear you do actually have a transformed limb. You could also compare this with the arm: upper arm and lower arm, although the 'anvil' would be missing from that picture since the 'kneecap' part is not properly developed in the arm. Just as your two legs negotiate the ground and sense it, so the 'foot' in your ear, that tiny ossicle, senses the eardrum. The difference is only that the earthly foot you walk on is coarser in form, and you use it to sense the ground in a fairly rough and ready way, whereas the hand or foot you have in your ear is continually sensing the fine resonance of the eardrum. If you continue inwards you come to the 'cochlea', filled with fluid. All this is necessary for hearing. What the 'foot' senses at the eardrum has to be conveyed inwards into the cochlea lying in the auditory chamber. Above our femur lie our innards or intestines; and this cochlea in the ear is in fact a very finely developed kind of intestine. In this way you can actually picture a human being in the ear, whose head is embedded in our brain. In fact we bear within us a whole number of more or less metamorphosed human forms, and this one inside the ear is just one of them.

What is actually at work here? You see, someone who studies human development with more than the coarse, sensory means employed by modern science, and who knows that this human embryo forming in the womb is an image of a life preceding earthly life, will also know that the initial stages of embryonic development essentially form the incipient head. The rest of the embryo consists of small appendage organs. These appendages, little stumps that become the legs and feet, could equally well become a kind of ear if it were only a matter of the embryo's own inner capacities in the womb. The appendages have the potential to become an ear. In other words, the human foetus could certainly grow an ear down below there, as well as here and here. This seems paradoxical but it is absolutely true. We could also grow an ear where our limbs are. Why does this not happen? It does not because, at a certain stage of development in the womb, the embryo falls under the sway of earthly gravity. Gravity, which makes a stone fall earthwards, encumbers it with weight, bears down on a part of the embryo seeking to become ear, and reconfigures the whole of our lower organism from it. Under the sway of earthly gravity the ear that seeks to grow below becomes instead our lower body. And why does the ear itself not grow its ossicles into pretty little legs emerging from the right and left of our head? This is simply because the whole position of the human embryo in the womb protects the ear from succumbing to the realm of gravity in the same way as the leg appendages. For this reason the ear retains for longer the predisposition it acquired in pre-earthly existence in the world of spirit; it is a pure image of these worlds of spirit. But what lives in these spiritual worlds? Well, I have often spoken of the reality of the music of the spheres; and as soon as we enter the world of spirit that lies beyond the soul world, we find ourselves in a world that lives altogether in sounds and tones, in melody, harmony and tonal accords. And from this realm of tones and sound the human ear forms. We can say therefore that our ear preserves a memory of our spiritual, pre-earthly existence, which we have forgotten in our lower human organism, instead adapting the latter to earthly gravity, to all that originates in weight. If we understand the human form properly, the way we are shaped and configured, we can always discern how one organ system has adapted more to the earth while another remains more in tune with pre-earthly existence. Consider, after all, that even after we're born we perpetuate the predisposition implanted in our embryo. Only after we are born do we learn to stand upright and walk, to integrate ourselves fully into gravity and orientate ourselves in the three directions of space. But the ear removes itself from these three dimensions and retains its affinity with the world of spirit. As human beings our form is partly always a living memorial to the work we undertook with higher beings between death and a new birth; and partly also it bears witness to the fact that we incorporate ourselves into earthly existence which is subject to the sway of gravity, of weight.

But such reconfigurations do not just happen in the direction I have now described. The reverse is true also. You walk around on the earth by using your legs, and they carry you—forgive me—into good, better and worse actions. Ultimately it is all one to the legs themselves whether they are walking into good or evil deeds with you. Yet as true as it is that the lower human organism arises through metamorphosis of a potential ear, so that we can stand upon earth with our legs, so it is equally true that all morality enacted by our capacity for movement—whether you walk towards good deeds or bad—is transformed after you pass through the gate of death into tones and sounds: not immediately, but after some time.

Let us assume, therefore, that someone has been carried away into a bad action. Here on earth all we can see is that his legs have carried him for this purpose. But the bad deed attaches to these leg movements when you pass through the gate of death. After laying aside the physical body and also the ether body, everything embodied in such leg movements is transformed into a discord or dissonance in the world of spirit. And the whole of our lower organism is reconfigured back into head organization. The way you have moved upon earth becomes head organization after death, and is imbued with a moral nuance. And then you hear with these new ears how you behaved morally in the earthly world. Your moral actions become beautiful music, your immorality becomes ugly discord. And from these harmonious or dissonant tones you hear emerging the words of judgement as spoken by the higher hierarchies upon your deeds.

Thus by observing the human being himself we see how a transition occurs from the world of spirit into the sense world and from the sense world back into the world of spirit again, through one transformation after another. Your head organism is used up, exhausted in your present incarnation, in this earthly life where it is fitted to perceive the spirit within the sensory realm. But after death this head falls away and the other part of your being—everything other than the head—transforms after death into a spiritual head, a head organism; and this other part of you will become your head in your next life. You see, the very form of the human being expresses the reality of recurring lives on earth. No one can understand the human head if he does not regard it as a transformation of the body a person had in his previous life. And no one can understand the body as it appears now without seeing in it the seed of a head in a person's next life. To fully comprehend the human being we have to permeate what we perceive through our senses with perceptions of, and insights into the supersensible realm.

There are various other specific things we can outline in connection with this. Last time I spoke here I said that in the period between death and rebirth we experience a state in which we become fully united inwardly with the beings of the higher hierarchies. Basically, we forget ourselves, actually *becoming* the higher hierarchies. We would never come back to ourselves if we could not extinguish this feeling of the higher hierarchies within us. Precisely by going out of ourselves we return to ourselves again. By contrast, here on earth we come to ourselves when we disregard the outer world and focus upon our inner experience, whereas between death and a new birth we come to ourselves when we disregard what is within us—the higher hierarchies. The powers that later remain available to us from the return to ourselves are the powers of memory, while the powers that remain with us from our union with the beings of the higher hierarchies are those of morality and love—all that enables us to lovingly extend our own being on earth to other beings. In our earthly capacity to love we must see an echo of our life in union with the higher hierarchies; and in our memory we have an echo of the other state when, during the life between death and a new birth, we release ourselves from the higher hierarchies and come back to ourselves.

A little while back I suggested that this resembles the process of breathing. We have to breathe in to enliven ourselves; and then we breathe out the 'air of death', one might say, since what is exhaled is not something we can live in. In the same way, we breathe spiritually in the world between death and rebirth, uniting ourselves with the beings of the higher hierarchies, then departing from them again. On earth we have an after-echo of this heavenly breathing. The fact that we can walk upon earth means that we adapt to earth's gravity. This is the experience of weight—through the transformed ear, as I said. And if we see things in the right light we can discern how in our organs of speech and singing we possess a metamorphosis of the predisposition we have in the world of spirit as we pass through pre-earthly existence. Here on this earth we adapt our speech organs to human language. Between death and rebirth we assimilate the Logos, the cosmic word, incorporate it into ourselves; and our whole organ of speech and singing is elaborated from this cosmic language. In the same way—though less strongly—that we transform this downward-extending ear into our limbs for our directional walking, so we also transform our organ of speech and singing. In the case of the ear, we have only a faithful copy, if you like, of what developed in the world of spirit in pre-earthly existence, whereas the organ of speech occupies a middle position in this regard. We only learn to speak after birth of course. But that is really just an illusion. In truth the cosmic language, the Logos, forms our larynx and our whole speech and singing organ. We forget the universal Logos as we incline towards earth and pass through the embryo stage, but what has pushed itself down into the unconscious realm is refreshed and reawoken when we acquire human language.

But in this human speech basically we can hear both earthly qualities and what the spirit has shaped. We would be unable to form consonants if we could not adapt to external, earthly things. If you have some sense of these things, you will be able to feel that one consonant is reminiscent of something angular while another recalls something seedlike. In the consonants we adapt ourselves to the forms, the configurations which the external world presents us with. In vowels, on the other hand, we voice our inner experience. If you say 'Ah' you know that something like wonder or amazement lives in you, which this vowel expresses. 'Oh' likewise voices an inner experience: each vowel expresses an inner quality.

You see, one day science will be imbued with spiritual science, and will be all the more interesting: it will discover that in cultures whose languages have a greater preponderance of consonants, people cannot so easily be held to account for their moral actions since they are less responsible for these actions than are people who speak languages more fully endowed with vowels. The vowels are an echo of our community with the spiritual hierarchies. We bring this with us, bear it into earthly conditions, and it remains in us as the manifestation of our own being. In consonants, on the other hand, we adapt to the outer world. The world of consonants is an earthly one. If we could imagine a language consisting only of consonants, it would be a language which an initiate would tell you relates to the earth. If you wish to have more of a heavenly element, you would need to add the vowels. But watch out, for then you become responsible to the divine realm, which cannot be treated so profanely as the consonantal realm.

In recognition of this, the ancient Hebrews only indicated the vowels in their script, writing the consonants alone. Basically, heaven and earth resound together in our speech; and here once again we see how we have something that belongs to our middle realm and is, as it were, oriented in two ways—towards both the heavenly and the earthly. The head is entirely oriented to heaven, the lower organism to the earth; but the latter strives towards heaven, and to such a degree that it actually becomes it once we have passed through the gate of death. Our middle sphere, which includes breathing, along with speech and song that are carried on the flow of breath, connects heaven and earth. This is why this middle sphere is in every respect the disposition in us primarily inclined to artistic expression, to the uniting of heaven and earth. And so we can sum up by saying the following. As we observe the developing human being we find he is born without any orientation in the world; he cannot yet walk or stand. He is born with the potential to relate to gravity, something he acquired prior to birth when gravity prevailed over his organism, apart from the head. Organs of sight and hearing are wrested free of gravity. We then develop spatial orientation and learn to stand upright and walk. This is a capacity we acquire after birth of course, since the world of spirit has not yet configured us to master spatial orientation. If we did already possess this orientation, while we might be able to sleep on the earth—since, after all, the auditory ossicle that represents the foot has a horizontal orientation—we would be unable to walk. Something similar is true of the eye. You see, one thing we only learn fully on the earth is to adapt what we acquired in pre-earthly existence to the earth's gravity. The second thing, as we learn to speak and sing, is to adapt to our earthly surroundings. And then we also learn to think. We are born without any orientation towards walking or standing; we are born without speech, and we are also born without thoughts. One cannot, you see, say that infants can already think. These three things we learn fully only on earth—and all three are the metamorphosis of other capacities we possessed in pre-earthly existence. All three of them are living memorials to the spiritual disposition laid down in us in pre-earthly life.

Now last time I described how memory here on earth is the echo of our self-awareness in the world of spirit, while love in all forms is the echo of our experience of being poured out into the world of the higher hierarchies, and merging with this world. And now we have our physical abilities, walking, speaking, singing and thinking. To think that earthly thinking is a spiritual capacity is mistaken, for it is certainly tied to the physical body, just as walking is; and so we have our most outstanding corporeal abilities as a transformation or metamorphosis of something spiritual. What spiritual attribute do we have on earth? Sensory perception! The fact that we can hear, smell, taste and so on, everything involved in sense perception, relies on organs lying at the outer periphery of our organism which are elaborated from the highest spiritual regions. The ear originates in the harmony of the spheres. It is formed so strongly from the harmony of the spheres that it remains safe from gravity. And the way the ear is embedded in its fluid is to protect it from gravity, so gravity cannot get a purchase on it. The ear is really not a citizen of the earth but a citizen rather of the loftiest spiritual world. So are the eye and the other sense organs. If we consider the body in walking, speaking, singing and thinking, we find a metamorphosis there of the spiritual realm in pre-earthly existence. In the soul domain, memory and love are a transformation of spiritual life in pre-earthly existence. And the senses, lastly, are metamorphoses of the most sublime spiritual realm of pre-earthly existence.

Here our anthroposophic science of the spirit connects with Goetheanism, with things Goethe was already aware of; but it also takes it further, entirely in keeping with the spirit of Goethe. I have often quoted Goethe's phrase about the eye being formed 'by light for light'.[56] This is true—but it is not formed by and for the light we actually see. The light we see could never create the inner formative powers for an eye. Take a human countenance—its noble brow, the jutting nose, the eyes and whole physiognomy. Then add gestures. We might record all this by some device but this would only give us its shapes and forms. But if we look at a person before us we are not content with the spatial discernment of form; instead we look through the spatial forms and movements of a person's gestures to the soul at work in them. Sunlight reaches us. There is the sun outside us and sunlight shines down. That is the external aspect, behind which is hidden the other aspect, the spirit of the sunlight. And it is in this soul and this spirit that we dwell between death and rebirth, where light is something different. When you speak of someone's glance or look and are speaking of a soul quality that reaches us through their eyes, you are really speaking of something that lies behind the eyes in the realm of soul. And if I speak of the spiritual quality in light, this is the soul of light. An eye that already exists sees the external aspect of light, its physical property. But the eye itself is formed by the spirit, the soul of light, by what underlies or lies behind it. And so if we have really understood what Goethe means we ought to say: the eye sees the light but is formed, created by the soul and spirit of the light, before it acquires physical corporeality here on the earth.

The whole human being presents us with reconfigured spiritual essence that passes back again into a spiritual condition. At death you pass back your physical sense organs to the earth. But what lives in the physical sense organs shines forth between death and a new birth and actually becomes your inner community with the spiritual beings of the higher hierarchies. And now you will understand the extent to which the resonant earthly world is a physical reflection of the harmony of the heavenly spheres, and how we are not an outcome of these earthly powers but of the heavenly powers, and integrate ourselves into earthly powers. We have seen how we do this. Our lower organism would become ear if we remained heavenly, and could not walk but would have to acquire a different means to move—would move upon the waves of cosmic harmony instead, just as, in a small reflection of this, the ossicle moves on the waves of the ear drum. We learn to hear with our ears, and with our larynx and the organs situated around the mouth we learn to speak and sing.

Let us imagine that you hear a particular word, say 'tree'. You can speak this word yourself, and connect a meaning with it. Hearing the word 'tree' means that what you utter in the simple word 'tree' lives in your ear in the way I have just described, in organs formed as the embodiment of heavenly activities. When you utter the word 'tree' this means that earthly air passes through the larynx and the instrument of your mouth in a shape and formation which manifests this word, which you also hear. But there's more than this—something not generally perceived sufficiently. When you hear the word 'tree' your etheric body quietly says 'tree' as well. This is something you do not do with your physical body but your etheric body. Through the Eustachian tube, which passes from mouth to ear, etherically the word 'tree' rises from within to meet the word 'tree' coming from outside you; they resonate together. The two meet and by virtue of this you understand the word. Otherwise you would hear it and it could be anything. You only grasp it, understand it, because, through the Eustachian tube, you say back the word coming from without. And as the vibrations from without meet those from within and interweave, inwardly we understand what comes towards us from without.

You see how wonderful is the interplay of things in the human organism. But something else is connected with this. Imagine that you wish to enquire into the nature of the human ear, eye, nose and so forth. Fine. You tell yourself that science has made wonderful advances and that although such progress is expensive it is worth it. So we purchase ourselves a large volume on physiology or anatomy; or we sign up for a university course and attend lectures on the eye or ear. You can learn a great deal in this way—and yet I think it is true to say that your soul will remain unmoved. Your sensibility will stay cold. Listen to how physiology describes the ear; your feelings will not be engaged. In this sense the account is very objective. But when I describe things to you as I now have done, how we understand the word 'tree', how the ear is an image of heavenly activity, I would like to meet the person who feels no stirring of feeling, who fails to sense the wonderful nature of these phenomena. As I gave the description today, it is incomplete, and needs to be rounded out. But one would have to be inwardly arid to feel no sense of wonder at such things, at the way we human beings emerge from the world of spirit and incorporate ourselves into the physical world.

Anthroposophic spiritual science has this quality. It presents these things with as much objectivity as mainstream science. There is nothing subjective mixed in with my account of the ear formed from the heavenly spheres, but at the same time one's feelings and sensibility are engaged. The second aspect of our being, our soul life, which is intimately connected with the whole of our human nature, is also engaged. In other words, what the head acquires through such a science at the same time involves the heart. Anthroposophic science draws on the human heart and is therefore not just 'head' knowledge. It not only fills the head but fills us fully, the whole of us with our blood circulation and heart as well. If you take seriously what I have said then you can apply this in turn to the movement of the legs, study the mechanism of leg movements from this perspective. If you read up on the physiology of leg movements as mainstream science describes this, you will certainly not feel any stirring of your sense of responsibility. But the moment you learn that the good or bad actions into which you are carried by your legs resound towards you after death as harmony or discord, then your knowledge about the human being will immediately be associated with a sense of responsibility, one that henceforth accompanies your will actions. Not only our feelings but our will too is invoked by what our head initially assimilates in just as objective a way as in empirical science; but then it reaches beyond the head, pushes further into our feelings and will. For this reason anthroposophic science speaks to the whole human being, contrary to the increasingly current view that knowledge is only worthy of the name if it addresses the head alone. What speaks only to the head leaves the soul and sensibility cold, and does not begin to impinge on our will.

We do face a crisis at present, and this means it is essential to acquire knowledge of supersensible worlds through our whole being. Even at the first stage of this, knowledge gained through Imagination, we have to actively develop this faculty. We develop ordinary knowledge in certain academic circles that are particularly suited to it: we load ourselves up with this knowledge like beasts of burden, commit it to memory, fill our minds with it. By contrast, if we practise exercises such as those I described in *Knowledge of the Higher Worlds* and thereby acquire imaginative perception, or if we have the inner disposition to see the world in spiritual terms as I described this capacity in my book on Goethe's world-view, then we are already practising etheric perception, which is, at the same time, a more direct form of experience. Then we no longer have to give ourselves up so passively to the world. You cannot cram yourself with spiritual science in the same way as theoretical knowledge, and those who are used to such a yoke will not take kindly to the liberation of spiritual science. But it has to be developed actively. You have to be inwardly active; and even then it is true that what we first acquire in Imagination is very fleeting and soon vanishes. It does not easily lodge in the mind or memory. After three days it will have faded, certainly—everything gained by exerting the faculty of Imagination will be gone. This is also why our memory in the ether body fades roughly three days after death. The length of time varies. You can read more about this in my book *Occult Science*. Our memories remain with us for about three days, until the etheric body dissipates. And in the same way, someone who has developed the ability to perceive etherically knows that, without all the efforts needed to bring down this knowledge into ordinary concepts, it will have evaporated after three days.

You can already see from this that imaginative thinking addresses the whole person, and that this whole person must live in such imaginative perception. In still higher forms of knowledge this is so to an even greater extent. There is no cause for surprise at this. We can also come to recognize that a great deal more exists in the world than the outer senses can perceive. Above all, we can discover the possibility of living in a world in which the dimensions of space no longer have any meaning. Music gives us a foretaste of this, of a non-spatial realm. Physical space is outside us, really, externally present, whereas within us, in the sphere where music is realized, space only plays a role, at most, as a kind of after-image. In imaginative perception, the spatial element gradually ceases entirely and everything becomes temporal. In the realm of Imagination, time has the role which space has in the physical realm. And this now leads us to another thing: to the realization that temporal things remain. The temporal realm is in fact an enduring realm. If you develop the capacity for imaginative perception you will gradually learn to perceive every moment of the life on earth you have had so far—you can become 18 again even when you're very old. You can perceive your youth with the same vividness as you perceived it when you were 18. Imagine that when you were 18 you lost someone you loved a great deal. Try to picture the vividness of your grief at the time. Then think how pale the memory of such an event will have become after 30 years, or not even 30—less will do. Memories fade even in the most deeply feeling person, and this is inevitable in ordinary outward life on earth. But precisely because a memory fades as time passes, it remains within you as a real part of your human nature. And we can indeed transport ourselves back, and *are* transported back after death, experiencing what occurred with the same intensity once more. This is part and parcel of our human nature; what we have experienced remains and is only 'past' because of how we perceive things.

If you were born at the age of 7—living, say, in some different form of existence, in some kind of embryonic condition—and were then born, and got your second teeth straight away (so that you had already had your first teeth in the embryo) you could never develop a religious sensibility. A disposition to be religious could no longer take effect in the further course of your life on earth. All the religious sensibility you possess is present because the first seven years of your life are still there in you. You do not perceive them as being present and yet they are there and present in you. In our first seven years we are entirely surrendered to the outer world. The religious mood is embodied in this, and we transfer it to other things. In these first seven years we have an urge to imitate everything around us; and later this same mood flows into devotion to the soul-spiritual realm.

If we were not born until we were 14, entering immediately into puberty, we would never develop morality since this is something we have to acquire through the inner development of rhythm between the ages of 6 and 14. This is why we have such influence on a person's moral education in primary school, as something we later carry in us. We always carry everything in us. If you cut your big toe, this is a good distance away from your head, but the pain you feel is still experienced via the head. If you have a religious sensibility today this is because something still works in you that you inwardly experienced up to the age of 6 or so, until the change of teeth, but at that time experienced only as devotion to your outer surroundings. In the same way that you feel pain in your big toe through the activity of your head, what you experienced up to the age of 6 or 7 is still active in you when you are 40. It is present.

This has an important consequence. There are a great many people who say that anthroposophic spiritual science is fine in its way, and it's nice to hear about supersensible worlds; but they wonder why they need to know about experiences between death and a new birth since they will find out soon enough when they die. If we meet these worlds between death and rebirth, they think, why should we learn about them now? Why bother making such effort to learn about the spiritual world while still alive on earth?

Well, dear friends, this is not how it is. The temporal realm is real. Just as the spatial realm is reality here in the physical world, so the temporal realm, and even the super-temporal, is reality for the supersensible world. Here, later in your life, the child still lives in you. When you pass through the gate of death, the whole of this life is present in you in a single moment, belongs to you, to your organization. As a person here in physical space you might just as well ask why you need an eye, since light is all around you, as ask why we need spiritual science on earth. Light exists everywhere, but we need an eye to perceive it. When we enter the realm of spirit, we have the light of spirit all around us; and what we learn through anthroposophic spiritual science is not lost but becomes the eye with which we perceive spiritual light after death. If, at our current stage of human evolution, we do not cultivate a science of the spirit, we will have no eyes for the world of spirit when we come there and will be as if blind to what we experience.

In ancient times, as a consequence of their pre-earthly life, people still possessed an instinctive clairvoyance. This capacity faded and disappeared, and we no longer have it. Humankind had to acquire a sense of freedom in an interim phase of evolution. But it has now entered a further phase where it needs an eye for the spiritual world into which we enter at death. And people will not develop this eye if they do not acquire it here on earth. Just as a physical eye must be acquired in pre-earthly existence, so an eye for perceiving supersensible reality after death must be acquired here through spiritual science, through spiritual perception. This does not mean one has to become clairvoyant—which is a matter for each individual—but the eye for spiritual reality can be developed too by using our healthy common sense to understand the results of spiritual-scientific research. It simply is not true to say that we all have to gain perception of the world of spirit in order to believe what clairvoyants say. No, this is not so. If you use your healthy powers of reason you will see that the ear is really a heavenly organ. The reality of this can only be discovered by clairvoyant research but once discovered it can be understood. One need only allow oneself to think it through and feel one's way through it. And this recognition through healthy powers of reason of what has been discovered about the world of spirit—not clairvoyance itself—is what gives people clear vision after death. This eye of spirit is something the clairvoyant must also develop like anyone else. What we perceive through the faculty of Imagination, what we see clairvoyantly, fades after a few days; and we can only retain it by bringing it down into the perspective of ordinary comprehension. Then we are compelled to grasp it in the same way as understood by someone to whom we impart it. You see, clairvoyance as such is not humankind's immediate task on earth. Clairvoyance need only exist in order to discover supersensible truths. Our real task on earth is to comprehend supersensible truths with our ordinary healthy powers of reason.

This is extraordinarily important, and is not acknowledged even by subtler modern minds. In Berlin a little while ago, when I was explaining these things in a public lecture,[57] someone stated it was very wrong of me to say that spiritual science can be understood through healthy powers of human reason. He asserted dogmatically that the inherently healthy faculty of reason can grasp nothing spiritual, and that someone who does perceive spiritual things is for that reason unhealthy. He criticized me in those very terms. Such things are highly characteristic of our times—the idea that anyone who proposes the reality of the spirit must be in some way mentally ill. No greater wisdom than this is needed apparently, and such wisdom is, sadly, very widespread today. You can see from this how true it is, as I always say, that the time has now come again when humanity depends on assimilating spiritual understanding, integrating it and living with it. Anthroposophic spiritual science ought not to be something we acquire only theoretically. Those who do acquire it in a real sense must be aware that they are forming a core of humanity, of spreading numbers of people who know that to be fully human requires knowledge of their connection with the spirit. A magnificent feeling comes over us if we know this—and we must, above all, instil this knowledge into pedagogy and education. Ordinary head knowledge is morally neutral, really. As soon as we rise to spiritual realms we discover they are imbued with morality. You need only recall what I said: in community with the higher hierarchies we develop love; and morality on earth is only a reflection of our experiences in heavenly spheres. But how do we experience what we call 'good'? We make this our lived experience by recognizing that the human being is not just a physical but also a spiritual being. If we really live our way into the world of spirit, we learn to absorb the good through our spirit.

This is also the fundamental idea in *The Philosophy of Freedom*. We learn to absorb the good through the spirit, and if we do not do so we are not whole human beings. Then we are crippled or maimed. It is like losing both your arms. If your arms are amputated you will be physically crippled. If you lack the good, you are crippled in soul and spirit. Take this idea and employ it, and its effect on feeling and will, in education. Give people a *living sense* by the time they enter adolescence that they are only whole, only have the right to call themselves fully human, if they are good, then you will achieve real moral education, one fit for humanity—whereas all tub-thumping moral sermons will achieve nothing at all. If you educate people to regard morality as belonging intrinsically to their individual being, and to consider themselves as crippled in some way if they do not have a moral compass, are therefore not whole, they will discern moral qualities entirely within themselves rather than as outward exhortations. No doubt many schools of thought will think this an abomination, un-German[58] and so on, although it is in fact the purest outcome of German thinking. It is something that brings the spirit as close as possible to human beings, to each individual. And this is essential today, because only the single and separate human being, the human individual, can take on his own full sense of responsibility in our present age.

NOTES

Original texts: The lectures in Dornach, London and The Hague were transcribed by the professional stenographer Helene Finckh, and then typed out by her. The original shorthand transcripts are extant and were checked in relation to a few unclarities in the text. It is not known who was responsible for the shorthand transcripts of lectures given in Stuttgart and Berlin.

For the 3rd edition in 1992, Anna-Maria Balastèr checked through the text once more, adding a more comprehensive list of contents and notes, as well as an index of names.

Notebook entries by Rudolf Steiner relating to his lectures in London are published in *Beiträge zur Rudolf Steiner Gesamtausgabe*, no. 106, 1991.

The title of this volume (in German), chosen by H.W. Zbinden, is the same as that of the 1945 edition of the lectures of 20, 22 and 23 October 1922.

The titles of the lectures in London on 18, 19 and 20 November 1922 correspond to their prior announcement in *Das Goetheanum* periodical of 29 October 1922, and must have originated with Rudolf Steiner. When first published in *Das Goetheanum*, the lecture of 19 November 1922 was given the title 'Questions of Education and Teaching', and this was adopted also for the book edition. For the new edition of 1922, the original title was used. The titles of all other lectures in this volume originated with the editors of earlier single-lecture editions.

The board drawings: The original board drawings and captions by Rudolf Steiner for the lectures in Dornach have been preserved, with the exception of the second drawing for the lecture of 22 October 1922, as they were done on black paper pinned to a board. They have been published in reduced format in a separate supplementary volume in the series *Rudolf Steiner, Wandtafelzeichnungen zum Vortragswerk*. Drawings based on these representations were added to the text of earlier editions, and these drawings have been retained here.

1. See the second lecture in this volume.
2. See the first lecture in this volume.
3. Genesis 1:27.
4. Galatians 2:20.
5. See I Corinthians 15:14 ff.
6. After the lecture had ended, Rudolf Steiner spoke the following further words to his listeners:
   My dear friends, I need to add something at this point, and have often had to say something similar here in Stuttgart. This has nothing directly to do with the lecture. I am sorry that it has not been possible for me, as was once a kind of normal part of my presence here, to hold meetings in person with indivi-

duals. The fact is that my work here in Stuttgart has assumed such proportions that it completely fragments my powers. It has become necessary to try to ensure that as this work increases and expands I should only carry as much of it as is really dependent on me, and that the growth of the work does not lead to immeasurable new tasks for myself. You will therefore have to excuse me, my dear friends, that I had to give this lecture in a state of exhaustion and tiredness that I do not usually experience, but which is increasingly affecting me whenever I am here because the necessary help and support does not keep pace with the growth of the work in Stuttgart. I will therefore have to decline any private conversation or meeting with individuals during my stay here on this occasion. If things change, we can reinstate these individual meetings. But if things continue as they have been so that an increase in the work here confronts me increasingly with a whole host of diverse and unconnected demands, my day is filled from morning to night, and really everyone will understand if I have to excuse myself from offering the opportunity for personal conversations.

7. Rudolf Steiner, *Die Grundimpulse des weltgeschichtlichen Werdens der Menschheit*, GA 216.

8. The sculpture in wood of the 'Representative of Humanity' carved by Rudolf Steiner. This was to have been placed in the first Goetheanum and now stands in a special room in the second Goetheanum. At the end of this lecture Rudolf Steiner said: 'This is to happen in the next few days. But as I cannot be in Dornach from tomorrow, please bear with me if I give these two lectures on Sunday and Monday at 8 o'clock. I don't want to renege on any lecture commitment, but I can't be back soon enough tomorrow to be sure I can give the lecture.'

9. Lili Kolisko (1893–1976), *Milzfunktion und Plättchenfrage*, Stuttgart 1922.

10. Wolfram von Eschenbach, *c.* 1170–1220.
Hartmann von Aue, *c.* 1165–1260.
Gottfried of Strassburg, lived at the end of the twelfth century and beginning of the thirteenth.

11. Psalm 16:7.

12. Legend in verse composed by Hartmann von Aue.

13. Hippocrates of Kos, *c.* 460–377 BC.

14. Johann Gottlieb Fichte, 1762–1814. He stated this: 'Once they were over 30 one would have wished them to die for their own honour and the good of the world. From then on they lived only in a way which did increasing injury to themselves and their surroundings.' This passage comes from the fragment entitled 'Episode on our age, by a Republican author' (winter 1806/07) which was published by Fichte's son in the first complete edition of his works as volume VII, pp. 519 ff.

15. In the words spoken by Baccalaureus: 'If someone's reached the age of thirty / already he's as good as dead. / 'Twere best to kill him in good time.' *Faust* II, Act 2, Gothic Chamber.

16. Oswald Spengler, 1880–1936, cultural philosopher. *Der Untergang des Abendlandes*, Munich 1922.

17. At the end of this lecture Rudolf Steiner said: 'I have to break off this series of

lectures now for a while. The next lecture, after my return, will be announced in due course my dear friends.'

18. The lectures Steiner gave in Holland in The Hague, Rotterdam and Delft between 31 October and 6 November 1922 have not yet been published in the Collected Works. They were published in *Das Goetheanum*, 1941, nos. 35–48.

19. Galatians 2:20.

20. Lectures given in London: Rudolf Steiner lectured in German and divided each lecture into two or three parts, each of which was translated into English after he had given the respective section. The interruptions to allow for this are marked in the text by spaces.

21. In the lecture of 30 August 1922 on 'The Human Being's Experience of Sleep and the Life Between Death and Rebirth' In: *Das Geheimnis der Trinität*, GA 214. (*The Mystery of the Trinity*, SteinerBooks 1991.)

22. On 14 and 15 April 1922, included in CW 211, *The Sun Mystery and the Mystery of Death and Resurrection*, SteinerBooks 2006.

23. At the end of the lecture Steiner said: 'I wished to introduce our reflections here in this way, and we will continue them next time when we meet again.'

24. 'Guru' referred to a person who guided a pupil's esoteric development in oriental schooling, while 'chela' indicates the guru's pupil.

25. See the previous lecture in this volume, 12 November 1922.

26. See pp. 110f. in this volume.

27. See Steiner's comments in the semi-public lecture on 17 November 1922 on pp. 143f of this volume.

28. See the lecture of 30 August 1922 in *Das Geheimnis der Trinität*, GA 214, pp. 173 ff.

29. See pp. 148f. of this volume.

30. In Scene 6 of the fourth Mystery Play, *The Soul's Awakening*. The Guardian says: 'Know thy cosmic midnight hour!' *The Four Mystery Plays*, Rudolf Steiner Press 1982.

31. John 18:36.

32. At the end of the lectures given to members of the Anthroposophical Society in London, Rudolf Steiner concluded with these words:
And now my dear friends, as I take my leave of you I must say a few things which I beg you to regard in a sense as communications to branch members. Firstly I wish to thank the dear friends here very warmly for making these lectures possible. However, I also feel a duty to draw your attention to one or two other things so that no misunderstandings arise in relation to our anthroposophical movement.

This movement, you see, should not be some kind of vague, mystical, nebulous and theoretical movement that seeks to turn people away from life but should be one that enables us to lead the spirit into all spheres of life in practical ways. It certainly gives one the greatest pleasure to see, for example, that the educational movement has been initiated here. This is one of the streams through which anthroposophy can flow into the world, and there can be various others by means of which we must seek a connection with the rest of the world. But there is one thing we ought not to forget: that we can achieve nothing with all these movements arising as consequences of anthroposophy *if* we do not energetically cultivate the anthroposophical impulse itself, whose aim is to realize in the world the teachings of anthroposophy, the powers at work in it. Then people will increasingly recognize and understand what anthroposophy is, and it will spread ever further. It is this impulse we need chiefly to focus on, and I have a sense that we have here a good soil in which anthroposophy as such can thrive, so that real receptivity develops for anthroposophical ideas and thoughts.

Imagine that, miraculously, we succeeded in founding a great many schools. But what do we need for these schools? We need anthroposophically trained teachers; and if we initiate anything else too, it must be done fully out of anthroposophy. And so before we can even conceive of schools having a good effect more broadly, we need active anthroposophists. There would be a good soil here for direct propagation of the anthroposophic impulse itself. And we must regard this as the thing of most importance. Of chief importance is what introduces spiritual life into human sensibilities.

For instance, people think it is good for eurythmy if it is introduced into schools; and some may think that it will be less obvious there somehow, that eurythmy can slip in through education, without drawing much attention. But it is better if we make a public show of eurythmy rather than hiding it away, for it arises directly from anthroposophy. It should be seen in the world. Here again you will find good soil if you will only take in hand what is already there in the way of anthroposophic initiatives—whether this be in the artistic domain or the teachings of anthroposophy itself—and really carry it out into the world as anthroposophy.

For this to happen it may perhaps be necessary for our dear friends here to work together still more consciously, to carry anthroposophy itself out into the world, particularly here, in a more living way.

Consider, dear friends, what I once said in Dornach: the English-speaking peoples of the world have a particular and great responsibility that fell to them after the terrible war: to spread the life of spirit first and foremost. And this can really be done by taking the anthroposophic impulse strongly in hand. The Society here may be small—believe in ideal magic!—but it will be able to grow large, precisely because there is a great longing here for spiritual life. Underlying all the terrible decadence that you will certainly acknowledge, many people do nevertheless perhaps harbour a very unconscious yearning for a life of spirit. And if there is a great deal of enthusiasm, a great deal of vitality here in the anthroposophic impulse, specific aspects of anthroposophy could also make very good progress here.

I have the impression that people try to push anthroposophy itself into the background, and instead emphasize and cultivate secondary movements. I would not like it to be thought that *I* condone this. These secondary streams will only thrive if a powerful impulse works within anthroposophy itself. And for this to happen the friends who have so kindly supported these three lectures need to work together still more intensively. I hope no misunderstandings will arise because I have expressed these views here now.'

33. See the following lectures of 18 and 19 November 1922.

34. See the lecture in London on 14 April 1922, 'Knowledge and Initiation', and on 15 April 1922, 'Knowledge of the Christ through Anthroposophy', published in CW 211, *The Sun Mystery and the Mystery of Death and Resurrection*, SteinerBooks 2006.

35. An English edition of *Knowledge of the Higher Worlds*, CW 10.

36. See the previous lecture in this volume.

37. Galatians 2:20.

38. Matthew 18:20.

39. See the two previous lectures in this volume.

40. *The Philosophy of Freedom* (CW 4) was published in 1893.

41. See the next lecture in this volume, 20 November 1922. This public lecture, addressed in particular to teachers, was organized by the 'Educational Union for the Realization of Spiritual Values', an association that had formed in Oxford in August 1922 following Rudolf Steiner's lectures there on education.

42. This probably relates to an introduction given by someone from the 'Educational Union' before Steiner's lecture began.

43. Emil Molt, 1876–1936, director of the Waldorf-Astoria cigarette factory. He founded the Waldorf School in 1919, initially for the children of employees at his factory, asking Rudolf Steiner to take responsibility for its methods.

44. Rudolf Steiner, GA 305; some of these lectures are published in *Rudolf Steiner Speaks to the British—Lectures and Addresses in England and Wales*, Rudolf Steiner Press, 1998.

45. See note 41 above.

46. On 11 November 1922, a public eurythmy performance was given at the Royal Academy of Dramatic Art in London.

47. See the first and second lectures in this volume.

48. See *Geisteswissenschaftliche Erläuterungen zu Goethes Faust*, Vol. II, *Das Faust Problem. Die romantische und die klassische Walpurgisnacht*, GA 273, and the lecture of 21 December 1923 on 'The Mysteries of the Cabeiri of Samothrace' in *Mystery Knowledge and Mystery Centres*, Rudolf Steiner Press, 1973, CW 232.

49. In the poem 'The Artist'.

50. The Berlin branch, where this lecture took place, was founded by Rudolf Steiner and Marie Steiner-von Sivers in 1905. Here, until the beginning of the First World War, Steiner developed his science of the spirit in successive lectures.

51. *The Soul's Awakening*, Scene 6.

52. A tea made from the plant *Cetraria islandica*.

53. It has not been possible to find out which lecture this refers to, since not all of the lectures given in Berlin were transcribed.

54. Rudolf Steiner only gave a single further lecture at the Berlin branch, on 23 May 1923. This is published in *Die menschliche Seele in ihrem Zusammenhang mit göttlich-geistigen Individualitäten*, GA 224.

55. See the lecture of 4 December 1922 in this volume.

56. Goethe, in his introduction to the *Theory of Colours*.

57. The public lectures in Berlin were taken down in shorthand, but not the subsequent discussions, and we therefore do not know which lecture is meant here.

58. Opponents of Steiner had used this epithet to attack him.

RUDOLF STEINER'S COLLECTED WORKS

The German Edition of Rudolf Steiner's Collected Works (the *Gesamtausgabe* [GA] published by Rudolf Steiner Verlag, Dornach, Switzerland) presently runs to 354 titles, organized either by type of work (written or spoken), chronology, audience (public or other), or subject (education, art, etc.). For ease of comparison, the Collected Works in English [CW] follows the German organization exactly. A complete listing of the CWs follows with literal translations of the German titles. Other than in the case of the books published in his lifetime, titles were rarely given by Rudolf Steiner himself, and were often provided by the editors of the German editions. The titles in English are not necessarily the same as the German; and, indeed, over the past seventy-five years have frequently been different, with the same book sometimes appearing under different titles.

For ease of identification and to avoid confusion, we suggest that readers looking for a title should do so by CW number. Because the work of creating the Collected Works of Rudolf Steiner is an ongoing process, with new titles being published every year, we have not indicated in this listing which books are presently available. To find out what titles in the Collected Works are currently in print, please check our website at www.rudolfsteinerpress.com (or www.steinerbooks.org for US readers).

Written Work

CW 1	Goethe: Natural-Scientific Writings, Introduction, with Footnotes and Explanations in the text by Rudolf Steiner
CW 2	Outlines of an Epistemology of the Goethean World View, with Special Consideration of Schiller
CW 3	Truth and Science
CW 4	The Philosophy of Freedom
CW 4a	Documents to 'The Philosophy of Freedom'
CW 5	Friedrich Nietzsche, A Fighter against His Time
CW 6	Goethe's Worldview
CW 6a	Now in CW 30
CW 7	Mysticism at the Dawn of Modern Spiritual Life and Its Relationship with Modern Worldviews
CW 8	Christianity as Mystical Fact and the Mysteries of Antiquity
CW 9	Theosophy: An Introduction into Supersensible World Knowledge and Human Purpose
CW 10	How Does One Attain Knowledge of Higher Worlds?
CW 11	From the Akasha-Chronicle

Public Lectures

Lectures to the Members of the Anthroposophical Society

CW 88   Concerning the Astral World and Devachan
CW 89   Consciousness—Life—Form. Fundamental Principles of a Spiritual-Scientific Cosmology
CW 90   Participant Notes from the Lectures during the Years 1903–1905
CW 91   Participant Notes from the Lectures during the Years 1903–1905
CW 92   The Occult Truths of Ancient Myths and Sagas
CW 93   The Temple Legend and the Golden Legend
CW 93a   Fundamentals of Esotericism
CW 94   Cosmogony. Popular Occultism. The Gospel of John. The Theosophy in the Gospel of John
CW 95   At the Gates of Theosophy
CW 96   Origin-Impulses of Spiritual Science. Christian Esotericism in the Light of New Spirit-Knowledge
CW 97   The Christian Mystery
CW 98   Nature Beings and Spirit Beings—Their Effects in Our Visible World
CW 99   The Theosophy of the Rosicrucians
CW 100   Human Development and Christ-Knowledge
CW 101   Myths and Legends. Occult Signs and Symbols
CW 102   The Working into Human Beings by Spiritual Beings
CW 103   The Gospel of John
CW 104   The Apocalypse of John
CW 104a   From the Picture-Script of the Apocalypse of John
CW 105   Universe, Earth, the Human Being: Their Being and Development, as well as Their Reflection in the Connection between Egyptian Mythology and Modern Culture
CW 106   Egyptian Myths and Mysteries in Relation to the Active Spiritual Forces of the Present
CW 107   Spiritual-Scientific Knowledge of the Human Being
CW 108   Answering the Questions of Life and the World through Anthroposophy
CW 109   The Principle of Spiritual Economy in Connection with the Question of Reincarnation. An Aspect of the Spiritual Guidance of Humanity
CW 110   The Spiritual Hierarchies and Their Reflection in the Physical World. Zodiac, Planets and Cosmos
CW 111   Contained in CW 109
CW 112   The Gospel of John in Relation to the Three Other Gospels, Especially the Gospel of Luke
CW 113   The Orient in the Light of the Occident. The Children of Lucifer and the Brothers of Christ
CW 114   The Gospel of Luke
CW 115   Anthroposophy—Psychosophy—Pneumatosophy
CW 116   The Christ-Impulse and the Development of 'I'-Consciousness
CW 117   The Deeper Secrets of the Development of Humanity in Light of the Gospels

CW 200   The New Spirituality and the Christ-Experience of the 20th Century

CW 201   The Correspondences Between Microcosm and Macrocosm. The Human Being—A Hieroglyph of the Universe. The Human Being in Relationship with the Cosmos: 1

CW 202   The Bridge between the World-Spirituality and the Physical Aspect of the Human Being. The Search for the New Isis, the Divine Sophia. The Human Being in Relationship with the Cosmos: 2

CW 203   The Responsibility of Human Beings for the Development of the World through their Spiritual Connection with the Planet Earth and the World of the Stars. The Human Being in Relationship with the Cosmos: 3

CW 204   Perspectives of the Development of Humanity. The Materialistic Knowledge-Impulse and the Task of Anthroposophy. The Human Being in Relationship with the Cosmos: 4

CW 205   Human Development, World-Soul, and World-Spirit. Part One: The Human Being as a Being of Body and Soul in Relationship to the World. The Human Being in Relationship with the Cosmos: 5

CW 206   Human Development, World-Soul, and World-Spirit. Part Two: The Human Being as a Spiritual Being in the Process of Historical Development. The Human Being in Relationship with the Cosmos: 6

CW 207   Anthroposophy as Cosmosophy. Part One: Characteristic Features of the Human Being in the Earthly and the Cosmic Realms. The Human Being in Relationship with the Cosmos: 7

CW 208   Anthroposophy as Cosmosophy. Part Two: The Forming of the Human Being as the Result of Cosmic Influence. The Human Being in Relationship with the Cosmos: 8

CW 209   Nordic and Central European Spiritual Impulses. The Festival of the Appearance of Christ. The Human Being in Relationship with the Cosmos: 9

CW 210   Old and New Methods of Initiation. Drama and Poetry in the Change of Consciousness in the Modern Age

CW 211   The Sun Mystery and the Mystery of Death and Resurrection. Exoteric and Esoteric Christianity

CW 212   Human Soul Life and Spiritual Striving in Connection with World and Earth Development

CW 213   Human Questions and World Answers

CW 214   The Mystery of the Trinity: The Human Being in Relationship with the Spiritual World in the Course of Time

CW 215   Philosophy, Cosmology, and Religion in Anthroposophy

CW 216   The Fundamental Impulses of the World-Historical Development of Humanity

CW 217   Spiritually Active Forces in the Coexistence of the Older and Younger Generations. Pedagogical Course for Youth

CW 217a	Youth's Cognitive Task
CW 218	Spiritual Connections in the Forming of the Human Organism
CW 219	The Relationship of the World of the Stars to the Human Being, and of the Human Being to the World of the Stars. The Spiritual Communion of Humanity
CW 220	Living Knowledge of Nature. Intellectual Fall and Spiritual Redemption
CW 221	Earth-Knowing and Heaven-Insight
CW 222	The Imparting of Impulses to World-Historical Events through Spiritual Powers
CW 223	The Cycle of the Year as Breathing Process of the Earth and the Four Great Festival-Seasons. Anthroposophy and the Human Heart (Gemüt)
CW 224	The Human Soul and its Connection with Divine-Spiritual Individualities. The Internalization of the Festivals of the Year
CW 225	Three Perspectives of Anthroposophy. Cultural Phenomena observed from a Spiritual-Scientific Perspective
CW 226	Human Being, Human Destiny, and World Development
CW 227	Initiation-Knowledge
CW 228	Science of Initiation and Knowledge of the Stars. The Human Being in the Past, the Present, and the Future from the Viewpoint of the Development of Consciousness
CW 229	The Experiencing of the Course of the Year in Four Cosmic Imaginations
CW 230	The Human Being as Harmony of the Creative, Building, and Formative World-Word
CW 231	The Supersensible Human Being, Understood Anthroposophically
CW 232	The Forming of the Mysteries
CW 233	World History Illuminated by Anthroposophy and as the Foundation for Knowledge of the Human Spirit
CW 233a	Mystery Sites of the Middle Ages: Rosicrucianism and the Modern Initiation-Principle. The Festival of Easter as Part of the History of the Mysteries of Humanity
CW 234	Anthroposophy. A Summary after 21 Years
CW 235	Esoteric Observations of Karmic Relationships in 6 Volumes, Vol. 1
CW 236	Esoteric Observations of Karmic Relationships in 6 Volumes, Vol. 2
CW 237	Esoteric Observations of Karmic Relationships in 6 Volumes, Vol. 3: The Karmic Relationships of the Anthroposophical Movement
CW 238	Esoteric Observations of Karmic Relationships in 6 Volumes, Vol. 4: The Spiritual Life of the Present in Relationship to the Anthroposophical Movement
CW 239	Esoteric Observations of Karmic Relationships in 6 Volumes, Vol. 5

CW 291	The Nature of Colours
CW 291a	Knowledge of Colours. Supplementary Volume to 'The Nature of Colours'
CW 292	Art History as Image of Inner Spiritual Impulses
CW 293	General Knowledge of the Human Being as the Foundation of Pedagogy
CW 294	The Art of Education, Methodology and Didactics
CW 295	The Art of Education: Seminar Discussions and Lectures on Lesson Planning
CW 296	The Question of Education as a Social Question
CW 297	The Idea and Practice of the Waldorf School
CW 297a	Education for Life: Self-Education and the Practice of Pedagogy
CW 298	Rudolf Steiner in the Waldorf School
CW 299	Spiritual-Scientific Observations on Speech
CW 300a	Conferences with the Teachers of the Free Waldorf School in Stuttgart, 1919 to 1924, in 3 Volumes, Vol. 1
CW 300b	Conferences with the Teachers of the Free Waldorf School in Stuttgart, 1919 to 1924, in 3 Volumes, Vol. 2
CW 300c	Conferences with the Teachers of the Free Waldorf School in Stuttgart, 1919 to 1924, in 3 Volumes, Vol. 3
CW 301	The Renewal of Pedagogical-Didactical Art through Spiritual Science
CW 302	Knowledge of the Human Being and the Forming of Class Lessons
CW 302a	Education and Teaching from a Knowledge of the Human Being
CW 303	The Healthy Development of the Human Being
CW 304	Methods of Education and Teaching Based on Anthroposophy
CW 304a	Anthroposophical Knowledge of the Human Being and Pedagogy
CW 305	The Soul-Spiritual Foundational Forces of the Art of Education. Spiritual Values in Education and Social Life
CW 306	Pedagogical Praxis from the Viewpoint of a Spiritual-Scientific Knowledge of the Human Being. The Education of the Child and Young Human Beings
CW 307	The Spiritual Life of the Present and Education
CW 308	The Method of Teaching and the Life-Requirements for Teaching
CW 309	Anthroposophical Pedagogy and Its Prerequisites
CW 310	The Pedagogical Value of a Knowledge of the Human Being and the Cultural Value of Pedagogy
CW 311	The Art of Education from an Understanding of the Being of Humanity
CW 312	Spiritual Science and Medicine
CW 313	Spiritual-Scientific Viewpoints on Therapy
CW 314	Physiology and Therapy Based on Spiritual Science
CW 315	Curative Eurythmy
CW 316	Meditative Observations and Instructions for a Deepening of the Art of Healing
CW 317	The Curative Education Course

SIGNIFICANT EVENTS IN THE LIFE OF RUDOLF STEINER

1829:   June 23: birth of Johann Steiner (1829–1910)—Rudolf Steiner's father—in Geras, Lower Austria.

1834:   May 8: birth of Franciska Blie (1834–1918)—Rudolf Steiner's mother—in Horn, Lower Austria. 'My father and mother were both children of the glorious Lower Austrian forest district north of the Danube.'

1860:   May 16: marriage of Johann Steiner and Franciska Blie.

1861:   February 25: birth of *Rudolf Joseph Lorenz Steiner* in Kraljevec, Croatia, near the border with Hungary, where Johann Steiner works as a telegrapher for the South Austria Railroad. Rudolf Steiner is baptized two days later, February 27, the date usually given as his birthday.

1862:   Summer: the family moves to Mödling, Lower Austria.

1863:   The family moves to Pottschach, Lower Austria, near the Styrian border, where Johann Steiner becomes stationmaster. 'The view stretched to the mountains ... majestic peaks in the distance and the sweet charm of nature in the immediate surroundings.'

1864:   November 15: birth of Rudolf Steiner's sister, Leopoldine (d. November 1, 1927). She will become a seamstress and live with her parents for the rest of her life.

1866:   July 28: birth of Rudolf Steiner's deaf-mute brother, Gustav (d. May 1, 1941).

1867:   Rudolf Steiner enters the village school. Following a disagreement between his father and the schoolmaster, whose wife falsely accused the boy of causing a commotion, Rudolf Steiner is taken out of school and taught at home.

1868:   A critical experience. Unknown to the family, an aunt dies in a distant town. Sitting in the station waiting room, Rudolf Steiner sees her 'form,' which speaks to him, asking for help. 'Beginning with this experience, a new soul life began in the boy, one in which not only the outer trees and mountains spoke to him, but also the worlds that lay behind them. From this moment on, the boy began to live with the spirits of nature ...'

1869:   The family moves to the peaceful, rural village of Neudörfl, near Wiener-Neustadt in present-day Austria. Rudolf Steiner attends the village school. Because of the 'unorthodoxy' of his writing and spelling, he has to do 'extra lessons.'

1870:   Through a book lent to him by his tutor, he discovers geometry: 'To grasp something purely in the spirit brought me inner happiness. I know that I first learned happiness through geometry.' The same tutor allows him to draw, while other students still struggle with their reading and writing. 'An artistic element' thus enters his education.

1871: Though his parents are not religious, Rudolf Steiner becomes a 'church child,' a favourite of the priest, who was 'an exceptional character.' 'Up to the age of ten or eleven, among those I came to know, he was far and away the most significant.' Among other things, he introduces Steiner to Copernican, heliocentric cosmology. As an altar boy, Rudolf Steiner serves at Masses, funerals, and Corpus Christi processions. At year's end, after an incident in which he escapes a thrashing, his father forbids him to go to church.

1872: Rudolf Steiner transfers to grammar school in Wiener-Neustadt, a five-mile walk from home, which must be done in all weathers.

1873–75: Through his teachers and on his own, Rudolf Steiner has many wonderful experiences with science and mathematics. Outside school, he teaches himself analytic geometry, trigonometry, differential equations, and calculus.

1876: Rudolf Steiner begins tutoring other students. He learns bookbinding from his father. He also teaches himself stenography.

1877: Rudolf Steiner discovers Kant's *Critique of Pure Reason*, which he reads and rereads. He also discovers and reads von Rotteck's *World History*.

1878: He studies extensively in contemporary psychology and philosophy.

1879: Rudolf Steiner graduates from high school with honours. His father is transferred to Inzersdorf, near Vienna. He uses his first visit to Vienna 'to purchase a great number of philosophy books'—Kant, Fichte, Schelling, and Hegel, as well as numerous histories of philosophy. His aim: to find a path from the 'I' to nature.

October 1879–1883: Rudolf Steiner attends the Technical College in Vienna—to study mathematics, chemistry, physics, mineralogy, botany, zoology, biology, geology, and mechanics—with a scholarship. He also attends lectures in history and literature, while avidly reading philosophy on his own. His two favourite professors are Karl Julius Schröer (German language and literature) and Edmund Reitlinger (physics). He also audits lectures by Robert Zimmermann on aesthetics and Franz Brentano on philosophy. During this year he begins his friendship with Moritz Zitter (1861–1921), who will help support him financially when he is in Berlin.

1880: Rudolf Steiner attends lectures on Schiller and Goethe by Karl Julius Schröer, who becomes his mentor. Also 'through a remarkable combination of circumstances,' he meets Felix Koguzki, a 'herb gatherer' and healer, who could 'see deeply into the secrets of nature.' Rudolf Steiner will meet and study with this 'emissary of the Master' throughout his time in Vienna.

1881: January: '... I didn't sleep a wink. I was busy with philosophical problems until about 12:30 a.m. Then, finally, I threw myself down on my couch. All my striving during the previous year had been to research whether the following statement by Schelling was true or not: *Within everyone dwells a secret, marvelous capacity to draw back from the stream of time—out of the self clothed in all that comes to us from outside—into our innermost being and there, in the immutable form of the Eternal, to look into ourselves.* I believe, and I am still quite certain of it, that I discovered this capacity in myself; I had long had an inkling of it. Now the whole of idealist philosophy stood before me in modified form. What's a sleepless night compared to that!'

Rudolf Steiner begins communicating with leading thinkers of the day, who send him books in return, which he reads eagerly.

July: 'I am not one of those who dives into the day like an animal in human form. I pursue a quite specific goal, an idealistic aim—knowledge of the truth! This cannot be done offhandedly. It requires the greatest striving in the world, free of all egotism, and equally of all resignation.'

August: Steiner puts down on paper for the first time thoughts for a 'Philosophy of Freedom.' 'The striving for the absolute: this human yearning is freedom.' He also seeks to outline a 'peasant philosophy,' describing what the worldview of a 'peasant'—one who lives close to the earth and the old ways—really is.

1881–1882: Felix Koguzki, the herb gatherer, reveals himself to be the envoy of another, higher initiatory personality, who instructs Rudolf Steiner to penetrate Fichte's philosophy and to master modern scientific thinking as a preparation for right entry into the spirit. This 'Master' also teaches him the double (evolutionary and involutionary) nature of time.

1882: Through the offices of Karl Julius Schröer, Rudolf Steiner is asked by Joseph Kürschner to edit Goethe's scientific works for the *Deutschen National-Literatur* edition. He writes 'A Possible Critique of Atomistic Concepts' and sends it to Friedrich Theodor Vischer.

1883: Rudolf Steiner completes his college studies and begins work on the Goethe project.

1884: First volume of Goethe's *Scientific Writings* (CW 1) appears (March). He lectures on Goethe and Lessing, and Goethe's approach to science. In July, he enters the household of Ladislaus and Pauline Specht as tutor to the four Specht boys. He will live there until 1890. At this time, he meets Josef Breuer (1842–1925), the co-author with Sigmund Freud of *Studies in Hysteria*, who is the Specht family doctor.

1885: While continuing to edit Goethe's writings, Rudolf Steiner reads deeply in contemporary philosophy (Eduard von Hartmann, Johannes Volkelt, and Richard Wahle, among others).

1886: May: Rudolf Steiner sends Kürschner the manuscript of *Outlines of Goethe's Theory of Knowledge* (CW 2), which appears in October, and which he sends out widely. He also meets the poet Marie Eugenie Delle Grazie and writes 'Nature and Our Ideals' for her. He attends her salon, where he meets many priests, theologians, and philosophers, who will become his friends. Meanwhile, the director of the Goethe Archive in Weimar requests his collaboration with the *Sophien* edition of Goethe's works, particularly the writings on colour.

1887: At the beginning of the year, Rudolf Steiner is very sick. As the year progresses and his health improves, he becomes increasingly 'a man of letters,' lecturing, writing essays, and taking part in Austrian cultural life. In August–September, the second volume of Goethe's *Scientific Writings* appears.

1888:   January–July: Rudolf Steiner assumes editorship of the 'German Weekly' (*Deutsche Wochenschrift*). He begins lecturing more intensively, giving, for example, a lecture titled 'Goethe as Father of a New Aesthetics.' He meets and becomes soul friends with Friedrich Eckstein (1861–1939), a vegetarian, philosopher of symbolism, alchemist, and musician, who will introduce him to various spiritual currents (including Theosophy) and with whom he will meditate and interpret esoteric and alchemical texts.

1889:   Rudolf Steiner first reads Nietzsche (*Beyond Good and Evil*). He encounters Theosophy again and learns of Madame Blavatsky in the Theosophical circle around Marie Lang (1858–1934). Here he also meets well-known figures of Austrian life, as well as esoteric figures like the occultist Franz Hartmann and Karl Leinigen-Billigen (translator of C.G. Harrison's *The Transcendental Universe*). During this period, Steiner first reads A.P. Sinnett's *Esoteric Buddhism* and Mabel Collins's *Light on the Path*. He also begins travelling, visiting Budapest, Weimar, and Berlin (where he meets philosopher Eduard von Hartmann).

1890:   Rudolf Steiner finishes volume 3 of Goethe's scientific writings. He begins his doctoral dissertation, which will become *Truth and Science* (CW 3). He also meets the poet and feminist Rosa Mayreder (1858–1938), with whom he can exchange his most intimate thoughts. In September, Rudolf Steiner moves to Weimar to work in the Goethe-Schiller Archive.

1891:   Volume 3 of the Kürschner edition of Goethe appears. Meanwhile, Rudolf Steiner edits Goethe's studies in mineralogy and scientific writings for the *Sophien* edition. He meets Ludwig Laistner of the Cotta Publishing Company, who asks for a book on the basic question of metaphysics. From this will result, ultimately, *The Philosophy of Freedom* (CW 4), which will be published not by Cotta but by Emil Felber. In October, Rudolf Steiner takes the oral exam for a doctorate in philosophy, mathematics, and mechanics at Rostock University, receiving his doctorate on the twenty-sixth. In November, he gives his first lecture on Goethe's 'Fairy Tale' in Vienna.

1892:   Rudolf Steiner continues work at the Goethe-Schiller Archive and on his *Philosophy of Freedom*. *Truth and Science*, his doctoral dissertation, is published. Steiner undertakes to write introductions to books on Schopenhauer and Jean Paul for Cotta. At year's end, he finds lodging with Anna Eunike, née Schulz (1853–1911), a widow with four daughters and a son. He also develops a friendship with Otto Erich Hartleben (1864–1905) with whom he shares literary interests.

1893:   Rudolf Steiner begins his habit of producing many reviews and articles. In March, he gives a lecture titled 'Hypnotism, with Reference to Spiritism.' In September, volume 4 of the Kürschner edition is completed. In November, *The Philosophy of Freedom* appears. This year, too, he meets John Henry Mackay (1864–1933), the anarchist, and Max Stirner, a scholar and biographer.

1894:   Rudolf Steiner meets Elisabeth Förster Nietzsche, the philosopher's sister, and begins to read Nietzsche in earnest, beginning with the as yet unpublished *Antichrist*. He also meets Ernst Haeckel (1834–1919). In the fall, he begins to write *Nietzsche, A Fighter against His Time* (CW 5).

1895: May, *Nietzsche, A Fighter against His Time* appears.

1896: January 22: Rudolf Steiner sees Friedrich Nietzsche for the first and only time. Moves between the Nietzsche and the Goethe-Schiller Archives, where he completes his work before year's end. He falls out with Elisabeth Förster Nietzsche, thus ending his association with the Nietzsche Archive.

1897: Rudolf Steiner finishes the manuscript of *Goethe's Worldview* (CW 6). He moves to Berlin with Anna Eunike and begins editorship of the *Magazin für Literatur*. From now on, Steiner will write countless reviews, literary and philosophical articles, and so on. He begins lecturing at the 'Free Literary Society.' In September, he attends the Zionist Congress in Basel. He sides with Dreyfus in the Dreyfus affair.

1898: Rudolf Steiner is very active as an editor in the political, artistic, and theatrical life of Berlin. He becomes friendly with John Henry Mackay and poet Ludwig Jacobowski (1868–1900). He joins Jacobowski's circle of writers, artists, and scientists—'The Coming Ones' (*Die Kommenden*)— and contributes lectures to the group until 1903. He also lectures at the 'League for College Pedagogy.' He writes an article for Goethe's sesquicentennial, 'Goethe's Secret Revelation,' on the 'Fairy Tale of the Green Snake and the Beautiful Lily.'

1898–99: 'This was a trying time for my soul as I looked at Christianity. . . . I was able to progress only by contemplating, by means of spiritual perception, the evolution of Christianity. . . . Conscious knowledge of real Christianity began to dawn in me around the turn of the century. This seed continued to develop. My soul trial occurred shortly before the beginning of the twentieth century. It was decisive for my soul's development that I stood spiritually before the Mystery of Golgotha in a deep and solemn celebration of knowledge.'

1899: Rudolf Steiner begins teaching and giving lectures and lecture cycles at the Workers' College, founded by Wilhelm Liebknecht (1826–1900). He will continue to do so until 1904. Writes: *Literature and Spiritual Life in the Nineteenth Century; Individualism in Philosophy; Haeckel and His Opponents; Poetry in the Present;* and begins what will become (fifteen years later) *The Riddles of Philosophy* (CW 18). He also meets many artists and writers, including Käthe Kollwitz, Stefan Zweig, and Rainer Maria Rilke. On October 31, he marries Anna Eunike.

1900: 'I thought that the turn of the century must bring humanity a new light. It seemed to me that the separation of human thinking and willing from the spirit had peaked. A turn or reversal of direction in human evolution seemed to me a necessity.' Rudolf Steiner finishes *World and Life Views in the Nineteenth Century* (the second part of what will become *The Riddles of Philosophy*) and dedicates it to Ernst Haeckel. It is published in March. He continues lecturing at *Die Kommenden*, whose leadership he assumes after the death of Jacobowski. Also, he gives the Gutenberg Jubilee lecture before 7,000 typesetters and printers. In September, Rudolf Steiner is invited by Count and Countess Brockdorff to lecture in the Theosophical Library. His first lecture is on Nietzsche. His second lecture is titled 'Goethe's Secret Revelation.' October 6, he begins a lecture cycle on the mystics that will become *Mystics after Modernism* (CW 7). November–December: 'Marie von Sivers appears in the audience. . . .' Also in November, Steiner gives his first lecture at the Giordano Bruno Bund (where he will continue to lecture until May, 1905). He speaks on Bruno and modern Rome, focusing on the importance of the philosophy of Thomas Aquinas as monism.

1901: In continual financial straits, Rudolf Steiner's early friends Moritz Zitter and Rosa Mayreder help support him. In October, he begins the lecture cycle *Christianity as Mystical Fact* (CW 8) at the Theosophical Library. In November, he gives his first 'Theosophical lecture' on Goethe's 'Fairy Tale' in Hamburg at the invitation of Wilhelm Hubbe-Schleiden. He also attends a gathering to celebrate the founding of the Theosophical Society at Count and Countess Brockdorff's. He gives a lecture cycle, 'From Buddha to Christ,' for the circle of the *Kommenden*. November 17, Marie von Sivers asks Rudolf Steiner if Theosophy needs a Western-Christian spiritual movement (to complement Theosophy's Eastern emphasis). 'The question was posed. Now, following spiritual laws, I could begin to give an answer. . . .' In December, Rudolf Steiner writes his first article for a Theosophical publication. At year's end, the Brockdorffs and possibly Wilhelm Hubbe-Schleiden ask Rudolf Steiner to join the Theosophical Society and undertake the leadership of the German section. Rudolf Steiner agrees, on the condition that Marie von Sivers (then in Italy) work with him.

1902: Beginning in January, Rudolf Steiner attends the opening of the Workers' School in Spandau with Rosa Luxemberg (1870–1919). January 17, Rudolf Steiner joins the Theosophical Society. In April, he is asked to become general secretary of the German Section of the Theosophical Society, and works on preparations for its founding. In July, he visits London for a Theosophical congress. He meets Bertram Keightly, G.R.S. Mead, A.P. Sinnett, and Annie Besant, among others. In September, *Christianity as Mystical Fact* appears. In October, Rudolf Steiner gives his first public lecture on Theosophy ('Monism and Theosophy') to about three hundred people at the Giordano Bruno Bund. On October 19–21, the German Section of the Theosophical Society has its first meeting; Rudolf Steiner is the general secretary, and Annie Besant attends. Steiner lectures on practical karma studies. On October 23, Annie Besant inducts Rudolf Steiner into the Esoteric School of the Theosophical Society. On October 25, Steiner begins a weekly series of lectures: 'The Field of Theosophy.' During this year, Rudolf Steiner also first meets Ita Wegman (1876–1943), who will become his close collaborator in his final years.

1903: Rudolf Steiner holds about 300 lectures and seminars. In May, the first issue of the periodical *Luzifer* appears. In June, Rudolf Steiner visits

London for the first meeting of the Federation of the European Sections of the Theosophical Society, where he meets Colonel Olcott. He begins to write *Theosophy* (CW 9).

1904: Rudolf Steiner continues lecturing at the Workers' College and elsewhere (about 90 lectures), while lecturing intensively all over Germany among Theosophists (about 140 lectures). In February, he meets Carl Unger (1878–1929), who will become a member of the board of the Anthroposophical Society (1913). In March, he meets Michael Bauer (1871–1929), a Christian mystic, who will also be on the board. In May, *Theosophy* appears, with the dedication: 'To the spirit of Giordano Bruno.' Rudolf Steiner and Marie von Sivers visit London for meetings with Annie Besant. June: Rudolf Steiner and Marie von Sivers attend the meeting of the Federation of European Sections of the Theosophical Society in Amsterdam. In July, Steiner begins the articles in *Luzifer-Gnosis* that will become *How to Know Higher Worlds* (CW 10) and *Cosmic Memory* (CW 11). In September, Annie Besant visits Germany. In December, Steiner lectures on Freemasonry. He mentions the High Grade Masonry derived from John Yarker and represented by Theodore Reuss and Karl Kellner as a blank slate 'into which a good image could be placed.'

1905: This year, Steiner ends his non-Theosophical lecturing activity. Supported by Marie von Sivers, his Theosophical lecturing—both in public and in the Theosophical Society—increases significantly: 'The German Theosophical Movement is of exceptional importance.' Steiner recommends reading, among others, Fichte, Jacob Boehme, and Angelus Silesius. He begins to introduce Christian themes into Theosophy. He also begins to work with doctors (Felix Peipers and Ludwig Noll). In July, he is in London for the Federation of European Sections, where he attends a lecture by Annie Besant: 'I have seldom seen Mrs. Besant speak in so inward and heartfelt a manner....' 'Through Mrs. Besant I have found the way to H.P. Blavatsky.' September to October, he gives a course of thirty-one lectures for a small group of esoteric students. In October, the annual meeting of the German Section of the Theosophical Society, which still remains very small, takes place. Rudolf Steiner reports membership has risen from 121 to 377 members. In November, seeking to establish esoteric 'continuity,' Rudolf Steiner and Marie von Sivers participate in a 'Memphis-Misraim' Masonic ceremony. They pay forty-five marks for membership. 'Yesterday, you saw how little remains of former esoteric institutions.' 'We are dealing only with a "framework"... for the present, nothing lies behind it. The occult powers have completely withdrawn.'

1906: Expansion of Theosophical work. Rudolf Steiner gives about 245 lectures, only 44 of which take place in Berlin. Cycles are given in Paris, Leipzig, Stuttgart, and Munich. Esoteric work also intensifies. Rudolf Steiner begins writing *An Outline of Esoteric Science* (CW 13). In January, Rudolf Steiner receives permission (a patent) from the Great Orient of the Scottish A & A Thirty-Three Degree Rite of the Order of the Ancient

Freemasons of the Memphis-Misraim Rite to direct a chapter under the name 'Mystica Aeterna.' This will become the 'Cognitive-Ritual Section' (also called 'Misraim Service') of the Esoteric School. (See: *Freemasonry and Ritual Work: The Misraim Service*, CW 265). During this time, Steiner also meets Albert Schweitzer. In May, he is in Paris, where he visits Edouard Schuré. Many Russians attend his lectures (including Konstantin Balmont, Dimitri Mereszkovski, Zinaida Hippius, and Maximilian Woloshin). He attends the General Meeting of the European Federation of the Theosophical Society, at which Col. Olcott is present for the last time. He spends the year's end in Venice and Rome, where he writes and works on his translation of H.P. Blavatsky's *Key to Theosophy*.

1907: Further expansion of the German Theosophical Movement according to the Rosicrucian directive to 'introduce spirit into the world'—in education, in social questions, in art, and in science. In February, Col. Olcott dies in Adyar. Before he dies, Olcott indicates that 'the Masters' wish Annie Besant to succeed him: much politicking ensues. Rudolf Steiner supports Besant's candidacy. April-May: preparations for the Congress of the Federation of European Sections of the Theosophical Society—the great, watershed Whitsun 'Munich Congress,' attended by Annie Besant and others. Steiner decides to separate Eastern and Western (Christian-Rosicrucian) esoteric schools. He takes his esoteric school out of the Theosophical Society (Besant and Rudolf Steiner are 'in harmony' on this). Steiner makes his first lecture tours to Austria and Hungary. That summer, he is in Italy. In September, he visits Edouard Schuré, who will write the introduction to the French edition of *Christianity as Mystical Fact* in Barr, Alsace. Rudolf Steiner writes the autobiographical statement known as the 'Barr Document.' In *Luzifer-Gnosis*, 'The Education of the Child' appears.

1908: The movement grows (membership: 1,150). Lecturing expands. Steiner makes his first extended lecture tour to Holland and Scandinavia, as well as visits to Naples and Sicily. Themes: St. John's Gospel, the Apocalypse, Egypt, science, philosophy, and logic. *Luzifer-Gnosis* ceases publication. In Berlin, Marie von Sivers (with Johanna Mücke (1864–1949) forms the *Philosophisch-Theosophisch* (after 1915 *Philosophisch-Anthroposophisch*) *Verlag* to publish Steiner's work. Steiner gives lecture cycles titled *The Gospel of St. John* (CW 103) and *The Apocalypse* (104).

1909: *An Outline of Esoteric Science* appears. Lecturing and travel continues. Rudolf Steiner's spiritual research expands to include the polarity of Lucifer and Ahriman; the work of great individualities in history; the Maitreya Buddha and the Bodhisattvas; spiritual economy (CW 109); the work of the spiritual hierarchies in heaven and on earth (CW 110). He also deepens and intensifies his research into the Gospels, giving lectures on the Gospel of St. Luke (CW 114) with the first mention of two Jesus children. Meets and becomes friends with Christian Morgenstern (1871–1914). In April, he lays the foundation stone for the Malsch model—the building that will lead to the first Goetheanum. In May, the International Congress of the Federation of European Sections of the

Theosophical Society takes place in Budapest. Rudolf Steiner receives the Subba Row medal for *How to Know Higher Worlds*. During this time, Charles W. Leadbeater discovers Jiddu Krishnamurti (1895–1986) and proclaims him the future 'world teacher,' the bearer of the Maitreya Buddha and the 'reappearing Christ.' In October, Steiner delivers seminal lectures on 'anthroposophy,' which he will try, unsuccessfully, to rework over the next years into the unfinished work, *Anthroposophy (A Fragment)* (CW 45).

1910:   New themes: *The Reappearance of Christ in the Etheric* (CW 118); *The Fifth Gospel; The Mission of Folk Souls* (CW 121); *Occult History* (CW 126); the evolving development of etheric cognitive capacities. Rudolf Steiner continues his Gospel research with *The Gospel of St. Matthew* (CW 123). In January, his father dies. In April, he takes a month-long trip to Italy, including Rome, Monte Cassino, and Sicily. He also visits Scandinavia again. July–August, he writes the first mystery drama, *The Portal of Initiation* (CW 14). In November, he gives 'psychosophy' lectures. In December, he submits 'On the Psychological Foundations and Epistemological Framework of Theosophy' to the International Philosophical Congress in Bologna.

1911:   The crisis in the Theosophical Society deepens. In January, 'The Order of the Rising Sun,' which will soon become 'The Order of the Star in the East,' is founded for the coming world teacher, Krishnamurti. At the same time, Marie von Sivers, Rudolf Steiner's co-worker, falls ill. Fewer lectures are given, but important new ground is broken. In Prague, in March, Steiner meets Franz Kafka (1883–1924) and Hugo Bergmann (1883-1975). In April, he delivers his paper to the Philosophical Congress. He writes the second mystery drama, *The Soul's Probation* (CW 14). Also, while Marie von Sivers is convalescing, Rudolf Steiner begins work on *Calendar 1912/1913*, which will contain the 'Calendar of the Soul' meditations. On March 19, Anna (Eunike) Steiner dies. In September, Rudolf Steiner visits Einsiedeln, birthplace of Paracelsus. In December, Friedrich Rittelmeyer, future founder of the Christian Community, meets Rudolf Steiner. The *Johannes-Bauverein*, the 'building committee,' which would lead to the first Goetheanum (first planned for Munich), is also founded, and a preliminary committee for the founding of an independent association is created that, in the following year, will become the Anthroposophical Society. Important lecture cycles include *Occult Physiology* (CW 128); *Wonders of the World* (CW 129); *From Jesus to Christ* (CW 131). Other themes: esoteric Christianity; Christian Rosenkreutz; the spiritual guidance of humanity; the sense world and the world of the spirit.

1912:   Despite the ongoing, now increasing crisis in the Theosophical Society, much is accomplished: *Calendar 1912/1913* is published; eurythmy is created; both the third mystery drama, *The Guardian of the Threshold* (CW 14) and *A Way of Self-Knowledge* (CW 16) are written. New (or renewed) themes included life between death and rebirth and karma and reincarnation. Other lecture cycles: *Spiritual Beings in the Heavenly Bodies and in the Kingdoms of Nature* (CW 136); *The Human Being in the Light of Occultism, Theosophy, and Philosophy* (CW 137); *The Gospel of St. Mark* (CW 139); and *The Bhagavad Gita and the Epistles of Paul* (CW 142). On May 8, Rudolf Steiner celebrates White Lotus Day, H.P. Blavatsky's death day, which he had faithfully observed for the past decade, for the last time. In August, Rudolf Steiner suggests the 'independent association' be called the 'Anthroposophical Society.' In September, the first eurythmy course takes place. In October, Rudolf Steiner declines recognition of a Theosophical Society lodge dedicated to the Star of the East and decides to expel all Theosophical Society members belonging to the order. Also, with Marie von Sivers, he first visits Dornach, near Basel, Switzerland, and they stand on the hill where the Goetheanum will be built. In November, a Theosophical Society lodge is opened by direct mandate from Adyar (Annie Besant). In December, a meeting of the German section occurs at which it is decided that belonging to the Order of the Star of the East is incompatible with membership in the Theosophical Society. December 28: informal founding of the Anthroposophical Society in Berlin.

1913: Expulsion of the German section from the Theosophical Society. February 2–3: Foundation meeting of the Anthroposophical Society. Board members include: Marie von Sivers, Michael Bauer, and Carl Unger. September 20: Laying of the foundation stone for the *Johannes Bau* (Goetheanum) in Dornach. Building begins immediately. The third mystery drama, *The Soul's Awakening* (CW 14), is completed. Also: *The Threshold of the Spiritual World* (CW 147). Lecture cycles include: *The Bhagavad Gita and the Epistles of Paul* and *The Esoteric Meaning of the Bhagavad Gita* (CW 146), which the Russian philosopher Nikolai Berdyaev attends; *The Mysteries of the East and of Christianity* (CW 144); *The Effects of Esoteric Development* (CW 145); and *The Fifth Gospel* (CW 148). In May, Rudolf Steiner is in London and Paris, where anthroposophical work continues.

1914: Building continues on the *Johannes Bau* (Goetheanum) in Dornach, with artists and co-workers from seventeen nations. The general assembly of the Anthroposophical Society takes place. In May, Rudolf Steiner visits Paris, as well as Chartres Cathedral. June 28: assassination in Sarajevo ('Now the catastrophe has happened!'). August 1: War is declared. Rudolf Steiner returns to Germany from Dornach—he will travel back and forth. He writes the last chapter of *The Riddles of Philosophy*. Lecture cycles include: *Human and Cosmic Thought* (CW 151); *Inner Being of Humanity between Death and a New Birth* (CW 153); *Occult Reading and Occult Hearing* (CW 156). December 24: marriage of Rudolf Steiner and Marie von Sivers.

1915: Building continues. Life after death becomes a major theme, also art. Writes: *Thoughts during a Time of War* (CW 24). Lectures include: *The Secret of Death* (CW 159); *The Uniting of Humanity through the Christ Impulse* (CW 165).

1916: Rudolf Steiner begins work with Edith Maryon (1872–1924) on the sculpture 'The Representative of Humanity' ('The Group'—Christ, Lucifer, and Ahriman). He also works with the alchemist Alexander von Bernus on the quarterly *Das Reich*. He writes *The Riddle of Humanity* (CW 20). Lectures include: *Necessity and Freedom in World History and Human Action* (CW 166); *Past and Present in the Human Spirit* (CW 167); *The Karma of Vocation* (CW 172); *The Karma of Untruthfulness* (CW 173).

1917: Russian Revolution. The U.S. enters the war. Building continues. Rudolf Steiner delineates the idea of the 'threefold nature of the human being' (in a public lecture March 15) and the 'threefold nature of the social organism' (hammered out in May-June with the help of Otto von Lerchenfeld and Ludwig Polzer-Hoditz in the form of two documents titled *Memoranda*, which were distributed in high places). August–September: Rudolf Steiner writes *The Riddles of the Soul* (CW 20). Also: commentary on 'The Chymical Wedding of Christian Rosenkreutz' for Alexander Bernus (*Das Reich*). Lectures include: *The Karma of Materialism* (CW 176); *The Spiritual Background of the Outer World: The Fall of the Spirits of Darkness* (CW 177).

1918: March 18: peace treaty of Brest-Litovsk—'Now everything will truly enter chaos! What is needed is cultural renewal.' June: Rudolf Steiner visits Karlstein (Grail) Castle outside Prague. Lecture cycle: *From Symptom to Reality in Modern History* (CW 185). In mid-November, Emil Molt, of the Waldorf-Astoria Cigarette Company, has the idea of founding a school for his workers' children.

1919: Focus on the threefold social organism: tireless travel, countless lectures, meetings, and publications. At the same time, a new public stage of Anthroposophy emerges as cultural renewal begins. The coming years will see initiatives in pedagogy, medicine, pharmacology, and agriculture. January 27: threefold meeting: ' We must first of all, with the money we have, found free schools that can bring people what they need.' February: first public eurythmy performance in Zurich. Also: 'Appeal to the German People' (CW 24), circulated March 6 as a newspaper insert. In April, *Towards Social Renewal* (CW 23) appears— 'perhaps the most widely read of all books on politics appearing since the war.' Rudolf Steiner is asked to undertake the 'direction and leadership' of the school founded by the Waldorf-Astoria Company. Rudolf Steiner begins to talk about the 'renewal' of education. May 30: a building is selected and purchased for the future Waldorf School. August–September, Rudolf Steiner gives a lecture course for Waldorf teachers, *The Foundations of Human Experience (Study of Man)* (CW 293). September 7: Opening of the first Waldorf School. December (into January): first science course, the *Light Course* (CW 320).

1920: The Waldorf School flourishes. New threefold initiatives. Founding of limited companies *Der Kommende Tag* and *Futurum A.G.* to infuse spiritual values into the economic realm. Rudolf Steiner also focuses on the sciences. Lectures: *Introducing Anthroposophical Medicine* (CW 312); *The Warmth Course* (CW 321); *The Boundaries of Natural Science* (CW 322); *The Redemption of Thinking* (CW 74). February: Johannes Werner

Klein—later a co-founder of the Christian Community—asks Rudolf Steiner about the possibility of a 'religious renewal,' a 'Johannine church.' In March, Rudolf Steiner gives the first course for doctors and medical students. In April, a divinity student asks Rudolf Steiner a second time about the possibility of religious renewal. September 27–October 16: anthroposophical 'university course.' December: lectures titled *The Search for the New Isis* (CW 202).

1921: Rudolf Steiner continues his intensive work on cultural renewal, including the uphill battle for the threefold social order. 'University' arts, scientific, theological, and medical courses include: *The Astronomy Course* (CW 323); *Observation, Mathematics, and Scientific Experiment* (CW 324); the *Second Medical Course* (CW 313); *Colour*. In June and September-October, Rudolf Steiner also gives the first two 'priests' courses' (CW 342 and 343). The 'youth movement' gains momentum. Magazines are founded: *Die Drei* (January), and—under the editorship of Albert Steffen (1884–1963)—the weekly, *Das Goetheanum* (August). In February–March, Rudolf Steiner takes his first trip outside Germany since the war (Holland). On April 7, Steiner receives a letter regarding 'religious renewal,' and May 22–23, he agrees to address the question in a practical way. In June, the Klinical-Therapeutic Institute opens in Arlesheim under the direction of Dr. Ita Wegman. In August, the Chemical-Pharmaceutical Laboratory opens in Arlesheim (Oskar Schmiedel and Ita Wegman are directors). The Clinical Therapeutic Institute is inaugurated in Stuttgart (Dr. Ludwig Noll is director); also the Research Laboratory in Dornach (Ehrenfried Pfeiffer and Günther Wachsmuth are directors). In November–December, Rudolf Steiner visits Norway.

1922: The first half of the year involves very active public lecturing (thousands attend); in the second half, Rudolf Steiner begins to withdraw and turn toward the Society—'The Society is asleep.' It is 'too weak' to do what is asked of it. The businesses—*Der Kommende Tag* and *Futurum A.G.*—fail. In January, with the help of an agent, Steiner undertakes a twelve-city German lecture tour, accompanied by eurythmy performances. In two weeks he speaks to more than 2,000 people. In April, he gives a 'university course' in The Hague. He also visits England. In June, he is in Vienna for the East–West Congress. In August–September, he is back in England for the Oxford Conference on Education. Returning to Dornach, he gives the lectures *Philosophy, Cosmology, and Religion* (CW 215), and gives the third priests' course (CW 344). On September 16, The Christian Community is founded. In October–November, Steiner is in Holland and England. He also speaks to the youth: *The Youth Course* (CW 217). In December, Steiner gives lectures titled *The Origins of Natural Science* (CW 326), and *Humanity and the World of Stars: The Spiritual Communion of Humanity* (CW 219). December 31: Fire at the Goetheanum, which is destroyed.

1923: Despite the fire, Rudolf Steiner continues his work unabated. A very hard year. Internal dispersion, dissension, and apathy abound. There is conflict—between old and new visions—within the Society. A wake-up call is needed, and Rudolf Steiner responds with renewed lecturing vitality. His focus: the spiritual context of human life; initiation science; the course of the year; and community building. As a foundation for an artistic school, he creates a series of pastel sketches. Lecture cycles: *The Anthroposophical Movement; Initiation Science* (CW 227) (in England at the Penmaenmawr Summer School); *The Four Seasons and the Archangels* (CW 229); *Harmony of the Creative Word* (CW 230); *The Supersensible Human* (CW 231), given in Holland for the founding of the Dutch society. On November 10, in response to the failed Hitler-Ludendorff putsch in Munich, Steiner closes his Berlin residence and moves the *Philosophisch-Anthroposophisch Verlag* (Press) to Dornach. On December 9, Steiner begins the serialization of his *Autobiography: The Course of My Life* (CW 28) in *Das Goetheanum*. It will continue to appear weekly, without a break, until his death. Late December–early January: Rudolf Steiner re-founds the Anthroposophical Society (about 12,000 members internationally) and takes over its leadership. The new board members are: Marie Steiner, Ita Wegman, Albert Steffen, Elisabeth Vreede, and Günther Wachsmuth. (See *The Christmas Meeting for the Founding of the General Anthroposophical Society*, CW 260). Accompanying lectures: *Mystery Knowledge and Mystery Centres* (CW 232); *World History in the Light of Anthroposophy* (CW 233). December 25: the Foundation Stone is laid (in the hearts of members) in the form of the 'Foundation Stone Meditation.'

1924:   January 1: having founded the Anthroposophical Society and taken over its leadership, Rudolf Steiner has the task of 'reforming' it. The process begins with a weekly newssheet ('What's Happening in the Anthroposophical Society') in which Rudolf Steiner's 'Letters to Members' and 'Anthroposophical Leading Thoughts' appear (CW 26). The next step is the creation of a new esoteric class, the 'first class' of the 'University of Spiritual Science' (which was to have been followed, had Rudolf Steiner lived longer, by two more advanced classes). Then comes a new language for Anthroposophy—practical, phenomenological, and direct; and Rudolf Steiner creates the model for the second Goetheanum. He begins the series of extensive 'karma' lectures (CW 235–40); and finally, responding to needs, he creates two new initiatives: biodynamic agriculture and curative education. After the middle of the year, rumours begin to circulate regarding Steiner's health. Lectures: January–February, *Anthroposophy* (CW 234); February: *Tone Eurythmy* (CW 278); June: *The Agriculture Course* (CW 327); June–July: *Speech Eurythmy* (CW 279); *Curative Education* (CW 317); August: (England, 'Second International Summer School'), *Initiation Consciousness: True and False Paths in Spiritual Investigation* (CW 243); September: *Pastoral Medicine* (CW 318). On September 26, for the first time, Rudolf Steiner cancels a lecture. On September 28, he gives his last lecture. On September 29, he withdraws to his studio in the carpenter's shop; now he is definitively ill. Cared for by Ita Wegman, he continues working, however, and writing the weekly installments of his *Autobiography* and *Letters to the Members/Leading Thoughts* (CW 26).

1925: Rudolf Steiner, while continuing to work, continues to weaken. He finishes *Extending Practical Medicine* (CW 27) with Ita Wegman.
On March 30, around ten in the morning, Rudolf Steiner dies.

INDEX

A NOTE FROM RUDOLF STEINER PRESS

We are an independent publisher and registered charity (non-profit organisation) dedicated to making available the work of Rudolf Steiner in English translation. We care a great deal about the content of our books and have hundreds of titles available – as printed books, ebooks and in audio formats.

As a publisher devoted to anthroposophy…

- We continually commission translations of previously unpublished works by Rudolf Steiner and invest in re-translating, editing and improving our editions.

- We are committed to making anthroposophy available to all by publishing introductory books as well as contemporary research.

- Our new print editions and ebooks are carefully checked and proofread for accuracy, and converted into all formats for all platforms.

- Our translations are officially authorised by Rudolf Steiner's estate in Dornach, Switzerland, to whom we pay royalties on sales, thus assisting their critical work.

So, look out for Rudolf Steiner Press as a mark of quality and support us today by buying our books, or contact us should you wish to sponsor specific titles or to support the charity with a gift or legacy.

office@rudolfsteinerpress.com
Join our e-mailing list at www.rudolfsteinerpress.com

RUDOLF STEINER PRESS